THE ANCIENT NEAR EAST

221

Trapezus

CASPIAN

ARMENIA

Lake Van

Lake Urmia

HYRCANIA

ARAM NAHARAIM

Haran

Balikh R.

Habur R.

Nineveh

Mosul · Arbela

ASSYRIA

Asshur

Tigris

Euph

MEDIA

Ecbatana

Behistun

— 35°

events in the latter part of the same century.

The significant happenings in the Near East during the fifth-fourth centuries B.C. are examined with an overall view of the progress of thought and life during the conquests and the restoration and toward interconnections in cultural and historic developments as demonstrated by art, literature, and politics of the age.

Together with its detailed background material and its introduction to the age from Artaxerxes Cyrus II to the coming of the Greeks, this book provides an ideal commentary on the years of the conquests, the restoration, and the ultimate situation of the Jews in the period that followed.

· Der

ELAM

BONIA

Nippur

· Susa

Shuruppak ·

· Lagash

Ur ·

To Persepolis and Pasargadae

PERSIA

— 30°

Persian Gulf

00   200

LES

45°

PRENTICE-HALL

Backgrounds
to the
Bible Series

Editor
Bruce Vawter, C.M.

The Bible and Archaeology
George E. Mendenhall

The World of the Patriarchs
Ignatius Hunt, O.S.B.

The World of Moses
John E. Huesman, S.J.

The World of the Judges
John L. McKenzie, S.J.

The World of David and Solomon
Eugene H. Maly

The World of the Prophets
Dennis J. McCarthy, S.J.

The World of the Restoration
J. M. Myers

The World of Palestinian Judaism
Louis F. Hartman, C. Ss. R.

The World of the Diaspora
Roland E. Murphy, O. Carm.

The World of the Gospels
Myles Bourke

The Johannine World
(to be announced)

The World of the Apostles
Edgar M. Krentz

PRENTICE-HALL INTERNATIONAL, INC., *London*
PRENTICE-HALL OF AUSTRALIA, PTY. LTD., *Sydney*
PRENTICE-HALL OF CANADA, LTD., *Toronto*
PRENTICE-HALL OF INDIA (PRIVATE) LTD., *New Delhi*
PRENTICE-HALL OF JAPAN, INC., *Tokyo*

The
World
of the
Restoration

J. M. Myers
Lutheran Theological
Seminary

PRENTICE-HALL, INC.
Englewood Cliffs, N.J.

MS; Bible, O.T. —History of contemporary events
Jews —History—586 B.C. —70 A.D.

© 1968 by

PRENTICE-HALL, INC., *Englewood Cliffs*, *N.J.*

Current printing (last digit):
10 9 8 7 6 5 4 3 2 1

Library of Congress Catalog Card No.: 68-22073
Printed in the United States of America

To my Alma Mater

Gettysburg College

as a token of appreciation for the signal honor
conferred upon me June 4, 1967

Editor's Note

In his encyclical letter *Divino afflante Spiritu* of 1943, Pope Pius XII surveyed the currents of change in biblical studies since the earlier *Providentissimus Deus* written by Pope Leo XIII in 1893:

There is no one who cannot readily perceive how the conditions of biblical study and its auxiliary sciences have radically altered during these past fifty years. To mention only one thing, when our predecessor published his encyclical *Providentissimus Deus* hardly a single Palestinian site had been subjected to archaeological investigation. Now, on the contrary, excavations in ever increasing number carried out with all the methods and skills that have been developed through experience are continually giving us something new, something that is more certain. How much light has been drawn from these explorations for the better and more complete understanding of the sacred books is acknowledged by all experts and biblical scholars. Their importance is only enhanced by the periodic discovery of inscriptional materials which contribute greatly to our knowledge of the languages, literatures, history, customs, and religions of antiquity. No less important has been the discovery of the papyri, into which research is even at this moment being carried out, which have proved to be of such value especially for elucidating the language of our Savior's times as well as the institutions of both public and private life.

It is with matters such as these that this series of books is concerned. What was signaled out in 1943 as affecting the progress of biblical studies is still affecting it, perhaps in even greater measure, this short generation later.

"Archaeology" has become a somewhat inclusive term under which the layman thinks of the many sciences dealing with the past which set the tone of biblical study today just as "higher criticism" did that of the past century. Since he usually has but the vaguest notion of its methodology and processes, he is in danger of accepting its conclusions uncritically, or of making too much of them, or, in rarer instances, of regarding them with excessive scepticism. Some overenthusiastic popularization has, at times, given the impression that archaeology is intent on proving the Bible right at all costs, by turning scientific possibilities into religious certainties and by ignoring the many problems—far more numerous than the solutions—with which archaeology has confronted the biblical scholar.

The purpose of this series is to assist the educated but nonspecialized reader to understand what biblical study in the age of archaeology is all about. It will not provide commentaries on the biblical text, but it will attempt to relate it in its major divisions to the larger history of which it is a part by means of the geographical, linguistic, cultural, and religious data which modern studies have contributed to the understanding of the Bible. Under the guidance of the authors, who are specialists in the areas in which they have written, the reader should emerge with a clearer idea of the problematics of biblical history as well as of the direction taken by the scholarly consensus regarding these issues.

In this consensus all we who must be concerned here and now with the Book of our religious heritage have an obvious and vital stake.

This volume is concerned with a decisive era in biblical history— decisive not only for the Judaism whose rebirth it saw on Palestinian soil, but also, even if indirectly, for the Christianity that would later take its origin from this Palestinian Judaism. It is an age about which we are, for the most part, extremely well informed, though there exist significant and intriguing gaps in the documentation necessary for a satisfying reconstruction, and these, not surprisingly, have invited speculations often leading to quite contradictory conclusions. Professor Myers has tried to restrict himself to what is certain rather than to what is merely engaging; he is therefore a safe and trustworthy guide to anyone who wants to witness how the dynamism of the Semitic Old Testament reacted to and found a new life within the Aryan world of the Persian Empire. That new life was to be pre-eminently that of the Law, though the Israelite prophecy that came to an end in this period also produced figures not unworthy of its beginnings. A further volume has been reserved for the Sages of Israel, who also belong to this World of the Restoration.

BRUCE VAWTER, C.M.

Contents

Introduction

The subject of this book has been interpreted in its broadest sense in an endeavor to treat most of the historico-religious facets of the restoration period as they affected the fortunes of the Jews. There is doubtless some overlapping with other volumes of the series at both ends of this one. Without a brief account of the historical movements that led to the successive debacles of the Judean kingdom at the beginning of the sixth century B.C. and a sketch of the fate of their victims in Babylonia, the erstwhile homeland, and elsewhere, the whole story would be somewhat truncated. Similarly, it seemed necessary to spill over into the Greek period because the conquests of Alexander the Great marked the transition from Persian to Greek hegemony in the last half of the fourth century B.C.

This must not be regarded as a definitive portrait of the period of the restoration, because our sources are meager at many points; where they are more or less abundant there is often some question of interpretation. There may be some disagreement with the views herein expressed, but in most instances they follow a conservative pattern, with the possible exception of the dates and activities of Nehemiah and Ezra.

The aim is to present an over-all picture of the times and fortunes of the Jews, together with a broad outline of their religious experiences and adjustments to the changing circumstances of life in which they found themselves. There is a fair degree of factual certainty with respect to the general situation, but details are less subject to control.

Background

The motives for restoration and renewal following the exile are inherent in the old covenant faith of Israel combined with Yahweh's promise of the land to Abraham, Isaac, and Jacob (covenant with Abraham, Gn 15,1–6; with Jacob, Gn 28,13–14). To judge from the subsequent history of the nation, eternal possession of the promised land was taken for granted by people and rulers alike, who believed the presence of the temple to be an automatic guarantee of the permanence of their residence, irrespective of their conduct. The fall of the Northern Kingdom in 722 B.C. shook Judah to its foundations, as seen from the prophecies of Isaiah and Micah and the subsequent reformation under Josiah (640–609 B.C.). Zephaniah, Jeremiah, Habakkuk, and Ezekiel were genuinely alarmed by the flouting of the covenant under Jehoiakim (609–597 B.C.) and Zedekiah (598–587 B.C.). Jeremiah especially counseled submission to the yoke of Babylon as punishment for the nation's deviation (Jer 32,26–35).

The first onslaught of Nebuchadnezzar in 597 B.C. should have been ample warning to the authorities to mend their ways, but it only made them more wilfully resistant to the admonitions of the prophets, and matters grew worse. The headlong plunge toward disaster was not to be halted; in fact, it was to be accelerated in direct proportion to the application of political pressure from without and prophetic exhortation from within. The outside pressures were exerted, on the one hand, by Babylon, which demanded loyalty on the part of its vassal state, and on the other hand, by the princes of Moab, Ammon, Edom, Tyre, and Sidon (Jer 27), who did everything in their power to incite revolt against Babylon, probably at the instigation of Egypt (Jer 37), which was ever ready to create a disturbance without getting too deeply involved. Jeremiah counseled loyalty to Babylon (27,12–15) but was opposed by rulers and religious officials (27,16ff.). The more Jeremiah exhorted the nation to accept the yoke of Babylon as the will of Yahweh, the more frantically active became his opponents—all of which hastened the day of reckoning. Even after the final blow had fallen on Jerusalem, certain groups remaining in the land refused to accept the situation and continued the struggle against the inevitable (see Jer 41–44).

But as sacred history testifies, the Lord never ceases attempting to win back his own. Isaiah had already proclaimed the doctrine of the remnant—"a remnant will return, the remnant of Jacob, to God Almighty. Even though your people Israel be as numerous as the sand of the sea, a mere remnant will return" (Is 10,21–22a). Despite the devastation of three successive deportations from 597–585 B.C., Jeremiah was not without hope. More than once he spoke of restoration (Jer 27,22; 30,17; 31,31–34) after the purge. His letter to the first exiles in Babylon about 594–593 B.C. (John Bright, *Jeremiah, Anchor Bible,* XXI [New York: Doubleday, 1965], pp. 210ff.) promises categorically a return from captivity after the seventy years of exile have been completed (Jer 29,10). During the short interval in the final siege of Jerusalem when the Babylonian army withdrew to deal with the Egyptian army, Jeremiah, at great personal risk, set out to demonstrate his faith in ultimate restoration by redeeming his ancient patrimony at Anathoth (Jer 32,6–25; 37,11ff.). His prophecy of a new covenant (Jer 31,31–34) spells out in detail the prophet's hope for and faith in "the hound of heaven." The Lord would again redeem his people as he had done in the time of Moses, enter anew into a covenant relationship with them, and return them to the land as he promised the fathers.

Ezekiel's vision of the new Jerusalem (Ez 40–48) offered even more hope, and Deutero-Isaiah (Is 40–55) was ecstatic over the prospects for a return from captivity as the appointed time drew near and the political situation became more favorable to the Jews in exile.

The Captivities

Before proceeding to our main task, it is necessary to survey the historical position of the Jews in the exilic period as far as it can be determined from the sources available to us at present. The first captivity, according to Kings (2 Kgs 24,10–17; 2 Chr 36,9–10), consisted of the deportation of King Jehoiachin, the royal mother, the women of the harem, the officials of the court, provincial leaders, and others. The numbers of those taken to Babylon in 597 B.C. vary somewhat: 2 Kgs 24,14–10,000; 2 Kgs 24,16–8,000; Jer 52,28–3,023. Subsequent attitudes and activities under Zedekiah indicate the existence of little stability in Judah. The king was unable to exercise control or to enforce any semblance of direction among the refractory elements left in the land (Jer 38,5.14.24–26)—a sure sign of Nebuchadnezzar's effectiveness.

Worse was sure to come. The weakness of the king, with the dissidents now holding the upper hand, resulted in indecision and vacillation. The political and religious authorities refused to listen to the voice of Jeremiah and to accept the inevitable. In all probability the reason for the turmoil in Judah was that Zedekiah was looked upon as regent only, since Jehoiachin was still alive and regarded as the legitimate king. In fact, Babylonian texts (the so-called Weidner tablets—see Pritchard, *ANET* 308, and W. F. Albright, "King Jehoiachin in Exile," *BA* V [1942] 49–55) refer to him as king of Judah still. Jar-handles discovered in Palestinian excavations bore the stamp, "Eliakim, Steward of Jehoiachin" (from Tell Beit Mirsim, Beth-shemesh and Ramat Rahel—*RB* LXIX [1962] 402), which seems to indicate that Zedekiah's was only a caretaker government. Then, too, there was unrest among the exiles in Babylon, as seen from the attempt of Jeremiah to reconcile them to their lot (Jer 29). False prophets raised false hopes (Jer 28,2–4), and Egypt under Pharaoh Psammeticus II (595–589 B.C.) began once more to fish in troubled waters, fomenting rebellion among the Palestinian states. The pressures on Judah were thus building up to a climax, which came in 589–588 B.C. (2 Kgs 25,1; Jer 39,1; 52,4). The Babylonian army surrounded the city of Jerusalem and ravaged the provincial cities, as the Lachish letters and excavations demonstrate. Another deportation took place after the capture and destruction of the capital (2 Kgs 25,11.18–21; Jer 52,15.24–27). Only the poorest people were left in the land. Albright estimates that the population in the reign of Zedekiah declined to about half of what it was at the close of the eighth century B.C. (*BP* 84). The priests and "the keepers of the threshold" were executed so that now there was little religious leadership left. Only Jeremiah was permitted to remain behind, and with Gedaliah he offered the remnant some semblance of a holding force.

According to the Deuteronomic historian (2 Kgs 25,4 and Jer 52,7), the army of Zedekiah fled by night, some elements seeking refuge "in the way of the Arabah." This was the group who returned after the debacle to make trouble for those who attempted to make the best of their sad lot. Gedaliah was established at the provisional capital at

Mizpah. He urged the various parties to begin life anew as subjects of the Babylonian king (2 Kgs 25,24; Jer 40,9–10). But a scion of the royal family by the name of Ishmael slew the new governor, and as a result fear seized the leaders, who, although the assassins were driven out, compelled Jeremiah to accompany them in precipitate flight to Egypt (Jer 42–43). How the Babylonian authorities reacted is not known, but the historian of Jer 52 mentions a third deportation in the twenty-third year of Nebuchadnezzar (v. 30), which may reflect a somewhat belated reaction.

Condition of the Jews in Judah
After the Gedaliah Incident

To judge from literary reflections, the lot of the Jews in Palestine after the fall of Jerusalem was far from enviable. Only the "poorest of the land" were left to be vineyard workers and farmers. After the escapade of Ishmael, all semblance of order disappeared because no one capable of maintaining it remained. In short, a political vacuum unfilled by the authorities existed, and part of the former territory of Judah was added to the province of Samaria. A. Alt has shown that a portion of the former territory was given to Samaria, whereas another was occupied by Edom. (See "Die Rolle Samarias bei der Entstehung des Judentums," in Alt, *KS* II 316ff.) There was no settlement of other captive peoples in Judah to replace the exiled Jewish population as had been done by the Assyrians after the conquest of Israel nearly 135 years earlier.

Sources for the exilic period in Palestine are limited, but those we can identify with some certainty paint a gruesome picture of the situation. The unsettled condition immediately after the fall of the capital is portrayed in Jer 40–43. There we are told that certain Jewish military officers returned with their details from isolated or outlying posts to Mizpah when news of the establishment of a provisional government under Gedaliah reached them. They were advised against further resistance and to submit to Babylonian hegemony. They were urged to return to peaceful occupation of their villages and farms. And so they might have done had it not been for the conspiracy of those elements who had fled before the Babylonian army to the surrounding territory. At the behest of Baalis, king of Ammon (Jer 40,14), opposition against the local authorities was continued, possibly because the Jewish military officers objected to any collaboration with the Babylonians. Though warned, the credulous Gedaliah refused to take protective measures and consequently fell victim to their outrage. Thus the last hope of those Jews who attempted to hold on to whatever remained of their land and possessions vanished. After the murder of Gedaliah, and in sheer desperation, Johanan, the leader of those who had given their allegiance to the governor, and his supporters sought direction from Jeremiah, who advised them to remain in the land and to come to terms with reality. But possibly suspecting the prophet of pro-Babylonian sympathies, his counsel was rejected and they fled to Egypt, taking Jeremiah with them.

There is some indication that desultory sacrifices were still carried out at the Jerusalem altar site (Jer 41,5; Zech 7,2), but the comment of Zechariah, "Thus the land was left desolate, so that no one went about, for the pleasant land was in ruins" (Zech 7,14b), likely describes the true state of affairs. The best description of local conditions in Judah and Jerusalem is found in the five poems of Lamentations, whose subject, as Hans-Joachim Kraus (*Biblischer Kommentar, Altes Testament: Klagelieder* [*Threni*] [Neukirchen, Kreis Moers: Verlag der Buchhandlung des Erziehungsvereins, 1956], 9) has pointed out, is the destruction of the Jerusalem temple (for theological implications see N. K. Gottwald, *Studies in the Book of Lamentations* [London: SCM Press, 1954]). Whereas it is not absolutely certain whether the poems are all by the same author and whether they are the product of one who remained in the land or of one who was in exile, they do depict the sad disorder and confusion that befell the people and their institutions in the wake of the Babylonian conquest. What the poet (or poets) has to say does not differ from what we learn from the somewhat cryptic references in Jeremiah and Kings. If he operated in the land, there is some indication that not all the gifted and perceptive personalities had perished or had been removed from the tragic scene.

The structural art of Lamentations is significant. It consists of five poems, four of which are acrostics. Chapter I devotes three lines to each of the twenty-two letters of the Hebrew alphabet in the regular order. Chapter II also has three lines per letter, but the order of the *pe* and *'ayin*, the sixteenth and seventeenth letters of the Hebrew alphabet, are reversed. The same is true of Chapter III, which has the added feature of each of the three lines beginning with the same consonant. Chapter IV follows a two-line form, with only the first line beginning with a given letter of the alphabet, and has the same order of consonants as the preceding two chapters. Chapter V is not acrostic and is quite irregular in metric structure, which in the other chapters is *qinah* (i.e., three plus two beats, the meter of lamentation). Although the language is highly poetic, it does furnish a vivid portrait of the desolation of Judah. Jerusalem is pictured as a deserted city (Lam 1,1; 2,13.15). Where once there was mirth and song, jackals made their home (Lam 4,3; 5,18). The survivors were starving; food was exceedingly hard to come by (Lam 1,11; 4,3–5.9; 5,4.6.9.10). Erstwhile pilgrimages and religious feasts had come to an abrupt end (Lam 1,4; 2,6). Disorder and insecurity were rampant (Lam 4,18–19; 5,11), and there was no law and order. The neighbors of Judah now became her enemies and could vent their wrath upon the people at will (Lam 1,14.17; 2,16–17; 3,14.52). Especially strong enmity against the nations round about arose (Lam 1,21–22; 3,13–15.64–66; 4,21–22) and was to plague relationships for centuries. The situation was dismal indeed. Yet the poet, reflecting on it, was not without hope, and he voiced his prayer for restoration. He realized that what had befallen the land was not without justification. Judah had been a hotbed of transgression (Lam 1,5) and the embodiment of uncleanness (Lam 1,8–9), which had now found its reward (Lam 1,14.18; 5,16). The nation had been misled by its leaders (Lam 2,14; 4,13). The terrible calamity led the writer to call for a re-examination of the ways of the people and a return to the Lord (Lam 3,40). The final prayer (Lam 5,21) expresses an unfailing hope in restoration, a cardinal principle of Hebrew theology. Surely God had been good to Israel, his chosen people, and would not wipe them out completely (Lam 3,19–26.31–33). (For a different interpretation of Lamentations see E. Janssen, *Juda in der Exilszeit* [Göttingen: Vandenhoeck and Ruprecht, 1956], pp. 39ff.)

Another account of the catastrophe in Judah is the book of Obadiah —the work of a particularly heated critic of Edom's reaction to Judah's misfortune. The Edomites apparently participated in a significant way in the event. They not only gloated over Judah's destruction but waylaid refugees, headed off fugitives and handed them over to the invader, and even looted and plundered the unfortunate cities (Obd 12–14). Ez 33,23–29 speaks of the waste places, the desolate land, and the empty and forbidding mountains of Israel (cf. E. Klamroth, *Die jüdischen Exulanten in Babylonien* [Leipzig: J. C. Hinrichs'sche Buchhandlung, 1912], pp. 26f.).

Archaeology supports the above literary data. For example, James B. Pritchard (*Gibeon: Where the Sun Stood Still* [Princeton, N. J.: Princeton University Press, 1962], p. 163) reports that Gibeon (el–Jib) as a prosperous city ended with the Babylonian invasion and was never rebuilt. Lachish (Level II) everywhere bore signs of violent destruction and was not reoccupied until the middle of the fifth century (O. Tufnell, *Lachish III: The Iron Age* [New York: Oxford University Press, Inc., 1953], pp. 56f., 105, 111, 119). There is some indication that the same conditions applied at Beth–zur (O. R. Sellers, *The Citadel of Beth-Zur* [Philadelphia: The Westminster Press, 1933], p. 10), and also at Tell Beit Mirsim (ancient Debir) and probably Bethel. The situation at Bethel is not absolutely certain, although it was leveled by fire (*BASOR LVI* 14). Ramat Rahel was totally obliterated around 587 B.C. (Y. Aharoni, *Ramat Rahel: Seasons 1959 and 1960* [Rome: Università degli Studi, Centro di Studi Semitici, 1962], p. 49). Albright's study revealed that nearly all the Judean cities in the lower Shephelah and the Negeb (see Ez 20,45ff.; 36,3ff.) as well as a large number in the highlands were destroyed at the time and remained uninhabited during the exile (*The Archaeology of Palestine and the Bible*, 3rd ed. [New York: Fleming H. Revell Company, 1935], p. 171).

The biblical and archaeological evidence thus points to a bleak outlook (see Is 49,19; 51,3.19; 61,4; 64,10.11) for the immediate future in Palestine. The land was devastated; foreign elements hostile to the remnant overran the countryside; the sacred city lay in ruins; leadership for those who did remain was virtually nonexistent—if it did exist it was ineffective—and there seemed no possibility for the survival of Judaism existing in the population left in Judah. Consider, however, the argument of E. Janssen (*Juda in der Exilszeit*, pp. 39–46), who explains the Chronicler's emphasis on the vacuum existing in the land on the basis of the concept of prophecy and fulfillment. The prophets predicted exile because of the sins of the people but also promised restoration after a period of judgment (Jer 25,12; 29,10).

Although the catastrophic nature of events in Judah cannot be minimized, there is evidence that a modicum of worship continued. A temporary altar may have been put together soon after the destruction of the temple (Jer 41,5). There is possibly a hint in 1 Esdr 5,48b of an existent altar that was "prepared" for the presentation of burnt offerings by the first delegation of those who returned to Jerusalem after the exile, although that is by no means certain because verse 50 mentions the erection of an altar. Lamentations itself may imply some sort of mourning ritual carried out amidst the ruins (see Lam 2,7b.10; 3,55). The fixed possessions of the exiles were taken over by the people who remained in the land (Ez 11,15).

The Jews
in Babylon

According to Ez 3,15, a colony of Jews from the first captivity was settled at Telabib by the Canal Chebar. Later detachments occupied Telmelah, Telharsha, Cherub, Addan, and Immer (Ezr 2,59). There was another colony of Jews at Casiphia in the time of Ezra (Ezr 8,17). Rabbinical schools at Sura, Pumbeditha, and Nehardea since the second century A.D. seem to indicate earlier settlements there. The traditional location of the tomb of Ezekiel at Kefila near Birs Nimrud may also point to that of a colony of Jews. None of the biblical sites can presently be identified; they were probably not far from the capital. The morale of the captives was naturally quite low, as seen from Ps 137. They gathered by the tree-lined canals where they lamented their fate. The voice of harp and lyre was silent, the sound of joy and mirth gone, and the glad days spent in Jerusalem but an unhappy memory. Goading by their captors did not make their lot less painful. Josephus (*Against Apion*, I, 138f)* says that the captives were settled in the most appropriate places in Babylonia, which could mean the best places, the most convenient places, or the most suitable places for the tasks to which they were assigned.

One of the sources for our knowledge of the fate of the exiles is the now well-known Weidner texts dating from the thirteenth year of Nebuchadnezzar II (*Mélanges Syriens offerts à Monsieur René Dussaud*, II [Paris: Geuthner, 1939], 923–35), which contain a list of rations provided for Jewish and other captives living in or around Babylon. Mentioned by name is King Jehoiachin, who was doubtless not confined to prison but free to move about at will. Rations are listed also for his five sons, who are not named. Mentioned is a man by the name of Shelemiah, who was a gardener; also there are Semachiah, Keniah, Ur-melech, and Gaddiel. Some of these names occur in the Old Testament or on seals and in the Elephantine documents. The occupations of other captives from Philistia (sailors and musicians), the Phoenician cities of Tyre, Byblos, and Arvad (sailors and technicians), Egypt (sailors, horsemen, shipbuilders, monkey-handlers), and Greece (woodworkers, shipbuilders, carpenters) indicate a group of

---

* From *Josephus*, H. St. J. Thackeray, trans. (Cambridge, Mass.: Harvard University Press, 1926–1965), 9 vols.

elite artisans of various skills employed by the Babylonian authorities
for highly specialized work.

The first we hear of the deportation of 597 B.C. is the letter sent
(c. 594 B.C.) by Jeremiah, apparently in response to unrest among the
exiles fomented by false prophets and dreamers. It is not impossible
that they were inspired by the declaration of Hananiah (Jer 28,2–4)
to the effect that the yoke of the king of Babylon would soon be
smashed, and Jehoiachin would be restored to his throne within two
years. Jeremiah's reply to Hananiah was devastating. Jeremiah wore
an iron yoke that could not be smashed as easily as Hananiah had
smashed the earlier "wooden" yoke. He predicted Hananiah's death
within the year, and it so happened (Jer 28,15–17). He advised (Jer
29) the exiles to construct homes, plant gardens, marry so as to maintain the population at the existent level, even increase it, promote
the welfare of the land, and pray for its well-being. He said that they
must pay no attention to those prophets and dreamers whose only
desire was to put the Lord to the test by stirring up rebellion, their
prophecies being nothing but lies. He reminded the dissidents that
their predicament was brought on by themselves and that they were
now serving time for failure to obey the word of the Lord. Insurrection
could lead to even more dire judgment. If they accepted the discipline
of the Lord, after seventy years he would visit them, restore their fortunes, and bring them back to the homeland. From this correspondence
it is clear that so-called prophets were active in Babylon (Jer 29,15.21.-
31.32), working the kind of havoc among the people that Hananiah
did at home. Jer 51,59ff. tells us of a message sent by the prophet to
the exiles in the fourth year of Zedekiah. It was borne by a member
of the king's entourage going to Babylon on an official mission and
contained an oracle against Babylon.

One of the outstanding personalities among the *golah,* the exiles,
was the prophet Ezekiel, whose recorded oracles date from about 593–
571 B.C. This is not the place to argue the case for the locale of the
prophet (see C. G. Howie, *The Date and Composition of Ezekiel,*
Journal of Biblical Literature Monograph Series, IV [Philadelphia,
Pa.: Society of Biblical Literature, 1950]) or to give a detailed account
of his book. For our purpose, it is sufficient to call attention to the fact
that besides the dreamers noted above there was present among the
exiles in Babylon during the early years a true prophet of the Lord
whose activity in behalf of the people was in no way hampered by the
authorities. His work and the general atmosphere reflected in his writings indicate that Jeremiah's advice did not fall on deaf ears. Many

Jews occupied positions of significance (see the tradition voiced in the book of Daniel), whereas others soon achieved success by taking advantage of the incredibly rich opportunities offered by the land. Ezekiel had his own house (Ez 8,1), and certainly his fellows enjoyed the same privilege (Jer 29,5). They had plots of ground for their own use. They were, of course, required to render service to the government and pay taxes, but that was no more than was demanded of them in the homeland. Naturally they were subject to the local authorities and had to conform to the regulations and practices of the Babylonian community. Apart from temple privileges enjoyed at Jerusalem, they were apparently free to practice their religion as time permitted. The elders functioned, at least to the extent of being able to give advice to those who sought it (Ez 7,26; 8,1; 14,1; 20,1). They were free to meet as occasion required. On the other hand, there were doubtless innumerable hardships growing out of the demands laid upon the Jews by their captors or imposed upon them to curb their recalcitrance. There may have been some actual incarceration as the poetic literature of the period suggests (Is 43,14) and as the inscriptions attest concerning the methods employed by both Assyrians and Babylonians.

Although the voice of prophecy was quiescent for about thirty years after the last dated oracle of Ezekiel (Ez 29,17)—at least so far as we know—the fires of religion were not burned out. In about 560 B.C. Amel–Marduk released Jehoiachin from prison (Jer 52,31). Just when or why he had been confined is unknown; it may have been because of some unrest among the exiles sometime after the thirteenth year of Nebuchadnezzar II (592 B.C.) to which the Weidner texts refer. In any case, the fortune of the *golah* seems to have turned after the death of the great king. It is unlikely that the situation changed during the rapid succession of Babylonian kings between 561 and 555 B.C. when Nabonidus succeeded to the throne. It is not known what his attitudes toward the Jews were, but he was a deeply religious man as his concern for the sanctuaries of his kingdom shows, despite the derogatory statements recorded in the Cyrus cylinder (see Oppenheim's article in *The Interpreter's Dictionary of the Bible*, III [Nashville, Tenn.: Abingdon Press, 1962], 493f.). If the traditional story of Daniel is to be given any credence, the Jews occupied a favorable position during Belshazzar's governorship when the king was absent from the capital.

To the last years of Nabonidus' reign belong most of the oracles of Is 40–55. The Jews were still in exile, but the whole tenor of the chapters involved breathes the spirit of immanent return (Is 48,20). Jerusalem and other cities were still desolate, and the temple ruins were as they had been since 587 B.C. (Is 44,26–28). Cyrus was to be the Lord's agent to release his people and restore their cities and sanctuary. The very fact that a prophet could for the most part speak openly to the Jewish community reflects its relatively favorable status at the time. It is not impossible that the prophet was active among his people for some time and that as the Babylonian situation became more desperate, he was led to speak out publicly. Certainly prophecies condemning Babylon (Is 43,14; 47,1.5; 48,14), degrading her religion (Is 44,9–20; 46) or extending invitations to flee (Is 48,20; 52,11f.) could not have been delivered publicly. Others sound very much like private, or at best semi-private, messages to groups of Jews, offering encouragement and hope to an increasingly dissatisfied people (see Josephus, *Ant.* XI, 1:3).

The Jews
in Egypt

Next to nothing is known about the Jews in Egypt before the beginning of the fifth century B.C. There has been much speculation as to how the Jews of Elephantine got there, but none is foolproof. (See Emil G. Kraeling, *The Brooklyn Museum Aramaic Papyri* [New Haven, Conn.: Yale University Press, 1953], pp. 41–48.) In any event the colony existed before the inception of Persian rule in Egypt, that is, before 525 B.C. The statement is made in one of the papyri (no. 30 in A. Cowley, *Aramaic Papyri of the Fifth Century* B.C. [New York: Oxford University Press, Inc., 1923]) that the temple was built in the time of the kings of Egypt and that when Cambyses arrived in Egypt "he found this temple built." Hence the Jewish community at Elephantine must have been established considerably earlier and in the construction of a religious edifice either violated the Deuteronomic injunction or knew nothing about it. On the basis of a study of the relation between the wisdom of Amenemope and Prv 22,17–24,22 (*Mélanges bibliques rédigés en l'honneur de André Robert* [Paris: Bloud and Gay, n.d.] pp. 254–80), Etienne Drioton makes the interesting suggestion that the former is a translation from a Hebrew original and that it came from a Jewish community in Egypt composed of refugees from Samaria and Bethel after the fall of the former in 722 B.C. (*A la rencontre de Dieu: mémorial Albert Gelin* [Le Puy: Editions Xavier Mappus, 1961], pp. 181–91; and A. Vincent, *La religion des Judéo-araméens d'Eléphantine* [Paris: Librairie Orientaliste Paul Geuthner,

1937], p. 357). That might account for the presence of a Jewish temple at Elephantine in opposition to the Deuteronomic code, which was a product of the Josianic reformation in the Southern Kingdom. (See C. H. Gordon, "The Origin of the Jews in Elephantine," *JNES* XIV [1955] 56–58.) But it has been shown fairly conclusively that the Elephantine colony of Jews was composed of mercenaries and was established in the time of Apries (588–566 B.C.) (Albright, *Archaeology and the Religion of Israel* [Baltimore: Johns Hopkins Press, 1942], pp. 168, 171ff.). It is now far more likely that it was peopled by a group of Jews who in the time of Josiah (2 Kgs 23,15–20) had been converted to the Jerusalem cult and who had fled to Egypt after the destruction of Bethel toward the end of the neo-Babylonian period (Albright, *ibid.*, pp. 172f.). The only direct biblical information of Jews in Egypt during this period is found in Jeremiah, who warned the men around him not to flee there (Jer 42). They refused his advice, compelled him to accompany them (Jer 43), and finally resided at Tahpanhes (Daphnai, present-day Tell Defneh) where the prophet continued his oracles against Egypt, insisting on his view that Jews in Egypt would suffer annihilation. Specifically mentioned (Jer 44,1) are the Jews at Migdol (Pelusium), Tahpanhes, and Memphis in Pathros, which was in the Thebaid region of Egypt. Elephantine would thus fall within the Pathros district in Upper Egypt whence a delegation of Jews came to hear Jeremiah (Jer 44,15). But in all probability they were not of those who fled Judah after the murder of Gedaliah. Is 49,12 mentions people coming to the Lord from the north and west and "from the land of Syene." Albright thinks that some of the descendants of Jeremiah's group drifted south to Elephantine (*BP* 84). The prophet asserted that only a few of those in Egypt would ever return to Judah (Jer 44,28).

Hints of Jews
in Other Places

Doubtless Babylon and Egypt were not the only places to which Jews fled after the Jerusalem catastrophe. We know that the captive people of the Northern Kingdom were resettled in Mesopotamia (2 Kgs 17,6), some of them being employed in garrisons as far east as Media. Others may have escaped to Judah or to the surrounding principalities. It is reported in Jer 40,11–12 that *all* the Jews who had escaped to Moab, Ammon, and Edom to avoid capture by Nebuchadnezzar's army returned under the governorship of Gedaliah; it is likely, however, that some remained there in view of the attitude of Baalis, king of Ammon (Jer 40,14). There is a reference (Obd 20) to Jewish exiles at Sepharad (probably Sardis in Asia Minor), but the date of the prophecy is disputed. It is usually dated shortly after the exile because of the writer's intense hostility against Edom, which seems to have taken advantage of Judah's desperation. But the section of the little book involved here (Obd 19–21) is generally regarded as non-Obadian and therefore of uncertain date, probably later than the earlier part of the book. Even if a late post-exilic date should prove to be right, there is still a strong probability of a Jewish colony at Sardis.

It is impossible to go further with any certainty. Nothing conclusive can be drawn from the exalted poetic imagery of Deutero-Isaiah who sings of the gathering of "your offspring" from the east and the west, the north and the south (Is 43,5.6; 49,12), or from afar (Is 60,9). Is 66,19 mentions sending refugees or survivors "among the nations, to Tarshish, Put, Lud, Tubal and Javan." Zechariah refers to their being scattered "abroad as to the four winds of the heavens" (Zech 2,6), to the reclamation "of my people from the land of the rising sun and from the land of the setting sun" (Zech 8,7), and to coming days when "ten men from nations of every language shall seize the robe of a Jew with the importunity . . . Let us go with you, for we have heard that God is with you" (Zech 8,23). Ezekiel writes of the *countries* and the nations to which his brethren had been removed (Ez 11,16.17). The tradition recorded in Esther is to the effect that Jews were scattered through all the provinces of the Persian empire (Est 3,8). While serving at the Persian court at Susa, Nehemiah was visited by a delegation from Judah who may have been sent as representatives to affluent or important Jews then living at the capital. Though that happened nearly a century after the so-called exilic period, there is some reason to suppose that captives served at the capital for a long time. Josephus' *Against Apion*, I, 172–175 interpretation of a fragment from the Greek poet Choerilus (contemporary of Herodotus) to the effect that Jews served in Xerxes' expeditionary forces against Greece is gratuitous. It is highly probable that among the colonists settled in Arabia by Nabonidus were Jews, especially in view of the fact that in Muslim times Jewish communities (descendants of those colonists?) occupied five of the six centers mentioned in the Harran inscription (see *Anatolian Studies*, VIII [London: The British Institute of Archaeology at Ankara, 1958], pp. 58–59). Nabonidus had in his occupation forces people from "Akkad and Hatti-land," that is, from Babylonia and Western lands. In addition, attention may be called to the prayer of Nabonidus found at Qumran Cave 4 (J. T. Milik, *RB* 63 [1956], 407ff.), which refers to the healing of the king at Teima by a Jewish exorcist. The prayer reflects the same tradition as that current in Dn 4 (with the name of Nabonidus for Nebuchadnezzar; see D. N. Freedman, *BASOR* CXLV 31–32). Whatever may prove to be the historical worth of the story, it does transmit a Babylonian–Jewish tradition that Jews were present with Nabonidus in Arabia and thus supports the argument of Western and Muslim scholars that they are to be connected with one or another of the biblical stories (see C. J. Gadd, *Anatolian Studies*, VIII, pp. 86–89, and I. Ben-Zvi, "The Origins of the Settlement of Jewish Tribes in Arabia" in *Eretz-Israel*, VI [Jerusalem: Israel Exploration Society, 1960. Hebrew, pp. 130–48; English summary, pp. 35*–37*]).

The Religion
of Jews in Exile

The exile had profound consequences for the religion of the Jews. So long as the temple stood, the Lord was more or less confined to the institutions of religion in the land. To be sure the prophets had a larger view of the universality of Yahweh, but he still functioned from Jerusalem. One of the important revelations through Ezekiel concerned the distinction between "the glory of the Lord" and his dwelling place. The vision of the throne chariot (Ez 1,4–28; 11,22–23) echoes an earlier tradition associated with the exodus and wilderness period when the presence of the Lord was symbolized by the pillar of cloud and fire (Ex 13,21–22; Nm 14,14; Dt 31,15), pointing to his mobility. He was present with his people. Just where the prophet thought the throne chariot was during the interval between the destruction of Jerusalem and the reconstruction envisioned in Ez 40–48 is unclear, although it is said that it "came from the east" (Ez 43,2). The movement of the spirit of the Lord in the oracles of Ezekiel demonstrated that revelation did not come to an end with the overthrow of the temple and the deportation of the people. The Lord spoke to Ezekiel and Deutero-Isaiah in Babylon. Once more he showed himself as an immediate help to his people where they were. Thus, for the most part he functioned from Babylon during the exile (see, however, Klamroth, *Die jüdische Exulanten in Babylonien* [Leipzig: J. C. Hinrichs'sche Buchhandlung, 1912], pp. 60ff., on the persistence of the localization idea).

The *golah* now had time to reflect on the events that transpired between the Josianic reformation and the captivity. Why did Yahweh forsake his people? Why did he permit them to be driven from the homeland? Why did he see fit to destroy his temple, city, and land? Jeremiah had reminded the first detail of captives to seek their welfare in Babylon. To agitate against that land would be useless until they had fulfilled the allotted time inasmuch as they had been driven from Judah because they failed to listen to the persistent word of the Lord admonishing them concerning their iniquities (Jer 29,18–19). Ezekiel took up the same theme, accusing the people of being stubborn and rebellious (Ez 2,3ff.; 8,9–10). Granted that they were the victims of bad advice (Ez 13) and the prey of wilful rulers, priests, and prophets (Ez 22,23–31), they are nevertheless guilty. Actually the whole prophecy of Ezekiel is a study in the causes for the disaster that had befallen Judah. The picture presented there is one of instruction and guidance for a people in sackcloth and ashes. Wickedness had to be punished (Ez 16,43.58; 17,18; 20; 23,35). Thus we see the elders gathered in the prophet's house (Ez 8,1; 14,1) awaiting the Lord's word from his lips. We observe him more than once addressing the people (Ez 24,19; 33,2.12), either at their request or at the Lord's command.

Occupation with the torah now took the place of temple worship, partly perhaps as a substitute for it and partly as an attempt to discover how the community could avoid future catastrophes. The people in exile had been assured by the prophets that there would some day be a return to the homeland and the re-establishment of the sacred institutions; Ezekiel in his sermon on responsibility (Ez 18; 33,12ff.) enunciates the principle that only those directly guilty of sins and defection from the Lord would suffer. The new generation would be redeemed if they permitted themselves to learn from the bitter experiences of the past, accepted the discipline of the exile, employed the time to make amends, and followed the direction of the torah. This much is clear from the discourse on the exodus and wilderness experience of Israel (Ez 20). Although he was released from prison, Jehoiachin did not return: His son and grandson led the first contingent.

Although there is some doubt about the origin of some of the basic materials involved, it is fairly certain that the Holiness Code (Lv 17–26) was compiled in the time of Ezekiel (see O. Eissfeldt, *The Old Testament: An Introduction* [New York: Harper and Row Publishers, 1965], pp. 233–39). The Priestly strand of the Pentateuch, from the sixth or fifth century B.C. (Eissfeldt, pp. 204–208), was brought together in the exilic period. In fact, in all probability the whole Pentateuch was completed before or during the time of Ezra. The code of Deuteronomy (Dt 12–26) remained very much at the center of the thought and hope of the exilic community as demonstrated by the ethical demands of the prophets at the time and from the emphasis on the reconstruction of the old institutions with the operation of a holy cult. For example, the "glory" theology of Deuteronomy is everywhere apparent in Ezekiel (see G. von Rad, *Studies in Deuteronomy* [London: SCM Press, 1953], p. 42), to a lesser extent in Deutero-Isaiah but present nevertheless (Is 40,5; 58,8; 59,19; 60,1.2). Legal terminology itself is not so profuse as in pre-exilic prophets—*torah* = "law" occurs six times in Ezekiel, five in Deutero-Isaiah; *hoq* = "statute" occurs twenty-nine times in Ezekiel, once in Deutero-Isaiah; the root *špt* = "to judge," or "judgment" occurs eighty-two times in Ezekiel, twenty-one in Deutero-Isaiah; "covenant" appears eighteen times in Ezekiel, eight in Deutero-Isaiah; the name of Moses appears twice in Deutero-Isaiah and not at all in Ezekiel; and the name David occurs four times in Ezekiel and only once in Deutero-Isaiah; "righteousness," "right," or "to do right" occurs forty-six times in Deutero-Isaiah, thirty-eight times in Ezekiel; the term commandment (*miswah*) occurs in neither book.

The torah, then, was the last straw seized by a desperate community. Fortunate indeed that it had the staying power necessary to save it. The type of persons exiled was providential, for the priests and some of the prophets were well instructed in the torah, although they had handled it perfunctorily before. Now, however, they applied themselves to its organization, study, and application because it afforded the only rallying point available to them in a foreign land. Developments in Judaism since prove that something resulted from the exile besides the stress of captivity. The Jews now became the people of the book, and the contemplation of it probably saved them from a worse fate than that of exile in Babylon.

Along with the development of torah study went that of the so-called scribal function. The finished scribe about whom we read in Ezra and Nehemiah evolved out of the exile. Ezra is described as "skilled in the law of Moses" (Ezr 7,6), "learned in matters of the commandments of the Lord and his statutes for Israel" (Ezr 7,11), and as "scribe of the law of the God of heaven" (Ezr 7,12). His duty was to read and to interpret the torah to the people (see Neh 8,1f.; 8,4ff.; 8,13). The scribe had apparently not yet assumed the more restricted function of jurist. The significance of the scribes becomes evident when it is remembered that they were responsible for the selection and codification of Israel's laws as well as for their canonization. They were thus the custodians of the Scriptures and the textual scholars of the day.

Cultic rites did not vanish completely however; in fact, they are much in evidence in the literature of the period. Community services of worship could be carried on only where Yahweh had manifested himself in a special way. That requisite was met by his unique appearance to Ezekiel at the Canal Chebar. According to our sources, there is every reason to believe that a large part of cultic rites during the exile consisted of lamentation (see Ps 137). Zech 7,3–5 records the tradition of a fast held by the Jews in the fifth month (in commemoration of the burning of the temple, 2 Kgs 25,1; Jer 52,12) and in the seventh month (in lamentation of the murder of Gedaliah, 2 Kgs 25,25; Jer 41,1). Zech 8,18 mentions also the fourth month (the month in which the first breach was made in the walls of Jerusalem, 2 Kgs 25,3.4; Jer 52,6.7) and the tenth month (the month when the siege of Jerusalem began, 2 Kgs 25,1; Jer 52,4). (See also Is 58,1–9.) The reference to Casiphia as "a place" (Ezr 8,17) frequented by Levites does not of itself make it a cultic site. As R. de Vaux (*AI* 339) points out, the terminology may be explained on the basis of a Levitical family residence. But since a *wise man* by the name of Sherebiah with his sons and brothers (Ezr 8,18; Neh 8,8) responded to the plea of Ezra, it may be concluded that a well-established scribal school existed there. Some kind of devotional exercise may have been associated with other activities of the center.

The Sabbath acquired a new significance. References occur fifteen times in Ez (see especially Ez 20,12ff.). As Hans-Joachim Kraus (*Worship in Israel* [Oxford: Blackwell, 1966], p. 87f.) observes, the Sabbath now became a covenantal sign with confessional import. In the new community of Ezekiel it was featured as a day of sacrifice to be observed in connection with the temple liturgy (Ez 46,1ff.). How this developed in the post-exilic period may be seen from such passages as Is 56,2.4.6.; 58,13; 66,23. Along with the Sabbath, circumcision assumed an increasingly important role (see R. de Vaux, *AI* 46–48), as a distinguishing mark of the Jews among a foreign people.

Perhaps one of the most significant emphases of the period was on prayer. It is not beyond reason that the gatherings in Ezekiel's house were, to some extent, prayer meetings. The common Hebrew terminology for prayer and praying occurs almost exclusively in the late literature of Israel. With temple sacrifices no longer possible, the only way to communicate with the Lord was through prayer. Both Jeremiah and Ezekiel accentuated the place of the individual in the divine economy, and the most available avenue for him to approach God was through prayer. It may be no accident that the late section of Deutero-Isaiah states, "My house shall be called a house of prayer for all peoples" (Is 56,7). A psalmist expresses the conception of the pious Jew: "Let my prayer be incense before you, the lifting up of my hands an evening sacrifice" (Ps 141,2). Prayer posture is not stressed, at least in the sources. It may be that the exiles faced Jerusalem (see Dn 6,10). There may also have been the uplifted hands, as the above-quoted Psalm passage suggests. Other gestures were prostration, bowing down, and kneeling (see R. de Vaux, *AI* 458f.). No doubt there were both public and individual prayers.

As will be observed below in another connection, a new dimension was added to the religion of the Jews—one that was to prove both challenging and significant in later times. The faith of the nation had been mostly a matter of internal national devotion to the Lord expressed in local institutions and rites. It was thus by and large a domestic affair intended to manifest the community's loyalty to the covenant through sacrifices or other cult observances. But now they were no longer a free nation, and its national cult situation was gone. In place of the stately worship conducted in the Jerusalem temple, houses and open-air devotional assemblies took its place. Doubtless the devotees of the Lord were observed with curiosity, perhaps with genuine interest, by the local Babylonian populace (see Ps 137). That phenomenon did not escape the notice of at least one Jew who recognized the possibilities of appealing to these outsiders and who resolved to turn this to advantage with a definite and positive mission emphasis. He proclaimed the "aloneness" of Yahweh and the nonexistence of other gods. Furthermore, he began to think of Israel as the Lord's witness (Is 43,10.12; 55,4) and as a light to the nations (Is 42,6; 49,6). (See H. H. Rowley, *Israel's Mission to the World* [London: SCM Press, 1939].)

Jewish religious developments in Egypt were not the same as were those in Babylon and thus offer an interesting, if somewhat painful, contrast. As was observed above, it is not certain how the Elephantine community originated, but many of its religious beliefs and practices are known from documents referred to as the Elephantine Letters (see below). These papyri mention "the temple of the God Yahu" or simply "the God Yahu" many times (see A. Cowley, *Aramaic Papyri of the Fifth Century* B.C. [Oxford: Clarendon Press, 1923], nos. 2, 6, 13, 22, 25, 27, 30, 33, 44, 45, 56, and E. G. Kraeling, *The Brooklyn Museum Aramaic Papyri* [New Haven, Conn.: Yale University Press, 1953], nos. 3, 4, 6, 9, 10, 12). The most suggestive papyrus is no. 22

in Cowley (419 B.C.), which is a temple expense account listing contributions from the persons named to the shrine of Yahu divided between Yahu ("Yahweh"), Eshem-bethel, and Anat-bethel. It is clear from the text of the papyrus that we are concerned here with an Aramaic syncretistic phenomenon like that found at Bethel (2 Kgs 17,24–41) and Samaria later, although the garrison at Elephantine always regarded itself as Jewish or Aramaic. It did appeal to the authorities at Jerusalem and to Sanballat for help (Cowley, *Aramaic Papyri* no. 30), but it had no direct relation to the Samaritan cult. It is to be noted that Jedoniah the priest paid the sums indicated to the three deities who were apparently worshiped in the community. Such syncretism is precisely what post-exilic Jewish leaders feared and combated, as will be shown later.

Selected Readings

Albright, W. F., *The Biblical World from Abraham to Ezra*, Chap. 9. New York: Harper & Row, Publishers (Harper Torchbooks), 1963.

Bright, J., *A History of Israel*, Chap. 9. Philadelphia: The Westminster Press, 1959.

Ellis, P., *The Men and Message of the Old Testament*, Chap. 11, pp. 1–4. Collegeville, Minn.: The Liturgical Press, 1963.

Heinisch, P., *History of the Old Testament*, Chap. 42. Collegeville, Minn.: The Liturgical Press, 1952.

Ricciotti, G., *The History of Israel*, 2nd ed., II, 55ff. Milwaukee: Bruce Publishing Company, 1958.

Introductions and notes to the relevant biblical books in *The Jerusalem Bible* (New York: Doubleday & Co., Inc., 1966) should be consulted for details in connection with scriptural references.

II

The Last Years of the Babylonian Empire

The lot of the Jews in Babylon became more favorable with the accession of Evil-merodach (Amel-Marduk or Awel-Marduk of the inscriptions) to the throne (561–560 B.C.). He is said to have released King Jehoiachin from detention, given him a place of honor among the captive kings, and provided him with a regular ration allowance (2 Kgs 25,27–30; Jer 52,31–34). Berossus reports Evil-merodach to have been "an arbitrary and licentious" ruler (Josephus, *Contra Apion*, I, 20) who was soon overthrown. Nothing more is known at present about the successor of Nebuchadnezzar, nor do we have any further information about the former king of Judah. But events were now moving forward at a very rapid pace. Little wonder then that the prophet (Deutero-Isaiah) was enthusiastic a few years later about the prospect for fulfillment of the word of the Lord (Is 55,10–11). Evil-merodach may have endeavored

21

to imitate his father, who at the beginning of his reign showed generosity to the Jewish captives. In any case, he must have incurred the opposition of the officials, for he was overthrown in an uprising after two years by one of the old functionaries of Nebuchadnezzar, Neriglissar (559–556 B.C.). He was one of the "princes of the king of Babylon" (Jer 39,3.13) sent by the great king to make arrangements for handling affairs at Jerusalem after the fall of that city. Despite his age, he must have been a vigorous person because he undertook a difficult and dangerous military campaign into Asia Minor (557–556 B.C.) to deal with Appuašu, the king of Pirindu, who had invaded part of his territory— Hume, the region of eastern Cilicia. At first successful in his venture (see D. J. Wiseman, *Chronicles of Chaldean Kings* [London: British Museum, 1956], pp. 75–77), his enemy finally escaped capture, and Neriglissar appears to have suffered a serious reverse (H. W. F. Saggs, *The Greatness that Was Babylon* [London: Sidgwick and Jackson Ltd., 1962], pp. 144f.). Soon after his return to Babylon he died and was succeeded by his son, Labashi-Marduk (556 B.C.), who was a weakling (the Nabonidus stele refers to him as an ill-behaved adolescent; Pritchard, *ANET* IV 309) and was soon deposed by his own officials. In his place they enthroned Nabonidus, the son of a Babylonian peer and the lady Adda-guppi, who was a devotee, perhaps high priestess, of the moon god Sin at Harran.

Nabonidus (555–539 B.C.) *

Nabonidus was confronted with two problems with which he had to deal with resolution. The more serious of the two concerned religion. The inscriptions are replete with lamentations over the sorry state of the ancient gods (see *ANET* 309ff.; C. J. Gadd, *Anatolian Studies*, VIII [London: The British Institute of Archaelogy at Ankara, 1958], pp. 57ff.) and their consequent resentment against the land. Nabonidus apparently attributed the current economic depression to the neglect of the old religion of the Babylonians. In a dream was revealed to him by Sin—probably under the influence of his mother who was a priestess of the god—the reason for the wrath of the gods, which could be appeased only by the rebuilding of E-ḫul-ḫul, his temple at Harran. It appears that one of the causes of the prevalent attitude toward the gods was the presence of foreign groups in the country,

* See B. Meissner, *Königen Babyloniens und Assyriens* (Leipzig: Verlag Quelle & Meyer, 1926), pp. 276–285.

notably Jews and Medes. Deutero-Isaiah proclaimed the doctrine of the Lord's people as his witnesses (Is 43,10.12; 55,4), even as a light to the nations (Is 42,6; 49,6). Other foreign groups doubtless witnessed for their deities too—all of which made for confusion and uncertainty in the devotion of the native population. Just how soon Nabonidus set about his task is not known. The inscriptions differ about the completion of his restoration at Harran, which could not be undertaken until the withdrawal of the Medes, who controlled the city at the time of his investiture. Upon his accession, Nabonidus relates a dream in which Sin (Marduk in the Babylonian version) appeared to him and urged him to rebuild his sanctuary at Harran, to which the king replied, "It is still in the hands of the Ummanmanda" (= Medes?). But the god hastens to add that they were no longer present and that Cyrus, king of Anshan, would rout them in "the third year coming." (On the complex series of events following the dream vision, see K. Galling, *Studien zur Geschichte Israels im persischen Zeitalter* [Tübingen: Mohr, 1964], pp. 11–17.) However that may be, it is possible that he endeavored to deal with the situation by attempting to innovate— excavations at Ur disclose alterations in the temple of the moon god's wife, which doubtless meant also an updating of the ritual—and he was accused by his enemies of doing precisely that (see "Nabonidus at the Clergy of Babylon" in Pritchard, *ANET* 312–315). The Harran inscription, reported by Gadd (p. 49), affirms that Nabonidus restored the forgotten rites of Sin, Nin-gal, Nusku, and Sadarnunna and renewed and rebuilt the temple of Sin, for which the grateful god granted long life to his mother (she died at the age of 107).

Actually the building enterprises at Harran were incidental, for early in his reign Nabonidus, in connivance with Cyrus, king of Anshan, planned a campaign against the Medes, who apparently abandoned Harran by virtue of the threat to their supremacy—by the rebellion of Cyrus. That left Nabonidus free to occupy himself with the reconstruction of the religious institutions at Harran. Then suddenly he withdrew from his capital, undertook a campaign in Arabia, and established residence at Teima in northwest Arabia. Why did he withdraw from Babylon? The answer to that question is far from clear (see R. P. Dougherty, *Nabonidus and Belshazzar* [New Haven, Conn.: Yale University Press, 1929], Chap. XI, for possible solutions). In the Harran inscription, Nabonidus says that the inhabitants of the great Babylonian cities acted impiously against Nannar and fomented treason, and that famine and pestilence overtook them and threatened them. He remained at Teima ten years while his son

Belshazzar handled affairs at the capital. Babylonian legal documents are extant for each year from the first to the seventeenth year of Nabonidus, indicating that he retained his authority over the kingdom. Moreover, there are other documents such as oaths and tribute receipts attested in the name of the king and Belshazzar, his son (Dougherty, *Nabonidus and Belshazzar*, pp. 96ff.). Finally there is evidence of frequent communication between the capital and Teima at the time.

It would seem, therefore, that the king was sorely troubled by two problems—one religious, the other economic. Both were probably intimately related. Perhaps the nation was brought to this extremity by some instability due to the rapid turnover of governments since the demise of Nebuchadnezzar and the expenditures incurred by the building programs of Neriglissar. Nabonidus would naturally attribute conditions to the slighting of the god to whom he believed he owed his throne. So he moved in two directions to remedy the situation: one to restore the religious institutions at Harran, as noted above; the other to seek economic aid by securing the desert trade routes that converged at Teima, about 700 miles due south of Harran and some 450 miles southwest of Babylon, on the old caravan trail between Babylon and Egypt. (For location, description, and history, see Jaussen and Savignac, *Mission archéologique en Arabie II* [Paris: Geuthner, 1914], pp. 109–165, and H. St. John Philby, *The Land of Midian* [London: Benn, 1957], pp. 72–103, for a modern description.) Spreading out from Teima he established centers in five other places, all of which were on important trade routes or road junctions (Harran Inscriptions of Nabonidus H2, A and B, Col. I, lines 24–25). After the ten years spent in Arabia, Nabonidus' fortune improved, the homeland territory prospered, and when he returned he continued to improve the Harran temple of Sin (Harran 2, A and B, col. III, lines 21, 22). Whereas these inscriptions were literary devices attempting to preserve or justify the actions of a king by reciting his deeds and recounting his concern for the gods and people (A. L. Oppenheim, *Ancient Mesopotamia* [Chicago: University of Chicago Press, 1964], pp. 147ff.), they must not be discounted as of little or no historical import. Historical order cannot always be determined without other evidence, but the main facts can hardly be denied. The tradition of Nabonidus as an eccentric was current in his time, and these inscriptions were set up by the temple scribes to show his real character and to proclaim the truth of his piety for which he was thus duly praised. Dn 4 may actually refer to Nabonidus rather than to Nebuchadnezzar (Gadd, pp. 87–91; Saggs, p. 149).

Why did Nabonidus return from Arabia after "ten years" or when "the appointed time" arrived? It must be remembered that Babylon was itself in no great peril from without during a part of that period. There may have been some agreement between him and Cyrus against the Medes (A. T. Olmstead, *History of the Persian Empire* [Chicago: University of Chicago Press, 1948], pp. 36f.). Evidently Nabonidus was to secure the west, and Cyrus was to take care of the east and Asia Minor. The latter lost no time in solidifying his power over the Persian tribes and then took on Astyges, the cruel Median king, whom he defeated in two battles, and thus became ruler of all the territory between Upper Mesopotamia and Cappadocia. Although there was now a certain conflict of interest between Cyrus and Babylon (in addition to the alliance of Croesus with Babylon, which did not escape the notice of Cyrus, see *Herodotus* 1:77), the time for it to come to a head had not yet arrived. Considering the state of affairs in Babylon, he decided to deal with what appeared to be a greater threat to his claims that arose in Asia Minor in the wake of the suppression of the Medes, that is, the ambitious Croesus of Lydia who lost no time crossing the Halys river and, without opposition, claiming for himself the former Median lands there. Meanwhile Cyrus was on the march through Armenia, Cappadocia, and Cilicia, all of which accepted him as their king but at the same time were permitted to retain their own rulers as vassals. These lands became satrapies of the growing empire of the great king. Cyrus engaged the Lydian forces at Pteria who, defeated by him, retreated to their capital at Sardis. There Croesus hoped to gain time to summon allies under the protection of the winter season. He failed, however, to reckon with the determination of Cyrus, who pressed on, meeting the famous Lydian spear corps just east of the capital. With the help of his general, Harpagus, he pushed them aside and in short order laid siege to Sardis, which fell after a fourteen-day assault (*Her.* 1:84). By 547 B.C. Cyrus was master of Lydia, which he at once made into a satrapy—Saparda. One by one the other Greek states of Asia Minor were taken over until the whole of it fell under the rule of the Persians.

When Cyrus turned his attention toward the east, the Babylonians reacted at once because his move constituted a serious threat to them and made them forget their hostility against Nabonidus, who returned from his Arabian capital at Teima. Not only was the eastern territory of Babylonia imperiled, but raids on what before was a safe region in the south became more frequent. The west was regarded as fairly secure because of an alliance with Egypt. It is not certain whether Cyrus subdued, in one way or another, *all* the outlying provinces of Babylon before he directed his attention to the capital. Berossus, a priest of Belus at Babylon, who lived in the time of Antiochus II (261–246 B.C.), states that Cyrus attacked Babylon after subjecting "all the remainder of the kingdom" (Josephus, *Contra Apion* 1:20). Xenophon reports that Cyrus "in advancing on to Babylon subjugated greater Phrygia and Cappadocia, and brought the Arabs into subjection" (*Cyropaedia* 7:4:16). But the barrel inscription of Cyrus affirms that among others "all the kings of the westland who dwell in tents" brought tribute to him and offered formal submission at Babylon, implying that it was after the conquest. Nabonidus probably came back to defend his country, which it was believed could be done not only by force of arms but also by the favor of the gods. Dougherty (p. 65, note 241) conjectures that Nabonidus may have remained in Arabia until he was forced out by a Persian invasion. Being a man of strong religious inclinations, he set himself to the renewal of the temple of Sin at Harran. In fact, he was so absorbed in his devotion to the gods that he failed to notice the propaganda of Cyrus that was flooding the area. Cyrus proclaimed his leniency to conquered peoples as well as his concern for their religious institutions. It is possible that the "Verse Account of Nabonidus" vilifying the king was composed by the Babylonian priests after his death in order to soften the blow of Persian sovereignty over Babylon. In any event Nabonidus was censured for all sorts of shortcomings, and Cyrus was praised for his attitude and demolition of the religious monuments erected by the former. The barrel inscription of Cyrus (*ANET* 315f.) speaks of the support of Marduk, who directed him to march against Babylon; indeed, the god is said to have been at his side "like a true friend." Babylon, having been thus prepared, fell without a struggle, despite the fact that the gods of the southern cities were brought to the capital to bolster morale. No looting was permitted, and the religious and civil institutions were left undisturbed except that a Persian governor was appointed. The New Year festival saw Cyrus' son Cambyses receiving the investiture of Marduk, thus exercising the authority of kingship by divine right as his father had exercised it by right of conquest. Henceforth, so far as we are concerned, Babylon remained under the jurisdiction of the Persians.

Effect
Upon the Jews

The spirit of the Jews in exile must have soared more than once during the final decade of the neo-Babylonian empire. Those who were most vitally concerned to keep their faith alive in the promises of the Lord not only prayed earnestly, studied the torah, and observed such festivals as they could, but eagerly watched for signs of impending deliverance. As has been said above, very little is known about them until around 550 B.C. and after, when a veritable flash of light streams forth from the great prophet of the exile and from fragments from other prophets. Most scholars today accept the following as coming from the period under consideration: Is 13,1–14, 23, 21,1–10; Jer 50,1–51,58; Is 40–55. There can be no reasonable doubt that the prophets were opposed to Babylon and said so in no uncertain terms. Jeremiah, recognizing the necessity for a Babylonian captivity, predicted better days for his people when they had learned their lesson. His prediction no doubt was remembered by the *golah*, especially by the religious enthusiasts who never could adapt themselves to the life and culture of the metropolis. As we know from other sources, many Jews followed Jeremiah's advice (Jer 29,4–7) and adjusted only too well to their new home. It was now more than half a century since the first contingent of captives was settled in Babylon, and the less scrupulous of them entered wholeheartedly into the task of establishing themselves and their families. Moreover, the second generation, perhaps a third, was assuming new responsibilities and tended to ignore the sterner ideals of the past. They never had the glorious experience of worshiping the Lord in his holy temple at Jerusalem and could hardly comprehend the exhilaration associated with it. Theirs was, in a sense, taught religion, certainly not one fully cognizant or appreciative of the meaning of the praises of Israel.

Oracles
Against Babylon (Jer 50,1–51;58)

The faith of the prophets in the persistence of the Lord's covenant never wavered. They believed that he would carry out his purpose for Israel no matter how remote it might appear to the time for which they spoke. Of none of them is that more true than of Jeremiah. He envisaged a return of the exiles of the old Northern Kingdom (Jer 3,12; 30,4–31,37) and was even more positive about the restoration of Judah (Jer 3,14ff.; 24,6; 29,10.32). But he regarded the Babylonian captivity as inevitable and urged his people to submit to it because it was the will of Yahweh (Jer 20,4–6; 21,4–7; 27,8.17; 28,14; 32,3.4.36; 34,2.3.21; etc.). Speaking in the name of Yahweh, he declared Nebuchadnezzar to be "my servant" (Jer 25,9 [in the Hebrew Bible but not in LXX]; 27,6; 43,10), although, as already observed, he looked forward to the time when the yoke of Babylon would be snapped (Jer 25,12) after seventy years (Jer 29,10) or after three generations, when Babylon would itself become subject to "powerful nations and mighty kings" (Jer 27,7).

Turning, then, to the great oracle against Babylon, and noting its ceremonious language, it does not appear that Jeremiah himself would have uttered such a diatribe in his own time. Coming from a person of his standing in Judah and in the sight of the Babylonian authorities, it would, to say the least, have been quite injudicious. What we have here is a series of pronouncements drawing on Jeremiah's ideas, perhaps isolated expressions of his here and there, brought together by the editor of the book to elaborate the genuine prophecy of Jer 51,59–64. It is interesting that the prophet commanded that this scroll, after being read, was to be sunk into the depths of the Euphrates, perhaps with more than the symbolic purpose attributed to it in verse 64. We shall return to this below. Such prophecies as this, uttered in the days of Jeremiah, might easily have undermined the prophet's advice to the people in exile to accept the discipline of the Lord (Jer 29). Premature hopes could ruin later prospects as well as bring greater hardships to the *golah,* of which he was not oblivious (for a discussion of the date of these oracles see O. Eissfeldt, *The Old Testament: An Introduction* [New York: Harper and Row, Publishers, 1965], pp. 362–64; W. Rudolph, *Jeremiah* [Tübingen: Mohr, 1947], pp. 256f.; J. Bright, *Jeremiah, Anchor Bible,* XXI [New York: Doubleday, 1965], pp. 359–360).

This rather long passage appears to be a collection of oracles from various sources, with some genuinely Jeremianic material and thought, but dating from some time around the middle of the sixth century B.C. The author was a resident of Jerusalem (Jer 50,4–5) but his speeches were meant for the Jews in Babylon (Jer 51,49–57). Communication between the two locations was frequent, as we know from Jer 29, and it is not difficult to imagine a continuity of relationship between the two groups. It is quite difficult, as commentators suggest, to determine the exact limitations of most, if not all, of the sections of the series. For the sake of convenience the divisions of Artur Weiser, with modification (*Das Alte Testament Deutsch 21: Der Prophet Jeremia,* Kap. 25:15–52:34 [Göttingen: Vandenhoeck and Ruprecht, 1955]) are followed. *Oracle* 1 (Jer 50,2–3) sounds like the proclamation of a herald announcing to the nations that Babylon with her gods,

Bel and Merodach (= Marduk), had fallen, destroyed by a nation from the north. It could have arisen in the wake of news that Sardis had fallen under the sledge-hammer blow by Cyrus (547 B.C.) and the prophet's certainty that Babylon would be the next to feel the weight of his power. In fact it may have been that event that shook Nabonidus loose from his desert capital, which, if so, reflects the gravity of the situation. *Oracle* 2 (Jer 50,4–5) speaks of the return of the exiles from Judah and Israel—the second of the two themes running through these sections. It sounds very much like an adaptation of Jeremiah (Jer 3,18; 31,7.31), with emphasis on the covenant theme. *Oracle* 3 (Jer 50,6–7) also reflects the declarations of Jeremiah concerning the nation's guilt and the prophecy of Ezekiel against the shepherds of Israel (Ez 34). It answers the question that must have been asked by children of their elders in Babylon, perhaps elsewhere, too, as to the reason for exile. *Oracle* 4 (Jer 50,8–10) is in prose; here the prophet calls upon the Babylonian exiles to flee from the city and the land of the Chaldeans because of the impending disaster. *Oracle* 5 (Jer 50,11–16) is a highly poetic pronouncement of doom upon Babylon with a summons to the attackers to carry out their desire upon her. Both the haughty, tyrannical nation and her conquerors are addressed. *Oracle* 6 (Jer 50,17–20) states that Israel, hounded by Assyria, then Nebuchadnezzar, would be restored. The king of Babylon would suffer the same fate as did Assyria. Then Israel would again inhabit Carmel and Bashan, Ephraim and Gilead, and both she and Judah, redeemed, would be pardoned of sin. *Oracle* 7 (Jer 50,21–32) begins with a clarion call of the Lord to the opponents of Babylon to the task of her destruction and continues with holy glee at the opening of the arsenal of the Lord as his hosts are ordered to battle. The attack is viewed as already in progress with escapees fleeing to announce in Zion the vindication of Yahweh. There follows a command to the archers to finish the job so that none of the defenders escape. At last the judgment of the Lord has fallen upon the proud city. None such as arrogant and haughty Babylon can escape retribution when the Lord of Hosts has his day. *Oracle* 8 (Jer 50,33–34) has to do with the consolation of Israel and Judah in the wake of Babylon's destruction. Their redeemer has come to their rescue, to plead their case and pronounce sentence upon the oppressor. *Oracle* 9 (Jer 50,35–38) is a sword song calling upon that weapon to execute the punishment of the Lord upon inhabitants, rulers, diviners, soldiers, treasures, and images. The two verses preceding *Oracle* 10, based on Is 13,19–22, simply voice the desolation that will overtake the once teeming city when her enemies are finished. *Oracle* 10 (Jer 50,41–46) identifies the invader as people from the north, cruel, merciless, and skilled horsemen upon whose approach the king of Babylon panicked and remained utterly helpless. It came like a lion into the flock whose shepherd could only look on in dismay. The land of the Chaldeans would be crushed, its little ones dragged away, and the news of their fall would spread like a tremor throughout the earth. *Oracle* 11 (Jer 51,1–19) pictures Yahweh's judgment upon Babylon. The most dire threat thus far is expressed in this series of prophecies. The Lord is portrayed as sending forth against the Chaldeans the destroyer who is to winnow them until the land is empty and desolate. At the same time those in her midst are urged to flee before requital strikes fully, for Babylon has already fallen with none to lament her fate. Once again the vindication of the Lord is to be declared in Zion. In a prose verse (v.11) the agents of Yahweh's condemnation proceedings are the Medes, which here may refer to the Persians, as in Is 13,17 (the Greeks also referred to the Persians as Medes). Moreover, a large part of Cyrus' army was Median. Though possessed of productive land and great riches (see Aeschylus, *Persians,* line 62 in Everyman Edition, and on the defenses of the city *Her.* 1:190,191), Babylon could not survive because "he who made the earth by his strength and established the world by his wisdom" had "uttered his voice." Against him the images of gods were a worthless delusion. His mighty power was brought into play for Jacob and Israel. *Oracle* 12 (Jer 51,20–26) continues the invective hurled in the sword passage above. The five-fold thrust of the sword is against Babylon. Here the poet-prophet describes the use Yahweh made of Babylon to achieve his purpose among the nations. The theme of Jer 50,23—Babylon "the hammer of all the earth"—may here be carried further, although different terms are used in the Hebrew for the hammer figure. In the preceding chapter the word employed means a forge-hammer, here it means the "smasher," the war-club, as may be seen from the nine-fold repetition of the verbal root *šbr* ("to shatter, break in pieces") in depicting its effect in carrying out Yahweh's will. Babylon crushed nations, kingdoms, cavalrymen, charioteers, whole populations, old men, young men, maidens, shepherds, flocks, farmers, governors, and generals. Now, however, tables are turned, and the destroyer is himself to be destroyed. Jeremiah would hardly have spoken like this in his time; he did predict the vindication of Zion in the distant future with the ultimate overthrow of Babylon. As Assyria was once the instrument in the Lord's hand to chastise his people (Is 10:5.15) but suffered eclipse when he was finished with her, so it would be with Babylon (Jer 24). The very severity of the demolition—an everlasting waste—points to a time of massive threat such as did not exist in the prophet's time. *Oracle* 13 (Jer 51,27–33) calls for the mobilization of the nations under the leadership of the Medes (Persians) for the conquest of Babylon. Again utter desolation is prognosticated. The defenders are seen withdrawing from the field of battle into the fortress of the city paralyzed with fear and trepidation. From all angles, messengers arrive with bad news. The city, surrounded, without hope for escape, is like a threshing floor upon which every straw is trodden by the feet of oxen and chopped by the threshing sledge. *Oracle* 14 (Jer 51,34–40) recounts Jerusalem's humiliation at the hands of Nebuchadnezzar. Jerusalem was left in ruins, "the haunt of jackals, a horror and hissing"; now it was Babylon's turn to be made an ash heap and Jerusalem to be vindicated. Verses 41–43 of *Oracle* 15 (Jer 51,41–48) are a kind of joyful lamentation for fallen Babylon. The upholder of Babylon is its god Bel, whom Yahweh will now punish, removing from him what he has swallowed, that is, freeing his captives. Because of the insolence and effrontery of Bel, his images will be punished and his land put to shame, all of which bring rejoicing in heaven and earth. Surely, says the prophet in *Oracle* 16 (Jer 51,49–58), Babylon must pay for "the slain of Israel," reiterating what he said in Jer 51,24–35. He bids her recall Jerusalem and what she did to her. No tower of Babel can save her from the onslaught of the Lord. Already the speaker hears the noise of battle, the furious beating of the waves of destruction, and he visualizes the faltering movements of the fear-intoxicated garrison. Confusion and panic have seized her leaders and it is well, for everlasting sleep will envelop them. The mighty wall will be leveled, the high gates consumed by fire, and thus it is that proud nations labor for nothing and people expend their energy for that which does not abide.

What a series of devastating oracles! The sentiment expressed may have been influenced by the bloody visions of Nahum describing the siege and downfall of Nineveh in 612 B.C. But the prophet was in error when he predicted the utter ruin and desolation of Babylon. It was not destroyed by Cyrus; rather it was carefully spared, its buildings and institutions and temples preserved, even magnified and strengthened. Nevertheless he took advantage of the far-reaching and momentous political developments to reassert the hope expressed by Jeremiah because he believed that the time was at hand, the seventy years two-thirds passed, and that the signs of the times pointed to the beginning of the anticipated movement of Yahweh to deliver his people. There must have been a tremendous outburst of expectation in the wake of the conflict that raged first between Cyrus and Astyges, followed by the former's victory over the Medes, Lydians, and Ionian Greeks. The prophet was convinced that in accordance with the righteousness of the Lord and in view of his covenant promises, justice and right would ultimately prevail. Just as Judah could not sin with impunity, Babylon with its greater sin of enslavement, ruthless destruction of peoples and nations, and unmitigated idolatry could not escape unscathed. If these oracles come from Judah, as intimated above, the Babylonian conquests had failed to extinguish the flame of religious zeal even amid all the wanton devastation. Hope for restoration burned just as brightly at home as it did among the zealots of the *golah*.

Other Oracles
Against Babylon (Is 13,1–14,23; 21,1–10)

Three passages from the book of Isaiah are attributed to the period under consideration. Each is a separately constructed piece centering on the coming downfall of Babylon and its king. In both Isaiah and Jeremiah oracles against Babylon stand in a collection of prophecies against foreign nations. Interestingly enough there is no such oracle among the similar collection in the book of Ezekiel, which at least suggests that those dealing with Babylon are later than the time of Ezekiel. A comparison between those in Isaiah and Jeremiah shows much similarity in content and especially in attitude. A rather striking feature is the fact that those in Jeremiah—as just noted—incorporate a genuine prophecy of his; the first two in Isaiah are constructed on the same pattern. Is 14,24–27 is directed against Assyria and in all probability is Isaian. Most scholars agree that the anti-Babylonian oracles in Isaiah date from the middle of the sixth century B.C., at the same time as those in Jeremiah (see Eissfeldt, pp. 319–20, 321f.; J. Fischer, *Das Buch Isaias: Die Heilige Schrift des Alten Testamentes*, Bd. VII, Teil 1 [Bonn: Hanstein, 1937], pp. 110–22, 146–52; E. J. Kissane, *The Book of Isaiah*, Vol. 1 [Dublin: Browne and Nolan, 1941], 153–56—Kissane thinks a date later than Isaiah hinges on rather slender evidence, pp. 227ff. On the date of the third passage in Isaiah Kissane agrees with the others).

The prophetic vision recorded in Is 13 falls naturally into three parts. First (vv. 1–5) the prophet hears the summons of the Lord to raise the standard of war, mobilize his warriors (i.e., the Medes as we learn from v. 17), and direct them to "the gates of the nobility" of the city. The noise of the heralds delivering the summons rings ever louder in his ears, followed by the clatter of arms and the reverberation of marching feet until it becomes a tumultuous multitude rushing into the fray from every point of the compass. From a faraway land come the hosts of the Lord "to devastate the whole earth." Truly this is "the day of the Lord" around which the second part of the vision revolves (vv. 6–16). The eschatological emphasis of the present text is unmistakable. It will be a day of such cataclysmic consequences that the hearts of people will grow faint, seized by pangs of terror, aghast with horror. Even forces of nature are convulsed by the mighty movements of the Lord's army. The effect of the terrible day of the Lord extends beyond the scope contemplated in other portions of the prophecy. Not only will tyrants be humbled, but mankind will become rarer than Ophir gold. Instead of Babylon alone feeling the power of Yahweh's wrath, the world will have its wickedness punished. More horrible than the visitation of death will be the sight of their babes dashed to bits, their ancestral homes wiped out, and their wives violated (see also Ps 137,9). Whatever may be one's view of the sweeping cruelty of such a conception, it must be remembered that the imagery is poetic and is meant to express conviction that the consequences of sin fall upon innocent and helpless people. From a disquisition on the day of the Lord, the prophet returns to the main theme of his sermon (vv. 17–22), that is, the overthrow of Babylon at the hands of the Medes. Unless "Medes" here stands for Persians, the oracle could not have been delivered after about 550 B.C. when Cyrus outwitted Astyges, the Median king, whose army then joined his forces. The opponents of Babylon are pictured as a ruthless people destroying their enemies without pity, and they could not be bought off with silver and gold. Verse 19, with its reference to the overthrow of Sodom and Gomorrah, reminds us of Jer 50,40. So complete will be the devastation of Babylon that she will remain without inhabitants forever. Not even a nomadic Arab will set up his tent there, nor will shepherds pasture their flocks amid its ruins. Its location will be the habitat of jackals, ostriches, hyenas, and wolves, and satyrs will perform their nocturnal dances there. Once more it must be emphasized that although Babylon was the victim of Cyrus in 539 B.C., such desolation as the prophet predicted did not come to pass at the time. Recall what was said about the pattern of Nahum, which may have been in the writer's mind.

Is 14 (vv. 1–23), whose primary theme is a taunt song on or satire

against the king of Babylon, is introduced by a word of consolation
for Israel (vv. 1–2). It may be regarded either as a conclusion to the
preceding oracle or a kind of preface to the one that follows. The
word with which it begins (ky = "for" or "but") would appear to connect it with the foregoing. Because of what has been done to Israel,
the Lord will have compassion upon her and choose (elect) her again
—a favorite expression of Deutero-Isaiah—and bring her once more to
the land that was her own. But there is added the much broader view,
stressed in the Servant Songs, of the stranger (ger) who will join the
congregation of Israel, indeed, become a member of "the household
of Jacob." Not only will outsiders associate themselves with the chosen
people as menservants and maidservants, but they will be given a place
in the land. Those who had once been captives of oppression in a faraway land will turn the tables on their captors and make them captives
of freedom in a land and among a people of their own choice. Verses
3–4a then serve as an introduction to the taunt song. In the day of
their deliverance from servitude, the liberated people will take up the
following *mashal* (= proverb, then satire), the writer's vision of the
rest spreading over the earth after the turmoil and confusion of the
final clash of arms against Babylon have settled down. Verses 4b–8
are filled with striking figures of speech celebrating the stillness that
has engulfed the land. The only voices heard are the songs of the
released, the chants of the cypresses, and the gentle overtures played
by the winds wafting through the cedars of Lebanon. Then begins
the actual taunt of the king of Babylon (vv. 9–21), in which his entry
into Sheol forms the main theme. The underworld rejoices at his coming, for there a new set of rules apply. As the other kings who had
preceded him remark, now he too has become as weak and powerless
as they are. Like the once mighty Lucifer (Day Star)—which at dawn
rose above other stars but vanished from sight with the rising sun (a
reminiscence of the Baal-Mot cycle, now known from Ras Shamra)—
who fell from heaven, the king of Babylon has been brought to the
lowest depths, to Sheol. The sensation of his earthly activities had
reached the underworld, and the residents of Sheol are portrayed as
gathering around him in curiosity—"Can this be the man who shook
the earth and made kingdoms quake?"—amazed that he had no tomb
and was rolled down to Sheol like a discarded stone. They conceived
of themselves as having come to Sheol honorably, but not so the king
of Babylon: He came like a loathsome abortion, clothed in the garb of
sword-slain men. Hence he will not be permitted to join the honorable
dead in Sheol, where it is elsewhere observed that there is not even a

distinction between man and beast (Eccl 3,17f.). This must be regarded as Oriental hyperbole, but it does reflect the depth of feeling
against the king and the nation responsible for the ravaging of Judah
and the exile of her people, in addition to the sorry spectacle of those
who remained in the land. If these passages come from a prophet in
Babylon, they could have been influenced by the local feeling of the
natives whose priests so violently denounced Nabonidus for the par-
tiality he showed toward the moon god Sin of Harran to the neglect
of the great god Marduk and his priests. The prose conclusion (vv.
22–23) serves as a summary inasmuch as it is directed against Babylon
itself with all its inhabitants. The fate of the people and its site is
related in the most sweeping terms: Every semblance of the population will be cut off, and the very land will revert to marshes.

The impassioned language of these prophecies makes it probable
that they originated in the exilic community at a time when Babylon
was in real danger of collapse. The author recognized that before there
could be freedom for the captives, the tyrant nation and its king would
have to be eliminated. With a kind of holy glee, the prophet rejoiced
in the course of events because he saw therein the work of the mighty
hand of God. So he announced the imminent fall of the captors, which
would be followed by the escape or release of the Jews. His predictions
were meant for the ears of his fellows and may have been circulated
among them orally in the hope of alerting them to maintain their faith
in Yahweh who had not forgotten them; he was about to act on their
behalf as was clear from the turn of events.

Preparation
for Deliverance (Is 40–55)

The relatively restrained prophecies of Is 40–55 are products of one
of the greatest minds produced by Israel. He ranks with the foremost
writers, thinkers, and religious leaders of all time. It is not difficult to
see in his writings seeds that sprouted later and produced fruits that
have remained ever since. Some of these will be considered in later dis-
cussions and observations. Babylon had not yet fallen, but if the Cyrus
poems are authentic and the name of the Persian king has not been
interpolated, Cyrus had not just begun the march to world hegemony.
The whole tenor of the oracles of Deutero-Isaiah is that deliverance
from exile was imminent (Is 46,12–13), that Cyrus was knocking at
the gates of the city. The prophet was inspired by the approach of the

Persian with his armies, whom he saw as Yahweh's servant called to open the way for the deliverance of the *golah*. He believed that the time for deliverance had arrived and that the conjunction of historical events was brought about by the Lord, and hence he sought to prepare the people for Cyrus' advent. It may be that our author was influenced somewhat in the timing of his message by the Cyrus propaganda disseminated by the priests of Babylon (S. Smith, *Isaiah Chapters XL-LV: Literary Criticism and History* [London: The British Academy, 1944], note 126, pp. 108f.), but for an entirely different reason. He was operating from a different theological standpoint because he hoped not merely to win the favor of the conqueror but much more to stress the fulfillment of the Lord's promise to redeem his people and demonstrate that he was the motivating force behind Cyrus.

These addresses were directed primarily to the members of the Jewish community. They were not meant for public consumption or to impress the Persians (but see Morton Smith, "II Isaiah and the Persians," *JAOS* LXXXIII [1963], 415–421). Ushered into the heavenly council by vision, the prophet heard the Lord say, "Comfort, comfort *my* people" (Is 40,1). The allotted time of servitude was over; the debt was paid. Each messenger had a specific word to proclaim. The first one was to "speak to the heart of Jerusalem" (Is 40,2). The second was to call out that in the wilderness of hopelessness the way of the Lord was to be cleared, the mountains of difficulty brought low, and the valleys of despair lifted up. In the wake of the removal of those obstacles "the glory of the Lord" would be disclosed for all flesh to see. A third messenger was to proclaim the certainty and eternity of "the Word of our God" (Is 40,8). Other things would pass away; not so the Word of God. God was not inactive or unconcerned. The everlasting God, the Creator of the ends of the earth, was neither faint nor weary (Is 40,28). That he might appear hidden to the victims of the exile was a misconstruction of the whole situation (Is 40,27). Their condition was not being overlooked by the Lord. Compared to those around them and in their sight, Jacob might appear to be a mere worm, Israel a maggot (Is 41,14) but in God's sight his servant. Therefore the holy One of Israel would be their redeemer. He had not and would not forsake his people (Is 41,17). As the earlier prophets said, Israel forsook him (Jer 15,6); now he is pursuing them and in a short time they will be released from captivity, a sure sign that they have not been abandoned. He has long been silent, restrained (Is 42,14); yet Israel is still his, precious in his eyes (Is 43,4), his chosen people (Is 43,20). Beside him the gods of Babylon are nonexistent. They had to be borne around the city in religious processions. Not so Yahweh. He bears, carries, and saves his people (Is 46,4). They were to look to him alone, for were they not the descendants of Abraham and Sarah whom he called, chose, and blessed (Is 51,1–2)? Zion had been denominated by "my people" (Is 51:16), and salvation was now drawing near; it had gone forth and was already on its way (Is 51,5). Hence, like the exhortations of the earlier spokesmen of the Lord (a and b above), Deutero-Isaiah urges the captives to get out of Babylon, to flee from the Chaldeans (Is 48,20), for "the Lord has redeemed Jacob, his servant" (Is 48,20). (Jacob is a synonym of the conception of Israel.)

That the prophet was not an opportunist or simply a contemporary speaker or writer is shown in the tremendous advance in the articulation of Israel's philosophy of history and theology. It was emphasized above that the Jews in exile busied themselves with the study of the torah, a term that occurs only five times in Is 40–55. The word covenant is found only three times, and qualities associated with it are equally sparse—for example, *ḥesed* (= "lovingkindness," "loyalty," "devotion") occurs only four times, *'emeth* ("faithfulness," "sincerity") three times, and the corresponding verb (*'aman*), a favorite of Isaiah, only five times. Statutes and commandments are words not found at all here, although they are a significant part of the vocabulary of the pre-exilic prophets. The word for observe (*shamar*) appears only once, although the word for "hear," "hearken to" (*shama'*) occurs thirty-two times. The root for "judge," "judgments" (*shaphat, mishpat*) shows up only fourteen times. The name of Moses is wanting throughout. So are the words for "prophet" (*nabi'*) and "priest" (*kohen*), and the common word for "worship" (*'abodah*). The temple is mentioned only once (Is 44,28). On the other hand, the deuteronomic "name theology" persists; thirteen times *name*, referring to the Lord, is used. Nevertheless, just because the old language is for the most part missing, it does not mean an entirely new relationship is contemplated. Conditions of the moment required a different emphasis. Unless "the former things" and "the new things" can be more definitely identified, as North has done ("The 'Former Things' and the 'New Things' in Deutero-Isaiah," in *Studies in Old Testament Prophecy,* H. H. Rowley, ed. [Edinburgh: T. & T. Clark, 1950], pp. 111–26), we may have here a clue to the prophet's approach. Granting North's thesis, there is the clear implication that new times and circumstances require new procedures. Basic patterns such as the Lord's concern for his people and his determination to deal with them in still more wonderful ways are not upset or repudiated.

The leading theme is not castigation for failure to conform to the torah; it is rather mercy or pity (*rāḥam*), a term used no less than eight times. Out of pity for the condition of the exiles the Lord would redeem (*ga'al*) them (fourteen times) because they are his chosen people (three times; the root—*baḥar*—about twelve times). But along with the redemption of the Lord a broader role for the redeemed is emphasized. Yahweh is regarded as more than simply the God of Israel. He is the God of the world and the universe, and besides him there is no other god (Is 45,14.18). He is the Creator of heaven and earth. Bel and Nebo, gods of Babylon and Borsippa respectively, have no existence in fact; they are but idols riding on beasts and cattle (Is 46,1–2) and the product of the hands of men (Is 46,6–7) with only the intelligence and power men consign to them. They have no knowledge of the purpose or direction of history. Only Yahweh has the knowledge of the end and the beginning of things and is cognizant of things not yet done (Is 46,10). When he exerts himself to deliver his people, disaster will fall upon boastful Babylon that no amount of spells and enchantments will be able to prevent (Is 47,10–12). What then about stargazers and fortunetellers? On the one hand they are unable to save people "from the power of the flame" and on the other can offer no warmth to those who sit before the fire (Is 47,13–14). Yahweh alone is the living God who announces new and hidden things because he is the all-knowing one (Is 48,6). He is the first and the last, who laid the foundations of the earth (Is 48,12), and who has done nothing in secret. The evidence of his handiwork shouts to all men everywhere.

Deliverance for Israel is his doing, not that of any man or king. Cyrus is the agent of Yahweh, his shepherd, who will do only his will. When he issues the order for Jerusalem to be rebuilt and for the temple's foundations to be laid, he is but responding to Yahweh's prompting. To this end Cyrus is referred to as "his anointed one," "whose hand he has grasped" to level nations, to ungird the loins of kings, and to open the gates before him (Is 44,28–45,1). Cyrus is the one from the east who is greeted by victory after victory and makes kings bow before him, not by his own power but by that of the Lord (Is 41,2f.; 41,25). He has given Cyrus victory and started him on his way, and he has directed him to build [his] city and set [his] exiles free (Is 45:13). He has been summoned "from a faraway land" to execute Yahweh's purpose (Is 46,11), to perform his will (Is 48,14). "I, I myself spoke, indeed I called him, I inspired him to come and succeed in his way" (Is 48,15). Here we see another instance in Israel's history where Yahweh reaches out beyond his people to call to service one to fulfill his purpose (see Jer 25,9); and the whole world, in effect, becomes the arena of his activity for the sake of his people. As the universal God, he uses nations and peoples to fulfill his designs.

Along with this wider outlook, possibly motivated by such exalted conceptions as those voiced in Is 19,23–25 and Mi 7,11–12, arose a new role for Israel—that of being the Lord's servant. This is not the place to treat the stupendous concept of the suffering servant (see C. R. North, *The Suffering Servant in Deutero-Isaiah,* 2nd ed. [New York: Oxford University Press, 1956]). Suffice it to say that no theory is wholly satisfactory. The prophet may have had in view some person or persons, or even Israel itself, in exile upon whom he looked as the one or ones to carry out the Lord's specific purpose in the situation at the moment. Then, as such, the servant idea was uppermost in his mind, and the concept thus gained validity far beyond his purview—especially in Christ and his body, the Church. It is not accidental that the terms "servant" and "called" are the most characteristic words in the Deutero-Isaiah. The former occurs 19 times; the latter about 31 times. The function of the servant is as complex and varied as is the servant himself. It is to bring forth justice (*mishpat*) (Is 42,1.3), "to raise up the tribes of Jacob and to bring back the remnants of Israel" (Is 49,5–6), to take upon himself vicariously the afflictions of others (Is 53,4ff.), and thereby to justify many (Is 53,11). The lot of the servants of the Lord is to withstand all weapons directed against them and to confound every argument raised to discomfit them (Is 54,17). Most significantly of all, the servants are to be a testimony to the nations. No matter to whom the oracle in Is 42,6–7 refers, its far-reaching import is unmistakable—the Lord has made him "a covenant to people, a light to nations (see also Is 49,6; 51,4; the references to light may have been a deliberately chosen concept here) to open the eyes of the blind, to bring out prisoners from detention, from prison those who sit in darkness." If the servant here is Cyrus, his mission is not only to Jews in exile in Babylon but also to other peoples similarly in bondage there. Thus Yahweh's program of liberation extends to peoples and nations. That is the burden of such further passages as Is 43,9–10; 49,6; 52,15; 54,2–3; 55,4–5. There was a hint above that some of the exiles may have conceived of the idea of propagandizing their faith in the communities where they resided, despite the general reluctance voiced in Ps 137,1–6. The prophet emphasizes witnessing as may be seen from the servant's function as "a light to the nations." In the first place Israel is a witness to Yahweh, besides whom there is no other god. What he has done for his people in the past and what he is about to do now is testimony to that. No other nation has experienced what Israel has (Is 43,9–13; 44,8). The servant has been made by the Lord "a witness to the peoples, a leader and commander (one who gives direction) to peoples," summoning through them nations unknown as yet, and nations unaware of them will rush to them because of the Lord their God, the Holy One of Israel who has glorified them (Is 55,4–5). He is Yahweh's messenger (Is 42,19; 44,26) sent to do his will, announced and performed at his direction. The Lord's deliverance will be "an everlasting sign that shall not be cut off" (Is 55,13d).

What was about to transpire was the Lord's doing. To use a passage from Jn 1,3, "without him nothing was done that was done." It was he who called all generations from the beginning (Is 41,4), who caused Abraham to respond to his voice (Is 41,9; 51,2) so that Israel is under the divine vocation (Is 48,12; 45,3–4). The servant, too, was directly called by Yahweh (Is 42,6; 49,1); so was forsaken Israel (Is 54:6). What is even more remarkable, the deliverer who was to overthrow Babylon was ordained by the Lord (Is 41,2.25; 46,11; 48,15). Here is a philosophy of history of tremendous importance not only for the prophet's day but for the future. In the Lord's sight the vaunted nations were but "a drop from a bucket," "dust on the scales," "as nothing before him," "reckoned as less than nothing by him" (Is 40,15–17). They were making his creation into a chaos, whereas he had created it for a place of habitation (Is 45,18). What he had done before when he slashed Rahab to bits, when he dried up the sea and cut off the mighty waters to make a path for the redeemed to pass over (Is 51,9), he would do again. This time in the wilderness he would make a way by which his people could return to their land (Is 51,11). To this task he called his hitherto enslaved servants under the leadership of Cyrus, his anointed one. The apparent conspiracy of the nations was Yahweh's way of achieving his long-run purpose for Israel, which no power on earth could thwart.

The Chronicler, the great theologian of the post-exilic period, picked up some of the themes of Deutero-Isaiah. The latter had much to say about the chosen of the Lord, as noted above. That, too, was a favorite view of the Chronicler, which does not derive wholly from his sources. The two terms, Israel and Jacob, occur very widely in Deutero-Isaiah (forty-two for the former and twenty-two for the latter) in contrast to Judah, which appears only three times. I have elsewhere dealt with this idea (*Anchor Bible 12: I Chronicles* [New York: Doubleday & Co., Inc., 1965], LXXIV) in the work of the Chronicler. Finally there is the prophet's impression of Cyrus as in effect taking up the work assigned to David. He is spoken of as the Lord's anointed (Is 45,1; cf. Sydney Smith, p. 74), as David was, as a shepherd for his people (Is 44,28), the builder of Jerusalem, and the restorer of the temple (see 2 Sm 7 and 1 Chr 17).

Selected Readings

Albright, W. F., *The Biblical World from Abraham to Ezra,* Chap. IX. New York: Harper & Row, Publishers (Harper Torchbooks), 1963.

Bright, J., *A History of Israel,* Chap. IX. Philadelphia: The Westminster Press, 1959.

Ellis, P. ,*The Men and Message of the Old Testament,* Chap. XI, pp. 5–6. Collegeville, Minn.: The Liturgical Press, 1952.

Forster, W., *From the Exile to Christ.* Philadelphia: The Westminster Press, 1964.

Olmstead, A. T., *History of the Persian Empire,* Chaps. III–IV. Chicago: University of Chicago Press, 1948.

Snaith, N. H., *The Jews from Cyrus to Herod,* Chap. I. Wallington, Surrey: The Religious Press, Ltd., 1949.

Cyrus' Ascendancy to Power

The solid tradition of the Scriptures affirms that Cyrus II was the liberator of the Jews who had been taken captive to Babylon by Nebuchadnezzar II. There is not the slightest doubt of the basic historicity of the royal Persian rescript transmitted in Ezr 1,2–4 and repeated in 2 Chr 36,23. Cyrus' ascendancy to power heralded a new day in the ancient world, and a new outlook. Even his conquests were conducted differently and his treatment of subject peoples the opposite of that which characterized the practices of the great kings of Mesopotamia from the time of Tiglath-pileser III (744–727 B.C.) to Nebuchadnezzar II (604–562 B.C.). Hence it is necessary here to set forth as much as we know about the first important Persian king as a background against which the movement of the Jews must be understood. We have attempted to sketch their hopes and dreams exhibited in contemporary exilic literature so far as they can be determined. The materialization of the prophecies of Jeremiah, Ezekiel, Deutero-Isaiah, and other unnamed prophets was, they believed, due to the intervention of their God Yahweh, who was guiding history toward the achievement of his purposes and plans. It is incumbent upon us to see, so far as possible, the historical movements in which their destiny was wrought. The world of the return and restoration was a Persian world.

Cyrus
and His Conquests (559–529 B.C.)

The name of Cyrus occurs more frequently in the Bible than that of any other of the Persian kings (more than a score of times). What we know of the external events connected with his exploits can be related in short order. Our information comes from inscriptions, letters, business documents, the work of Greek historians such as Herodotus, Xenophon, Diodorus Siculus, Ctesias, and Arrian, and the Bible. In the few fragments of inscriptions attributed to the king himself, he refers to himself as the Achaemenian, which means that he claims descent from Achaemenes, who seems to have been the leader of the forces from Parsuash and Anshan who fought against the allies of Sennacherib at Halulina in 681 B.C. He was the son of Cambyses I, king of Anshan and Mandane, the daughter of Astyages, king of Media. Thus the blood of two nations coursed through his veins. (On his education see Xenophon, *Cyropaedia, I,* although it must be remembered that this is a type of historical novel and, while based on history, is fictionalized and often patterned on Greek models; cf. also *Her.* 1.108–130.) He succeeded his father on the throne of Anshan somewhere around 559 B.C.

The first solid historical fact about Cyrus is that he rebelled against Astyages of Media, who sought to deal with him by sending his general Harpagus against him. The latter, according to legend, had been grossly ill-treated by the Median king, who had slain his son. Perhaps because of that, Harpagus, instead of battling the rebel, defected to him. Apparently most of those under him followed suit. Astyages then led out a second force, which upon reaching the capital of Cyrus mutinied, arrested their king, and delivered him to Cyrus. The misfortune of Astyages thus laid open the whole country to Cyrus, who lost no time in capitalizing on his opportunity. In about 550 B.C. the capital of Ecbatana was taken and its treasures transported to Anshan. The country of the Medes probably was not too greatly distressed by the event because of the attitude of the army and because they knew and understood the Persians over whom they had ruled up to Cyrus' victory. In line with Persian principles few changes appear to have been made. Media became a satrapy of Persia, but its capital city remained a favored royal city. As was observed in the discussion of the kingship of Nabonidus, Cyrus may have sought and achieved an alliance with the Babylonian king, who was anxious to get the Medes out of Harran. Nabonidus' early years were devoted to a campaign to the west, possibly undertaken as his part of the deal. In any event, Cyrus by one fell stroke was now the ruler of a vast territory stretching from the eastern shores of the Persian Gulf to the Halys river in Asia Minor and east of the Tigris river. He had but two rivals: Croesus of Lydia and Nabonidus of Babylon. Aware of the latter's predilections toward religious and antiquarian interests, Cyrus resolved to take on the former first. Croesus ruled over the area extending from the Halys in the east to the Aegean sea in the west. When the news of Cyrus' victory reached him, he resolved to take what steps he could to secure his position. He made alliances with Amasis of Egypt and Nabonidus of Babylon and received some pledge of support from Sparta. The new entente cordiale freed Cyrus from any further obligation to Babylon, but he would deal first with Croesus, unless Nabonidus would somehow interfere—which he did not.

Cyrus was a man with purpose, rugged, and filled with determination. He was a restless person who had little patience with the ordinary affairs of state, which he usually committed to others while maintaining a watchful eye for any serious infraction of his plans or desires. So he would not be content with his newly won laurels. Besides, he would not give his opponents time to consolidate their position. Hence he set out at once for the northern borders of his empire to settle accounts with the fabled Lydian king. Though his march through his own territory entailed incredible difficulties—it would have been far easier to travel by the broad plains of northern Mesopotamia, but that might have invited a conflict with the Babylonian forces for which he was not ready—he resolved not to provoke his other rival. Meanwhile Croesus did not passively await the arrival of the enemy. He mustered all the available forces of his kingdom and then moved east across the Halys river into Cappadocia, which he apparently subdued. Cyrus, on his way to the west, entered Asia Minor through the Cilician Gates, where the people of Cilicia accepted his hegemony of their own accord, as did Armenia, which became a satrapy. For the latter it was really not much of a change because it involved only the exchange of the Median master for a Persian. Cappadocia, too, was given satrapal status. The relative ease with which Cyrus moved forward was in all probability due not so much to his military power and prowess—though that was impressive indeed—as to the consideration shown toward peoples whose territoroy he added to his empire. Native kings were retained in nearly all instances, and local pride and prejudices were played upon to foster loyalty and devotion to his empire. The armies of Croesus and Cyrus joined in a battle "in the district of Pteria" (*Her.* 1:76–77) that was indecisive, although the forces of the former were disbanded, and Croesus returned to Sardis. He was certain that Cyrus would not give up the struggle but was equally confident that the Persians would not strike immediately because of the impending winter during which he hoped to reorganize his troops and summon his allies, Nabonidus, Amasis, and the Greeks. Croesus, however, misjudged the determination of Cyrus, who, divining the plan of his enemy, allowed him no time to gather reinforcements. Before Croesus could act, Cyrus appeared with his army on the plain just east of the Lydian capital, at the juncture of the Hyllus and Hermus rivers (*Her.* 1:80) where the forces of Croesus were no match for the military tactics of Cyrus and his Median general, Harpagus. The remnants of Croesus' cavalry soon withdrew to the protection of the fortified city that Cyrus immediately laid under siege (*Her.* 1:80,81,84). Within the remarkably short time of a fortnight, the city was reduced and its king, who attempted to immolate himself, removed. Lydia was made into a Persian satrapy. Next Cyrus offered the olive branch to the Greek states formerly under Croesus, but all except Miletus refused. Hence they had to be induced by other methods to become subjects of Persia, mostly by Harpagus. The contempt of Cyrus for the Greek states was shown by his almost immediate withdrawal to Ecbatana and the placing into the hands of subordinates the task of subduing them. No sooner was he out of sight than Pactyas, who was charged with bringing the treasures of Croesus to Persia, revolted. With the gold in his charge, he procured mercenaries and seriously threatened Tabalus, the satrap left in command by the king. Relief was swiftly dispatched under Mazares, who relieved the satrap and once more brought the Lydian under subjection, and Harpagus continued his campaign against the recalcitrant Greeks.

The conquest of Lydia and the Ionian states was not the consummation of the task Cyrus had set for himself. Two major nations remained in the west—Babylon and Egypt. Since neither had responded to the request of Croesus, there seemed to be no immediate danger from their quarters, and Cyrus turned eastward—possibly because of the pressure from the Bactrians and Sacae or because he wanted to add the wild Iranian regions to his growing empire while waiting for other forces to assist him in the west. So much may be gathered from the stories of famine from Babylon and the defection of Gobryas, the Babylonian governor of Elam, with its capital at Susa. That was in 546 B.C. On his way to imperial expansion to the east, Cyrus added Hyrcania and Parthia, which he made into a satrapy over which its former king and a relative of his by the name of Hystaspes was made satrap. Then he continued on his journey eastward to the Oxus river, which he followed and made subject all the peoples between it and the Jaxartes and beyond. Here he introduced Persian methods of irrigation and cultivation. Continuing, he subjected the Bactrians and the fierce Sacae in the northwest corner of India—the land beyond the mountains.

Cyrus did more than extend his empire and secure its eastern and northern boundaries. He gained prestige, wealth, and manpower for his planned exploits in the west. (On the make-up of the Persian army see E. Meyer, *Geschichte des Altertums,* IV, 1, "Das Perserreich und die Griechen bis zum Vorabend des peloponnesischen Krieges," 5th ed. [Darmstadt: Wissenschaftliche Buchgemeinschaft, 1954], pp. 63–73). As we saw in the preceding chapter, the way was already being prepared for his advent by skillful propaganda spread by the priests of Bel and Marduk and certain of the Jewish prophetic circles. In the autumn of 540–539 B.C., the Persian army approached the Babylonian territory in Mesopotamia. Nabonidus, who had returned from his desert capital in a last minute effort to stave off the inevitable, followed his stubborn but ill-advised ideas of bringing the local city gods to Babylon both for their protection and for the salvation of his kingdom. A battle between the two armies took place on the Tigris river, and Nabonidus' forces were defeated. In October, 539 B.C. another battle was fought at Opir, where Belshazzar was again worsted and the residents burned. That harsh treatment evidently cast a scare over the whole of Babylon, and resistance faltered. A few days later Sippar fell without a struggle. By the thirteenth of October, Gobryas, Cyrus' general, entered Babylon without force. Nabonidus was later taken prisoner and Belshazzar was slain. What became of Nabonidus is not stated in the extant records. Berossos reports that he was humanely treated by Cyrus, who exiled him from Babylon to Carmania where he spent the remainder of his life (Josephus, *Against Apion,* 1:20). As was the custom of Cyrus, the city was not plundered, and business was permitted to go on as usual. Two weeks later the great king himself entered Babylon amid the plaudits of the populace, being received as a veritable messiah. Gobryas was made governor, but most of the lesser officials were allowed to retain their posts. Henceforth Cyrus refers to himself as "Cyrus, king of the world, the great king, the powerful king, king of Babylon, king of Sumer and Akkad, king of the four quarters (of the earth), son of Cambyses, the great king, king of the city Anshan, grandson of Cyrus, the great king, king of the city Anshan; great-grandson of Teispes, the great king, king of the city Anshan; eternal seed of royalty, whose rule Bel and Nabu love, in whose kingship they heartily rejoice" (Cyrus Cylinder, lines 20–22).

Organization
of Cyrus

Along with Pasargadae, Ecbatana, and Susa, Babylon was regarded as a royal city. Cyrus speaks of taking up "lordly residence in the royal palace" (Cyrus Cylinder, line 23); of guarding the city against all enemies; of caring for the needs of the people; of receiving tribute there from foreign princes and states; and of bringing back all the inhabitants of the city who fled either because of Nabonidus or because of the threatened disaster expected in the wake of the Persian conquest. For purposes of administration, the Persian empire was divided into twenty satrapies modeled somewhat after the Assyrian provincial system (see O. Leuze, *Die Satrapieneinteilung in Syrien und im Zweistromlande von 520–320* [Halle: Niemeyer, 1935], pp. 4–17). Over each was a satrap (Xšaçapavan = "kingdom protecting" or "protector"). Full organization was possibly accomplished only later, but certainly the beginnings must have taken place under Cyrus (Xenophon, *Cyropaedia* 8:6:1–15) as may be seen from his handling of the situation at Sardis, in Iran, and in Babylonia. The local satrap usually acted for the king and in his name and so had a full complement of officials—a virtual miniature court. But there were other royal officials who kept a constant check on affairs and reported directly to Cyrus. There were the king's secretary, always with each satrap (*Her.* 3:128), the financial secretary or treasurer, the military attaché (Xenophon, *Cyropaedia* 8:6:3), and the king's messenger, the king's eye (Xenophon, *ibid.,* 8:6:16), who could arrive any time for the annual inspection. No doubt his visit was awaited with fear and trembling. Such were the checks and balances whereby Cyrus kept the far-flung provinces of his empire under surveillance and control.

So far as the life of subject peoples is concerned, it went on much as always. From the archives of such cities as Susa, Babylon, and Erech have come a host of tablets bearing all kinds of contracts dating from Persian and pre-Persian times indicating no great change in the conduct of business or in the handling of legal transactions. They do, however, point to a much wider base of operation and exchange of goods (see F. E. Peiser, *Texte juristischen und geschäftlichen Inhalts* in *KB*, IV [Berlin: Verlag von Reuther & Reichard, 1896], pp. 207–294). Lawsuits in the time of Cyrus were just as intricate as they were in earlier times, even though appeals were carried through the satrapal tribunal (A. T. Olmstead, *History of the Persian Empire* [Chicago: University of Chicago Press, 1948], pp. 72f.). Social organization in Babylon also continued as it was in earlier times as may be seen from the documents in which contracts of various types were made—for example, the family of Egibi, of Iranu, and later of Murashu and the classes such as doctors, fishermen, herdsmen, smiths, weavers, and so on. These were really the citizens of the city who joined in a public assembly to transact the community's business presided over by the chief of the council with the king's representative as the advocate of the state. Routine cases appear to have been handled by the local officials and only special cases by the assembly court. The age-old system of forced labor was retained, although some modification was observed through monetary payment. There is no indication of tax reduction, which remained at from 20 to 30 per cent of the products of the land. Aside from his military and organizational ability, something of the larger vision of Cyrus may be gathered from the complex of constructions at the Persian capital of Pasargadae, which was composed of four groups of buildings—a citadel area, a palace with adjoining buildings, the tomb and its surrounding structures, and the so-called sacred precinct. (For a description of archaeological results see David Stronach, "Excavations at Pasargadae" in *Iran*, I [London: The British Institute of Persian Studies, [1963], 19–42; II [1964], 21–39; III [1965], 9–40.) Cyrus must have been an imposing personality as he appeared among his troops and people (see R. Ghirshman, *Persia: From the Origins to Alexander the Great* [London: Thames and Hudson, 1964], Fig. 179; and Georgina Thompson, "Iranian Dress in the Achaemenian Period," *Iran*, III [1965], 121–26).

The three main classes of people—aristocracy, citizens, which included artisans of all kinds, and slaves—continued. Undoubtedly the Jews were included in the latter two classes, to judge from the instances mentioned in the Bible and the inscriptions. At least this was the case in the early part of the Persian period. We know from the Weidner texts that Jews occupied important positions such as gardeners in the time of Nebuchadnezzar. Ezra, Nehemiah, and Daniel were no ordinary slaves. The fact that many wanted to remain in Babylon despite the Cyrus decree permitting such Jews as were so minded to return to their homeland indicates that their lot was far from oppressive. Presumably they were mostly regarded as citizens. Later on Ezra had an even harder time to convince some of his compatriots to return to Judah.

Cyrus
and the Religious Interests of His Empire

Xenophon, under the influence of Cyrus the younger, speaks glowingly of the piety of Cyrus the Great. He is said to have consulted the gods regularly and offered sacrifices (*Cyropaedia*, 1:5:6), inquiring of them about the most insignificant matters (1:5:14); prayed to Hestia and Zeus (1:6:1ff; 7:5:57); proceeded on campaigns only when the gods were favorable (6:2:40); presented gifts to them upon victory (4:5:14; 7:3:1; 7:5:57); and sung paeans to the gods before battle (3:3:58,59). Such inscriptions as we have seem to bear out, in general, this view of the great king. It will be recalled that in the "Verse account of Nabonidus" (Pritchard, *ANET* 312–15), after a devastating indictment of the innovations that were interpreted as impiety toward the traditional gods of Babylon, Cyrus is praised for returning them to their wonted places and reconstructing their sanctuaries. The introduction to the barrel inscription of Cyrus (*ANET* 315f.) tells us how, after Nabonidus' neglect of him, Marduk, the chief god of Babylon, looked around for one who might restore him to his traditional position and found the king of Anshan. To him he gave the power to destroy and supplant the guilty ones of Babylon. After the conquest, Cyrus proclaims himself the beloved of Bel and Nebo, who favored him because he "pleases their hearts." He goes on to tell how Marduk turned the hearts of the Babylonian people to him and what he did to those who failed to do the will of the gods; how well pleased the great god was with him, his son Cambyses, and his troops; how he restored the images and rebuilt the sanctuaries of the gods that had been exiled; and how he resettled, at the behest of Marduk, all the gods of Sumer and Akkad that had been brought to Babylon. Finally in a climactic outburst of devotion, he requests all those gods repatriated to their own cities to pray daily to Bel and Nebo for his position and welfare. More than once he speaks of his own worship of Marduk, Bel, and Nebo. Cyrus thus was careful to maintain the good will of the priests of the gods and had his son Cambyses officiate at the New Year festival when he was proclaimed king of Babylon. He ruled not simply by virtue of conquest but now by divine right.

Just what the personal religion of the king was is not certain. In fact little is actually known of his building activity outside of the excavations at Pasargadae, except what is mentioned by the ancient historians. Xenophon says he instituted the college of magi and regularly sang hymns to the gods at dawn and sacrificed daily to whatever gods the magi directed (*Cyropaedia* 8:1:23). He also describes a state religious ceremony that included an imposing procession beginning at the palace gate. First came four bulls for Zeus and the other gods, then horses to be sacrificed to the Sun, followed by a chariot drawn by white horses with golden yokes and garlands—all for Zeus. Next came another chariot similarly drawn by white horses, for the Sun. A third chariot followed, drawn by horses with purple trappings. The chariots were followed by men carrying fire on a huge altar. Last came Cyrus with his retinue. When they arrived at the sanctuaries, sacrifices to Zeus were offered, the horses put to the flames in worship of the Sun, and sacrifices offered to Earth and the tutelary gods of Syria. Following the ceremonies came a riding contest (*Cyropaedia* 8:3:11–24). As observed above, the construction at Pasargadae does contain a sacred precinct, which, however, does not tell us much as yet. We do know now that Herodotus was in error when he wrote that the Persians had "no temples nor altars" (1:131), for at the sacred precinct were found two fire altars (Stronach, "Excavations at Parsargadae," *Iran*, III [1965], pp. 24–29 and plates VI d, VII a, b). To whom these fire altars were dedicated is obscure, although there has been a good deal of speculation about it. That at least the initial work of construction comes from the Cyrus period appears fairly certain, although there is evidence of further work later. It may be that the great king did not have time to finish the work he began because he was so busy with the formation and solidification of his empire. Like David, he was a man of war, and most of his time was consumed with operations connected with its conduct and with organization and administration.

Cyrus
and the Jews

That Cyrus was a man of political sagacity is evident from all the documents, but his interest in the gods can hardly be entirely attributed to it. His concern for the restoration of the discredited deities also seems to be due to more than an attempt to win the plaudits of their devotees. He must have found something attractive about the religions of the peoples he had subjugated. At all events, he respected their religious beliefs. From what we have seen of his reaction to other religions, the Jewish historians and theologians may indeed be right in their belief that Cyrus really cared about their God. It is not beyond comprehension that he may have heard about the prophecies of Deutero-Isaiah, particularly those that referred specifically to him as the liberator of the Jews, the anointed of Yahweh. Had not the priests of Marduk said the same things about him with reference to Babylon? In view of the standing of many Jews in Babylon, it appears quite likely that the agents of the Persian king knew about their feelings, especially about the preachings of such a highly intelligent prophet whose religious faith was, at least superficially, much like his own— without images. All the biblical references speak of Cyrus regarding "the Lord, the God of the heavens" as the one who bestowed upon him all the kingdoms of the world (2 Chr 36,23; Ezr 1,2; 1 Esd 2,3; see also Josephus, *Ant.* 11:1:1). And inasmuch as Cyrus' policy was so generally favorable to religion and as he himself saw to it that altars and temples were rebuilt, it seems almost certain that the rescript cannot be an invention or the projection of a doctored Jewish document. Note that the divine name, Yahweh, is carefully qualified as the God of the heavens (Josephus refers to him as the "Most High God"), an expression that occurs only in the 2 Chr passage, in Ezr and Neh, and especially in the Aramaic sections of Dn and Ezr. After all, as Ghirshman (*Iran* [Baltimore: Penguin Books, Inc., 1954], p. 132) observes, there was some affinity between the religion of Persia and that of the Jews. Cyrus must have recognized that the religion of the Jews was closer to his own than were the beliefs and practices of the Babylonians or those of the other peoples with whom he came in contact. (See also B. Meissner, *Die Achämenidenkönige und das Judentum* [Berlin: Verlag der Akademie der Wissenschaften in Kommission bei Walter de Gruyter u. Co., 1938], p. 11.) And the Jews, too, saw something in Persian religion that reminded them of their own, and later on its influence was to become more pronounced. It can hardly be argued that the Jewish writers composed their treatises only for effect.

The Cyrus decree is repeated three times in the canonical literature of the Bible (2 Chr 36,22–23; Ezr 1,1–4; 6:3–5), once in 1 Esd 2,3–7, and in Josephus (*Ant.* 11:1:1–2). The Chronicles statement is, in substance, the same as that in Ezr 1, although the latter is somewhat embellished. The copy reposing in the Aramaic section of Ezra (6,3–5) is in general agreement with that in Ezr 1. The following features of the edict are to be observed. It was issued in two forms—by proclamation and in writing, regular practices in connection with royal decisions. The reference to Cyrus as king of Persia is a bit awkward since he refers to himself elsewhere as king of Anshan. However, in the Hamadan inscription of Ariaramnes, the king speaks of himself as king of Parsa. So does Arsames, his son. But both of these were earlier rulers of Parsa and would have no other way of identifying themselves. In the Behistun records, Darius says that he is, among other things, king of Persia. The "thus says Cyrus" is a form paralleled in the Cyrus Murghab B inscription and occurs in the Darius inscription just mentioned. The statement that "Yahweh has given me all the kingdoms of the earth" breathes the spirit of the Cyrus barrel inscription, where the Persian's hegemony is attributed to Marduk. It is interesting that this conception does not occur in the Aramaic document of Ezr 6. The official archival transcript could hardly contain such an introductory statement, and if it did its quotation there would be without purpose. In both documents (Ezr 1 and 6), the primary emphasis falls on the reconstruction of "a house" (= temple) in Jerusalem, later, in Ezr 1,3, defined as "the house of Yahweh, God of Israel who is the God in Jerusalem." In the Aramaic version it is simply called "a house of God in Jerusalem" (Ezr 6,3.5) and "the temple which is in Jerusalem" (Ezr 6,5, bis). It will be noted that the Aramaic copy calls for the foundations of the house to be retained and prescribes the method and materials of construction (vv. 3–4). The cost was to be defrayed by the royal treasury. The temple vessels and utensils carried off by Nebuchadnezzar were to be returned and restored to their place and function in the rebuilt house. No directive is given in the Hebrew account (Ezr 1,2–4) as to the method or building materials to be used, nor is there a reference to the contributions from the royal exchequer. The impression is that the emphasis here is on the release of those Jews who might be interested in going to Jerusalem to re-establish the old worship facilities and on the contributions to that end to be made by those who decided to remain in Babylon. Incidentally, "Wherever he may sojourn" (v. 4) may indicate a dissemination of Jews throughout the district of Babylon (see Ezr 2,59; 8,17).

The authenticity of the Cyrus edict can hardly be an ingenious contrivance of the Chronicler despite the arguments of Galling (*Studien zur Geschichte Israels im persischen Zeitalter* [Tübingen: Mohr, 1964], pp. 61–77). For weighty arguments in favor of authenticity see R. de Vaux, "Les Décrets de Cyrus et de Darius sur la reconstruction du Temple," *RB* 46 [1937] 29–57, and E. J. Bickerman, "The Edict of

Cyrus in Ezra 1," *JBL* LXV [1946] 244–75.) For one thing it corresponds perfectly with the attitude and temperament of Cyrus as revealed in his inscription noted above (see Pritchard, *ANET* 315–16) where it is stated that he returned the images that were once located there but had been removed lately by Nabonidus to the sanctuaries of the cities and regions listed. At the behest of Marduk, he resettled "all the gods of Sumer and Akkad," which delighted their devotees and the inhabitants of both places to which they were restored and the Babylonian priests—a not too subtle hint that the latter were unhappy because of the danger of religious subversion. Although it is true that there is no reference to the Jews or to the *golah* here, the unkind remarks about Bel and Nebo by Deutero-Isaiah (Is 46), if known to the Babylonian clergy, might have presented the same perils, particularly in local communities where zealous and outspoken Jews lived and conducted what religious ceremonies they could.

The list of the *golah* (Ezr 2; Neh 7; 1 Esd 5) who are said to have returned at the time can hardly have applied to the age of Cyrus (for possible purposes of the list, see my comments in *Anchor Bible: Ezra-Nehemiah,* pp. 15f.). It is probably a compilation of the names of families who had returned between Cyrus and the time of Ezra. The numbers given would point to a fantastically large response to the Cyrus edict, especially in view of the figures given for those taken into exile in the first place (see 2 Kgs 24; Jer 52,28–30)—nearly ten times the number taken into exile according to the figures given in Jer 52. What the immediate response to the decree of Cyrus was is unknown, but it was doubtless not too enthusiastic, at least at first. Many Jews were getting along quite well, and besides, the problems facing those who might want to return were enormous. It meant the disruption of family and community life, possibly the sacrificing of fairly lucrative positions on the part of the middle classes of artisans and the facing of serious perils in journeying across unsafe roads between Babylon and Judah. As Albright has pointed out (*BP* [1963], 87) it is not necessary to assume any great rush to return at once for reasons just stated. But there were certainly some who did take advantage of the opportunity: those who were extraordinarily zealous for the institutions of the fathers and those who were not doing too well in their present state.

The temple vessels were delivered to Sheshbazzar (Ezr 1,8) by Mithredath, the royal treasurer. The transfer was all very much in order, legally speaking, for Sheshbazzar is called "the prince of Judah." According to 1 Chr 3,18—where he is called Shenazzar—he was the fourth son of Jehoiachin. Both names may be corrupt spellings of the original Babylonian name, *šn'b'ṣr*. Sheshbazzar may have been acting as the oldest surviving son of the king of Judah or as regent for Zerubbabel, who was the son of Pediah, the oldest son of Jehoiachin, and who would normally have been the successor of his father. In delivering the temple objects to Sheshbazzar, Cyrus was following the practice he often did elsewhere—that is, establishing the returning community under its own native leadership operating within the satrapal system.

Cambyses (529–522 B.C.)

Cyrus had hoped to undertake a campaign against Egypt, whose king Amasis (570–526 B.C.) had an alliance with Nabonidus. But before he could get around to it, troubles on the northern and northeastern frontier of his empire required his attention. Before he left he made sure of his successor, who was to be Cambyses whom he made king of Babylon immediately after its conquest. No sooner had the latter ascended the throne than he was confronted with difficulties in which his brother Smerdis was involved (the story is told by Darius in the Behistun inscription, Col. I). Cambyses made short work of the problem by killing his brother, but for some reason he concealed his act. The way was then clear for him to undertake his father's unfulfilled dreams of the conquest of Egypt. Amasis was by now (526 B.C.) an old man, but one who had ruled well and a man who loved peace. He had earlier subjugated Cyprus and entered into a treaty of alliance with Cyrene. He was also a friend of Polycrates, the powerful chief of Samos. One of the interesting events of his reign was his handling of the Greek problem. The Greeks were becoming a menace in the delta region where many of them settled as merchants. To contain them, Amasis built and adorned the city of Naucratis, to which he confined them, apparently to their great satisfaction (see *Her.* 2:178). That city was to play a significant role later on along the lines laid down by the king. It became a great emporium.

Cambyses moved to the west three years after his investiture. On the way Phoenicia submitted without a struggle. That gave him the use of its fleet for such purposes as might require it. Cyprus also came to terms. Incidentally, Cambyses' campaign must have made roads across north Mesopotamia much safer, a situation probably turned to advantage by Jews intent upon returning to their homeland. The Persian king met the Egyptian army under Psammeticus III, who had by now succeeded his father, at Pelusium where a fierce battle ensued.

The Egyptians were finally defeated, and they fled in dismay to Memphis. After a comparatively long siege, the city finally capitulated. Cambyses seems to have followed the practice of his father in appointing an Egyptian to high office and instituting reforms for the people. He offered sacrifices in the temple of Neith at Sais and disallowed the lands and revenues of the priests who were made to fend for themselves. An Elephantine letter written in 408 B.C. by the Jewish colony there to Bigwai, the governor of Judah, boasts of the fact that in the time of Cambyses their temple remained untouched while those of the gods of Egypt were all overthrown (Cowley, *Aramaic Papyri of the Fifth Century B.C.* [New York: Oxford University Press, 1923], Letter 30, lines 13–14). His three further designs—a campaign against Carthage, his Ethiopian adventure, and the force sent to the Oasis of Siwa—came to naught. Herodotus (3:29) says Cambyses disfavored himself with the Egyptians by slaying the Apis bull and at the same time ridiculing their cult. But this is extremely doubtful inasmuch as the sarcophagus of an Apis bull with a dedicatory inscription to Cambyses has now turned up at the Serapeum (see Olmstead, *History of the Persian Empire* [Chicago: University of Chicago Press, 1948], pp. 89f., and G. Posener, *La première domination Perse en Égypte* [Cairo: Bibliothèque d'étude, 1936], pp. 30ff.). The failure of his plans is said to have preyed on the mind of the king to such an extent that he performed atrocious acts (*Her.* 3:30ff.), which is probably a fabrication by those who were responsible for the information given to the Greek historian. After installing Aryandes as satrap, Cambyses set out for Babylon. On the way he received word of the usurpation of Bardiya and soon afterward died in 522 B.C.

There is no further record of Cambyses' relationship with the Jews, and his name does not occur in the Bible. Aristeas (par. 14) speaks of many Jews having come to Egypt with the Persians. Josephus (*Ant.* 11,2:1) says Cambyses was the son of Cyrus but ascribes to him the activity attributed to Artaxerxes in Ezr 4,7ff.; 1 Esd 2:16ff. The garrison at Elephantine may have been strengthened by the king following his Ethiopian campaign. Although that cannot be proven, one could perhaps infer it from the colony's letter referred to above.

Darius (521–486 B.C.)

With the accession of Darius there is a change in family line, although the Achaemenian dynasty was to continue. While Cambyses was in Egypt, a revolt broke out in Persia and Media, to be joined by others as the news spread. The instigator was a man by the name of Gaumata, who passed himself off as the brother of the king, Smerdis. This he could do because he is said to have resembled the real Smerdis so closely that while the latter was still alive they were often confused. Moreover, Cambyses kept the death of his brother from the people, and, ignorant of the facts, they could easily be persuaded to follow the usurper. Perhaps because word of the failure of Cambyses in Egypt was brought to the homeland, dissatisfaction arose and Gaumata took advantage of the situation. In a comparatively short time virtually all the empire was won over, largely because Gaumata promised the people three years' remission of taxes and the institution of a religious reform. But he failed to reckon with the army, which remained loyal to the Achaemenian family. Seven so-called conspirators led by Darius, the son of Hystaspes, the Parthian satrap who had been with Cambyses during the Egyptian campaign, acted so swiftly that within two months after the demise of the king, Gaumata was captured and dispatched. Darius is said to have been chosen king in a contest with the others and then to have taken over the government.

The death of the imposter did not, however, conclude the matter of succession for the empire, which almost had to be won again by force of arms. It took Darius two full years to establish control over the rebels. The majestic relief at Behistun portrays Darius stepping on the prostrate body of Gaumata with nine kings standing before him awaiting his disposition. Around this portrait are cut the several columns telling the story of his victory over them as well as that of usurpation by the wretched Gaumata, who was the instigator of it all (see R. Ghirshman, *Persia*, p. 235, Fig. 283). The lengthy inscription is carved in three languages—Old Persian, Babylonian, and Elamite. One purpose seems to have been to impress the king's subjects with his power and determination and thus to serve as a warning to any person or province, who might, at present or in the future, contemplate rebellion. The decisive blow dealt every uprising, the savage cruelty of the punishment meted out to its leaders, and the close association the king claims with Ahuramazda, his great god, are factors pointing in that direction. In addition, copies were made of the content of the inscription in the appropriate languages and sent to all the provinces of the empire. A fragment of a cuneiform version was found at Babylon. A papyrus copy in Aramaic was discovered with the Elephantine documents (Cowley, *Aramaic Papyri*, pp. 248–71). There is some evidence that two or more such papyri existed in the Jewish colony in Egypt. There is an interesting possibility that the place for the name of the deity was left open in the copies sent to the different parts of the empire so that the proper epithet could be inserted. If true, this offers further evidence of the political sagacity as well as the religious sensitivity of the Persian kings. The inscription also served as a commemorative device celebrating the victories of the king, which led to the re-establishment of the empire at the behest of Ahuramazda, to whom such sweeping success was due. After the suppression of the Gaumata uprising, Darius claims to have restored the pastures, herds, domestic slaves, and houses that had been destroyed or confiscated by the upstart. He also repaired the temples that had suffered destruction. One of the reasons for repeated attempts to break away from the empire of certain provinces was the reimposition of taxes of various kinds, which had been lifted by Gaumata. Claus Schedl has recently made a strong case for dating the historical kernel of the book of Judith in the early years of Darius ("Nabuchodonosor, Arpakšad und Darius," in *ZDMG* CXV [1965] 242–54). If correct it would detail one more of Darius' troubles in which a brave Jewess assisted the Persians—a further indication of the Jewish feeling toward them.

Because of the involvement of the Jews in the events of Darius' exploits (see below), it is necessary to sketch, in brief, the major movements of this great and capable ruler. It was eminently clear to the king and his advisers that more stringent measures would have to be taken to maintain control of his far-flung empire composed of so many varied peoples with independent political and religious traditions. To that end the more lenient policy of Cyrus was, in part, abandoned and closer ties to the royal court established. The strong wave of nationalism revealed in a series of rebellions somehow had to be checked. This was done by replacing local officials by loyal Persian subjects, in some instances by members of the court—much as Solomon did in administrative reorganization (1 Kgs 4,7–19). In addition, Darius established a new system of common law, mostly after the pattern of the Hammurabi code, in which he set forth precedents by which local cases were to be judged and known among the Jews as the law of the king (*datha' di malka'*—Ezr 7,26). He proclaimed himself as one friendly to right and hostile to wrong and as concerned that neither the weak nor the strong suffer oppressions or injustice (Naqš-i-Rustam B. 5–11), that there be no "smiting" one of another in all his empire (Susa E, 30–41). Apparently he himself had a keen sense of justice (Behistun, col. IV, 61–67), which he expected to be the pattern for his subjects. On his visit to Egypt (see R. A. Parker, "Darius and His Egyptian Campaign," *AJSL* LVIII [1941] 373ff.) he undertook to do there what he had done for Western Asia. According to the Demotic Chronicle he summoned all the knowledgeable officials of Egypt—wise men, priests, scribes—to codify the laws of the land down through the reign of Amasis. They were to assemble the decrees of the Pharaohs, the religious regulations and those governing the populace, so that by the authority of the new king they might be applied and enforced. (For a discussion of Darius as lawgiver see Olmstead, *History of the Persian Empire*, Chap. IX.) In order to unify the provinces of the empire, Darius created a system of roads to maintain better communication with them. This network of roads was of such vital significance that it survived the downfall of Persia. The road from Susa to Ephesus was 1677 miles in length along which were 111 relay stations. Royal messengers could cover the distance in about a week. The old Babylonian-Egyptian route was rebuilt, with a connection to Hamadan to the east added. After later conquests of India, that branch was extended to the Kabul. Local branch roads were constructed to facilitate further the administrative contacts with centers of government and population in the various provinces off the mainline arteries and so brought the farthest points within easy reach. Exploration with the aim of conquest and trade seems also to have been engaged in. Herodotus (4:44) affirms the above to have been the purpose of the daring venture of Scylax of Caryanda, who sailed down the Indus to the sea, then westward along the coast, skirting the Arabian peninsula and ending at Suez. Such an expedition may have been behind Darius' plan to join the eastern branch of the Nile to the Red Sea. In any case, his Suez inscription celebrates the execution of the canal project and the passage of ships from Egypt to Persia. Thus, Darius appears to have been a commercial mogul as well as an astute military genius and government administrator. Herodotus (3:89) says the Persians called him a "huckster." This is further substantiated by his re-evaluation and standardizing of weights and measures and the introduction of coinage (see *Her.* 3:89; and E. Babelon, *Les Perses Achéménides* [Paris: Chez C. Rollin & Feuardent, 1893], pp. IV, XIV, 1–4). In fact the Persian daric, a gold coin weighing 8.41 grams, appears to owe its name to him. Business was accelerated everywhere, agriculture encouraged, and trades of all sorts promoted. From southern Europe to the Indus and from the region between the Black and Caspian seas to the sources of the Nile, by land and water, communication and commerce flourished. The great building projects of Darius reflect these wide contacts and influences as may be seen from the artistic designs and from various luxury items uncovered by archaeologists. The first eight of the Persepolis treasury tablets (G. G. Cameron, *Persepolis Treasury Tablets* [Chicago: University of Chicago Press, 1948], pp. 83–95) date from the last years of the reign of Darius I. They deal with economic matters—money to be paid to workers from a number of nations, including Egyptians and Persians.

Meanwhile the satrapal system was completed much along the lines laid down by Cyrus and Cambyses. Closer organization and surveillance on the part of imperial authorities increased the inflow of taxes to the royal treasury, which are calculated to have come to 14,560 talents (a talent was about 75½ pounds). Such revenues enabled the king to maintain both his military and civil organization and at the same time to engage in building projects on an elaborate scale. He erected a magnificent palace at Susa (DSf * in R. G. Kent, *Old Persian: Grammar, Texts, Lexicon* [New Haven: American Oriental Society, 1953], pp. 142–44) for which cedar was imported from Lebanon, gold from Sardis and Bactria, lapis-lazuli and carnelian from Sogdiana, turquoise from Chorasmia, silver and ebony from Egypt, ornamentation from Ionia, ivory from Ethiopia, Sind, and Arachosia, and stone pillars from Elam. Workmen from everywhere were employed on the project —Assyrians, Carians, Ionians, Sardinians, Medes, and Egyptians. At Persepolis he laid the foundations for one of the greatest monuments of the Persian empire, one which was extended and elaborated upon by Darius' successors. Two buildings were erected there—a palace and a huge audience chamber, the hall of a hundred columns. (For plans and archaeological remains at Susa and Persepolis see Ghirshman, *Persia*, pp. 138–209.) Some six miles north of his palace in the cliffs, he cut his tomb, whose facade appears in the form of a gigantic Greek cross. He decorated it appropriately, sculptured bas-reliefs depicting the nations who were his subjects, inscribed two columns of writing praising his god, telling of his exploits, and warning his fellow men not to rebel or to desert the right path. Before the portrait of the king with his bow is carved the winged symbol of Ahuramazda, the great god to whom he ascribed his success as warrior and ruler.

One other venture of Darius calls for brief notice here since it belongs to the story of Darius and as such is part of the world of his time. It is the well-known tale of his adventures with the Greeks. It began innocently enough with an attempt to deal with the Scythians in southeastern Europe. A combined sea and land expedition was undertaken at about the same time the canal near Suez was being dug. In

---

* See list of abbreviations at the back of the book.

513 B.C. he crossed the Bosporus on a ship-bridge while some 600 ships sailed through the Black Sea to the Danube delta. Darius had little difficulty in conquering the Thracian tribes, but the Scyths were another matter. When his land army reached the delta, another ship-bridge was thrown across for the troops, but the enemy had its own way of fighting, not by pitched battle but by the hit-and-run tactic. The Scyths destroyed their own land as they withdrew and led Darius' army into territory so sterile that it could not live. Darius was thus compelled to withdraw. Before leaving the shores of Europe he detached a force of some 80,000 soldiers under Megabazos to finalize operations in Thrace and Macedonia. The operations were successful, and a new satrapy was set up over which a Lydian, Otanes, was placed as satrap. Trouble arose in connection with one of the islands, Naxos, which the Persian general failed to bring to terms. That must have encouraged the Greeks, and the Persians were soon faced with a full-fledged revolt of the Ionians under the leadership of the Miletians supported by the Athenian navy. In 499 B.C. the Greek allies struck at Sardis, which was burned together with its temple of Cybele. The Greeks were finally defeated at Ephesus, but the aftermath of the revolt was tragic for Darius. Another attempt was made by the Greeks in a naval engagement at Miletus, where they were beaten by the maneuvers of the Persians. These machinations of the Greeks indicated to Darius that the Athenians had to be taught a lessen. The result was the invasion of Greece with Persian defeats at Plataea and Marathon in 490 B.C. However, Darius was now more determined than ever to subdue the Greeks and to that end began preparations for another expedition. Wars cost money and require taxation to pay for them. There are records of complaints coming from Babylon and elsewhere about the heavy burdens. Along with the growing tax burden are evidences of corruption such as that in the Aryandes case in Egypt, which consisted of imitation coinage. Despite the fact that the satrap was executed, dissatisfaction continued. The Egyptian revolt broke out in 486 B.C. because the people claimed they could no longer bear the heavy burdens imposed upon them by Darius. Before measures could be taken to quell the dissidents, the great king died.

A word is in order here about the religion of Darius. Only one god is mentioned in his inscriptions, that is, Ahuramazda, which occurs scores of times. The term means "wise lord" or "god." Darius claims this god as the one under whose aegis he operated. He was chosen by Ahuramazda when the earth was in turmoil to bring order thereto

(DNa, 30–41; DSf. 15–18). By the god's favor he carried out all his undertakings; by it he was made king over the lands and put down rebels, and people respected the king's laws by the grace of Ahuramazda. In the name of the god he invoked blessings or curses upon people (DB, V, 18–20). The royal house was established by his favor and to him he prayed for protection for it and himself. More than once Darius refers to himself as the worshiper of Ahuramazda (DB, V, 14–17; DS, k, 3–5) and promises divine blessings for those who follow his example. In fact, he calls upon men to accept the command of the god and never to regard it as repugnant (DNa, 56–60). At his behest he erected the building complex at Susa (DSo) and the palace at Persepolis (DPa), and set up the record and monument of his exploits at Behistun (DB, IV, 88–92). In effect Darius was a theoretical monotheist, for he attributed to Ahuramazda the creation of earth, sky, man (DNa, 1–8), the bestowing of wisdom and skillfulness upon the king (DNb, 1–5, 45–59), and the creating of excellence in earth, happiness for man, good horses and chariots (DSs). Ahuramazda was his inspiration for the establishment of the law against murder and oppression of the weak (DSe, 30–41) and for his bringing order where there had been disorder. Practically, however, Darius was wise enough to recognize that all the peoples in his empire did not share his religious views. So as a kind of afterthought he gives grudging recognition to them while retaining his own belief in Ahuramazda as the greatest of the gods (DPd, 1–5; DPh, 3–10; DSp). On one occasion he speaks of the aid borne him by Ahuramazda and the other gods who exist (DB, IV, 61). He urges prayer to Ahuramazda and the other gods of the royal household to protect the country (DPd, 12–24; DSe, 49–52). In DB, V, 14–20 he says that he worked his desire upon the Elamites because they were faithless and did not worship Ahuramazda and that whoever worships his god will enjoy blessings in life and death. Inasmuch as the inscriptions of Darius are monumental in character, it may be that they reflect the official religion of his empire and are not to be regarded as reflecting the unofficial, popular, or provincial cults. The continuance of temples in the time of Darius is attested to by archaeological remains at Pasargadae, Naqš-i-Rustam, and Persepolis. Particularly interesting is the exaggerated, protruding figure of Ahuramazda in the winged disc representation in the bas-relief at Behistun (Ghirshman, *Persia* Fig. 278, p. 229). The fire altars are also very much in evidence, but there is no indication of other divine statuary as there is later in the time of Artaxerxes II—of Anahita at Susa, Ecbatana, and

Babylon. Darius and his successors were not Zoroastrians, but it was under the Achaemenians that Zoroastrianism developed in the restless and insecure eastern provinces of the empire.

The Jews
in the Time of Darius

Other than in the Bible and works of Josephus, we have no specific information for this period about the Jews or events in Palestine. Even that information is exceedingly scanty and confused. Yet the entire activity of the *golah* in the homeland is based on the edict of Cyrus, which directed that the sacred vessels of the temple be given into the custody of Sheshbazzar, who was to take them to Jerusalem. The testimony of Ezr 1,11 is that Sheshbazzar carried out the decree, not only with reference to the temple utensils, but that he was accompanied by others of the *golah* who were charged with the task of rebuilding "the house of Yahweh, the God of Israel" (Ezr 1,3). Just when this took place is not clear from our present sources, although the implication is that it was done soon after the time of the issuance of the rescript. There is a possibility, however, that no significant movement took place before the Egyptian campaign of Cambyses because the roads were unsafe. Nevertheless not too much emphasis ought to be placed on that surmise because the western principalities hastened to bring their tribute to Cyrus immediately after the fall of Babylon and so would hardly have done anything overtly to oppose the directive of the great king. The question that arises at once is, what happened to Sheshbazzar? We don't know. It may be that he was deliberately downgraded by the Chronicler because he seems to have failed in his project whereas Zerubbabel succeeded. Certainly the present documents attest that Sheshbazzar and Zerubbabel were two persons and that both served as governor of Judah under the jurisdiction of the Persian authorities. In view of the later serious difficulties with the peoples of the land, probably both Jews remaining in it and others who had filled the vacuum after the debacle of 587 B.C., it could easily be that misunderstandings arose that for the moment could not be resolved (see Josephus, *Ant.*, 11:2:1; 11:4:4). It must be remembered that no serious attention was given by the Persians to the west before the reign of Cambyses, and hence matters were, so to speak, left to ride as they could. It is also possible that Sheshbazzar did carry out his commission, that he built an altar and laid the foundations of the temple, as Josephus asserts (*Against Apion*, 1:154), and delivered the temple vessels to Jerusalem to be kept until the building was finished. When he believed his work was done, he would then have returned to Babylon. He must, after all, have been no young man in 538 B.C., since he was born before 593 B.C., as we know from the Weidner Texts. In the light of the uncertainties prevalent in the interval between the death of Cambyses and the full accession of Darius, everything likely came to a standstill (see 1 Esdr 2,30). Conditions at the time may have enabled the local enemies of the Jews to undo the work of Sheshbazzar and his coworkers. In that event, a new attempt would have been necessary to carry out the Cyrus decree, which was undertaken under Darius under the leadership of Zerubbabel and Joshua, the high priest (see my remarks in *Anchor Bible, XIV: Ezra-Nehemiah*, pp. 45–6).

Josephus says that both Cyrus and Darius issued orders for the rebuilding of the temple (*Ant.*, 11:4:3; in *Ant.*, 11:4:1 it is said that the order was first issued by Cyrus and then carried out by Darius; in *Against Apion* [1:154] that the foundations of the temple were laid in the second year of Cyrus and that the work was completed in the second year of Darius; there were no doubt several returns from Babylon.) (See *BASOR* CXLV, 31 for a possible later one than any mentioned in the Bible.) Both 1 Esdr and Ezr simply say that reconstruction began under Cyrus and continued until the time of Darius. The Jewish historian further states that Zerubbabel, who came to Jerusalem before as governor, returned to the Persian court after Darius became king because he had struck up a friendship with him before his accession to the throne. The temple utensils, according to his story, were still in Babylon although promise of their transference to Jerusalem had been made by Cyrus. As a private citizen, Darius had vowed that if he were king he would have them brought to the Judean capital. The story of the banquet of Darius with its storytelling contest is probably apocryphal (*Ant.*, 11:3:1–7; 1 Esdr 3,4), but it affirms that after Zerubbabel had won it he reminded the king of his vow (11:3:7) in response to which the latter issued orders to his satraps in the west to escort Zerubbabel and his company and instructed the officials of Syria and Phoenicia to provide materials for the building operations. He also directed that those who had occupied the towns formerly belonging to the Jews surrender them and that a contribution of fifty talents (1 Esdr 4:51 says twenty plus ten talents yearly for its support) be given toward the project. Permission was also granted for the resumption of sacrifices, and provision was made for the sacred vestments of the high priest and the other priests (11:3:8). Everything was to be done in

accordance with the wishes that had been expressed by Cyrus. Josephus
then goes on to relate the details of what took place following the
Darius decrees, much as the story is unfolded in the Bible and in 1
Esdr. He does not list the names of the *golah* as we find them in Ezr
2 and 1 Esdr 5, though he does give some figures that are much higher
than the biblical ones. In the seventh month after leaving Babylon, an
assembly of the Jews and the people of the country was called and
an altar erected on the precise spot where the old one stood. Then they
celebrated the Feast of Tabernacles and began the building of the temple, with the aid of materials supplied by the Sidonians. During the
second year after the return to Jerusalem, the reconstruction was
launched. Supervision and work were executed with such zeal that consummation took place earlier than expected, when there was an enthusiastic service of thanksgiving. The product was not so pretentious
as the earlier one had been because of the poverty of the people, but
the people were nevertheless satisfied with their achievement. It was
in connection with the sound of the trumpets and the songs of worship
that the attention of potential enemies was attracted and troubles began (*Ant.*, 11:4:1–2).

1 Esdr 5 tells the same story, and Josephus obviously followed much
of it. A few details are added. For example, 1 Esdr says the *golah* were
joined by "some other peoples of the land" when they set up the altar
and that although they were unsympathetic toward them they supported them. Cooperation on the part of "the other peoples of the
land" together with their failure to press charges could have been because the *golah* were too busy building homes to threaten the existent
simple power structure. They brought sacrifices, observed the morning
and evening burnt offerings, kept the Feast of Tabernacles, and besides
the regular offerings, they presented such also on sabbaths, new moons,
and other festival occasions. There may be a subtle hint here of internal difficulties that afflicted the new movement. It is clear from the
work of the Chronicler that the *golah* regarded themselves as the true
community of Israel, an attitude that may well have been resented by
those Jews who never were in exile and who managed to survive despite the harassments to which they had been subjected in the interim.
Life was certainly difficult for them in the ostensibly pagan surround-
ings as indicated by the occupation of many of the old Jewish towns
and villages by Edomites and others. It is almost certain that these
homeland Jews maintained some semblance of cultic activity at the
old temple site, even offered sacrifices on the repaired altar and observed such other ceremonies as conditions permitted. Hence there

was bound to be misunderstanding, perhaps open hostility, as 1 Esdr says, between them and the *golah*. (See also E. Janssen, *Juda in der Exilszeit,* pp. 94–104.)

1 Esdr (5:47–65) is, in main outline, in agreement with Ezr 3. But in dealing with the Ezra chapter, it must not be forgotten that it is part of the story of the Chronicler, which has a distinct purpose. The sources he employed may well have come from temple archives. Taken as a whole the story reads as if the author were disregarding the story of Ezr 1, since Sheshbazzar is here replaced by Zerubbabel. Perhaps Sheshbazzar's responsibility is regarded by the writer as having ended with the delivery of the vessels of the temple to Jerusalem and the return of such of the *golah* as chose to follow him. There is no indication of the time that elapsed between the issuance of Cyrus' order, the preparations for the return, the time consumed in travel, and the actual inception of building operations. We have already noted that the list of the *golah* cannot contain those of the first return only; in fact, it may contain the names of those who came back over the years from Sheshbazzar to Ezra. What is of some import here is that a considerable period of time passed before the work of temple building began, for the *golah* are said to have been domiciled in their homes—the priests, Levites, and some of the people residing in Jerusalem and vicinity— while the musicians, gatekeepers, and temple slaves lived in their towns, and all the rest of Israel in their towns. This would seem to indicate that they first secured places of residence and then undertook the task for which they had come. That naturally took time and expense, because more was involved than simply the physical construction of homes. They had to be paid for, and that required other work. Then they had to support themselves and their families—and that, too, took time and effort. Possibly many of the *golah,* accustomed as they were to fairly good living conditions in Babylon, built more elaborately than the situation warranted. At least that is what the prophet Haggai complained about (Hag 1,2.3), and it was not until he began his agitation for temple building that anything significant happened. The word of Yahweh came to Haggai in the sixth month of the second year of Darius. (Hag 1,1). Then in the seventh month (Ezr 3,1) his preaching began to bear fruit (the dates in 1 Esdr 5,47.53.56.57 are confusing). Only the first one corresponds with Ezr 3,1 (1 Esdr 5,56 places the activity in the second year of Zerubbabel). However, it must be admitted that "the seventh month" may have a religious significance in Ezr 3,1. As is well known, that month was an important one in the religious calendar of Israel (see Nm 29; Lv 23,23–43). According to 2

Chr 5,3 festivities celebrating the dedication of Solomon's temple were conducted in the seventh month, a fact to be taken into consideration here. In addition, one of the great feasts requiring the presence of every male fell in that month. But when all is considered, it is striking that the Haggai sixth month fits in so well with Ezra's seventh.

That some festival occasion was responsible for bringing all the people to Jerusalem seems certain. Joshua, the high priest, and Zerubbabel then corralled the people and immediately set to work erecting the altar of burnt offering. It is important to observe that the altar was set "in its place," that is, precisely where it was before, to avoid any trouble from those who had sacrificed there during the exile. This fear (respect) of the peoples of the land reflects the caution taken by the *golah* leaders to follow exactly the pattern for reconstruction laid down by the Persian authorities. Josephus (*Ant.*, 11:1:3), probably overdoing it a bit, mentions the definite measurements included in the Cyrus rescript. It may also point to the relative position of the two parties in the early stages of the return. Erection of the altar was followed by sacrifices as prescribed in the Mosaic law. The Feast of Tabernacles was also celebrated with the specified offerings. All this took place before the foundation of the temple was laid (or relaid). Then they drew on the Persian account for materials and labor. In the second month of the second year after they reached Jerusalem, supervisory personnel were appointed and the work begun. It must have been an auspicious moment, for when the foundation stones were laid, a great ceremony took place. The priests appeared in their vestments with trumpets, the Levites with their cymbals, and their choir sang antiphonally with the congregation, "Praise and render thanks to Yahweh / For he is good / Everlasting is his devotion to Israel." A great shout rang out from the congregation when the first stone was put in place. There was weeping for joy. How the countryside must have echoed to the sound as it wafted across hills and valleys!

When news of the construction activity reached the rivals of Judah and Benjamin (Ezr 4,1–3), they immediately sought permission to participate on the plea that they were devotees of the same God to whom they had offered sacrifices since they were settled in the land by Esarhaddon (681–669 B.C.). There is no record of any resettlement of peoples in the west by that Assyrian king (there may be a hint of it in Is 7,8b), although he did campaign in the west (see *ANET* 290 and D. J. Wiseman, "An Esarhaddon Cylinder from Nimrud," in *Iraq* XIV [1952] 54–60). No outsiders were brought into Judah after the deportation by Nebuchadnezzar; a vacuum was created thereby but it is certain that descendants of the repatriates brought in after the Assyrian conquest of Israel moved south into the vacant towns and farms. It is doubtless to these elements that our author refers. Josephus calls them "Chuthaeans" (= Samaritans, in *Ant.* 11:4:4) who were brought from Media and Persia and settled in Samaria by Shalmaneser V when the Israelite population was deported (*Ant.* 11:2:1, 11:4:3). That explains the attitude of Zerubbabel and Joshua, whom the Chronicler regards as purists, toward the request of these people to share in the temple enterprise; they were syncretists and hence would have to be excluded from the sacred precincts. Josephus' comment in this connection is most interesting: He states that these people could not be permitted to participate in the building of the temple since no one but themselves had been commanded to do so (*Ant.* 11:4:3). That this was a strictly legal matter for him is shown by his further remark that they would be allowed to worship there (at the temple), but that the sole thing that they might, if they so desired, have in common with them and, indeed, with all other men, was to come to the sanctuary to worship God. These northerners had some precedent for their request in Hezekiah's invitation for people of their area to participate in the Passover (2 Chr 30), in Josiah's collection of funds for temple repairs from "Ephraim and Manasseh and from all the remnant of Israel" (2 Chr 34,9), and in the fact that Israelites were present at his Passover celebration (2 Chr 35,18).

Denial of the appeal of the peoples of the land brought reprisals, on their part, against the *golah* (Ezr 4,4), whose morale they immediately proceeded to undermine. According to Ezr 5,1–2, the leaders of the *golah*, with the inspiration and encouragement of Haggai and Zechariah, proceeded with determination to carry out their building program. However, they were soon to experience the power of the opposition (Ezr 5,3–6,15). Not only were the operations subverted by hindrances and delays—probably in the materials supplied from Lebanon—but the adversaries prompted the officials of the Syrian nations to demand cessation of building activities, just as Josephus says was done in the time of Cyrus and Cambyses (*Ant.* 11:4:4). Moreover, official intervention played its part in slowing down the work. Tattenai, the governor of the local district of the province Across the River (we now know that Tattenai was under the governor of Across the River as late as 502 B.C. —*JNES* III [1944] 46) and his secretary, Shetharbozenai, accompanied by representatives of the Samaritans, suddenly appeared on the scene to inquire about the legality of the construction activities of the Jews. These officials may have been genuinely worried about the situation

because of the unsettled conditions prevalent in the Persian empire
attendant upon the accession and establishment of Darius as king. And
they were concerned about imperial affairs because they were aware of
the heavy hand of the king should there be anything savoring of rebellion in their jurisdiction. But they were apparently satisfied by the
explanation of Zerubbabel and Joshua since they permitted the work
to go on while the investigation was conducted. In their official report
to the court they explained the type of building and listed the names
of the officials in charge. They included, also, their reply to the demand for credentials (Ezr 5,11–16). Finally they asked that a search
of the royal archives be made for the Cyrus decree. Apparently there
was no such decree among the records kept at Babylon, and so the
search was carried to Ecbatana, which was the repository for the imperial archives. Luckily there they found the official order of Cyrus,
which cleared up the whole matter. The result was an immediate directive from Darius to Tattenai and the other authorities reaffirming
the decree of Cyrus and demanding the discontinuance of obstruction
against the Jews (Ezr 6,6–12). The work was to be supported with
urgency so that it might be brought to consummation as soon as possible. The royal objective was the same for the Jews as it was for other
people of the empire—to assist them in their religious endeavors and
thus allay any religious discontent that might jeopardize imperial interests on the Egyptian frontier. Tattenai and his associates hastened
to comply. Josephus adds another story to the affair (*Ant.* 11:4:9) to
the effect that the Samaritans failed to convey the financial support
ordered by the king, which resulted in the Jews voting to send Zerubbabel and four other leaders to lodge a complaint against them in person. There is no other evidence to confirm this story. However, it is
possible that Zerubbabel, as governor of Judah, was summoned to the
court to explain after the report of Tattenai was received. If that is so,
he undoubtedly made counter-accusations against the obduracy of the
Samaritans.

Whatever may have been the sequence of events—moves and coun-
termoves between the parties involved—the net result was a gain for
the *golah*. They progressed in their work, thanks to the aid of Darius
and the exhortations of the prophets Haggai and Zechariah (Ezr
6,13–14). Success finally crowned their painstaking efforts so that on
the third of Adar (Ezr 6,15) of the sixth year of Darius the temple
stood completed. Dedication services naturally followed, and there was
great rejoicing (Ezr 6,16–18). Note the influence of the Chronicler in
the statement that "the people of Israel"—not the Jews—with the

priests, Levites, and the *golah,* participated in the service of dedication.
The priests and Levites appeared in their proper positions for the
service. Ezr 6,19–22 is the Chronicler's addition. While the Passover
was not celebrated in connection with the dedication of Solomon's
temple, it was held at the time of the rededication ceremonies conducted by Hezekiah (2 Chr 30,13ff.) and Josiah (2 Chr 35,1ff.). The
pattern of Hezekiah may have been followed here since the feast of
unleavened bread follows the Passover in both instances (see 2 Chr
30,21).

Prophets
of the Early Darius Period

Of the prophets Haggai and Zechariah (Zech 1–8) there can hardly
be a question, because we not only have their oracles but they figure
in the records preserved in Ezr (5,1; 6,14). As we have seen above,
they were intimately involved in the temple-rebuilding movement.
The first prophecy of Haggai precedes that of Zechariah by something
like two months—the day of the month is not given in Zechariah. The
five oracles of Haggai are dated and were delivered within a period of
about four months. The first is said to have been uttered on the first
day of the sixth month of the second year of Darius (520 B.C.). It was
directed to the governor and high priest, Zerubbabel and Joshua respectively, and dealt with the people's complaint about crop conditions
and their inability to get ahead in life. Everything seemed to go wrong,
and just when they thought they were on their feet another disaster
struck. At the moment a severe drought appears to have been plaguing
the land; even the normal dews failed, so that near starvation threatened, with severe shortages of grain, wine, oil, and pasture—a vicious
cycle that could end only in calamity. Doubtless many applied to the
community leaders for assistance. Perhaps in desperation they sought
the advice of the prophet who then delivered the word of the Lord.
Certainly, practical-minded people said, this is not the time to build
the house of the Lord. The prophet, however, declared the untoward
conditions to be a manifestation of Yahweh's displeasure at the delay
in carrying out the purpose for which the *golah* returned to Judah.
Lack of progress was due to procrastination, and the only way the
current misfortunes could be overcome was "to proceed to the hills,
bring timber and construct the house" (Hag 1,7). Then the Lord will
be pleased and appear in his glory, that is, not simply in effulgence

but in the blessings of life. The response of officials and people was sympathetic since they realized that Yahweh had sent him and they respected him. The reassuring word of Haggai was that the Lord was with them: Was not his spirit evident in the movement of all concerned when they came to work on the house of Yahweh? Preparatory work began on the twenty-fourth day of that very month. Haggai's sermon as the work was resumed after a long interval (see Josephus, *Ant.,* 11:2:2) is probably the shortest on record. It consists of only four words in Hebrew, two the actual words of the Lord, two its authentication: *'ᵃni 'ittᵉkem* (= I am with you); *nᵉ'um yhwh* (= is the oracle of Yahweh). The third discourse of the fiery prophet was delivered just a month later when invidious comparisons were heard between the rather shabby structure now going up and the glorious old Solomonic temple. The Zerubbabel temple seemed to many—according to Ezr 3,12, old men present at the dedication had seen the old temple —as virtually nothing. Such remarks had their effect and must have discouraged the builders. After all most of them were not skilled workers, and the tools and materials they had to work with were far from the best. It is significant that despondency set in after some work had been done and when it was possible to visualize what the end product would be. Once more Haggai came forward with the message of the Lord directed to strengthen the hands of Zerubbabel and Joshua and to encourage the people. The Lord's word to Israel as she departed from Egypt still stood, said Haggai, and the assurance voiced in the terse oracle when the building activity began was repeated—"I am with you." What is more, the spirit of the Lord was in their midst; therefore, they need have no fear—a clear reference to the undermined morale of the people and the troubles they were having with the political authorities. Meanwhile all were urged to persist, for help was soon to come from the nations, perhaps a hint of the outcome of the investigation carried out by the court with a prognostication of the directive of Darius to the effect that the Jews were to be financially and materially assisted by the government of Across the River. The poor and adverse beginnings must not impede the laborers; the end would bring satisfaction, for the future "splendor of this house will exceed that of the former one" (Hag 2,9). "In this place," says the Lord, "I will provide affluence." The fourth and fifth oracles were delivered on the same day—the twenty-fourth day of the ninth month, or nearly two months after the third. The first of the two is for general consumption and emphasizes the contagion of uncleanness. It is a striking recognition of the needs of the hour. The contamination of compromise is deadly in a community struggling for survival—a foreshadowing of the laws of Ezra and Nehemiah. The only way the little group of faithful devotees could endure and succeed in the re-establishment of their institutions was to keep themselves pure and their sacrifices undefiled. Already their condition had improved. Even if full prosperity was not yet evident, it was on the way. The seed had been sown; the vine, fig tree, pomegranate, and olive tree were showing signs of fruitage. "From this day forward, I will bless (you)," was the word of the Lord. The second of the last two prophecies is a private oracle for Zerubbabel. It reveals the strong nationalistic predilection of the prophet. The opposition facing Darius at the beginning of his reign may well be the basis for Haggai's declaration of the word of Yahweh: "I am about to overturn the throne of kingdoms and smash the kingdoms of the nations and overturn chariots with their riders, and horses and their riders shall go down, each one by the sword of his brother" (Hag 2,22). In the wake of this disorder he predicts that Zerubbabel, the servant of the Lord, would become like a signet ring, that is, be invested with messianic status. The order of the Haggai material, despite the fact that each section is carefully dated, is not certain, but it is beyond doubt that it belongs to the second year of Darius. (On Haggai's place among Israel's prophets, see below.)

The prophecy of Zechariah (Zech 1–8) falls into the same period as that of Haggai but continues for about two years more. Zechariah may have been the head of the priestly house of Iddo that is said to have been in the company of those who returned with Zerubbabel and Joshua (Neh 12:16). If so he was a priest-prophet or what is referred to in much modern critical literature on the prophets as a cult-prophet. His first message is dated in the eighth month of the second year of Darius and is an appeal to his contemporaries on the basis of history: Present predicaments were to be traced directly to Yahweh's displeasure with the fathers. So the prophet is directed to speak to his people now, imploring them not to act like the fathers. The simple but pungent word of the Lord is given a powerful thrust: "Return to me, and I will return to you" (Zech 1,3). Yet that was precisely the injunction of the former prophets who called upon the people of their day to "turn from your evil ways and your evil deeds" (Zech 1,4), but they refused to give heed. "Where are they?" The answer required no lengthy digression—the unheeded admonitions of the prophets overtook them. "What the Lord of hosts threatened to do with us is what he did with us" (Zech 1,6). The lesson was clear, the appeal to people now as urgent as it was to the fathers. This introductory exhortation is followed by a series of night visions that the prophet experienced in the eleventh month of the same year as the introductory oracle, according to the present arrangement of the book. The form of the night visions of Zechariah is interesting: It illustrates the use of apocalyptic imagery in the exilic and post-exilic periods and indeed, in the other oracles of Zechariah. The prophet does not see the Lord; he sees only the angel (*mal'ak*) who serves as the spokesman of Yahweh. In the first vision (Zech 1,7–17) he beholds a rider on a red horse by the myrtle trees in the glen. Behind him were other horses of different colors. They were in the service of patroling the earth and now reported to the angel: "the whole earth is quiet and subdued" (v. 11), reflecting the effectiveness of Darius' generals in quelling the rebellions raised against him when he took the throne. That seemed to augur ill for the people of the Lord in Judah and Jerusalem, as may be seen from the remonstrance of the angel (v. 12). The Lord replied that he had hired the nations for only a little punishment but they furthered the evil beyond his plan. He had, therefore, returned to Jerusalem with compassion; his house would be built again in it. The cities of the land would again become prosperous, Zion strengthened, and Jerusalem be the object of his choice as it was in the time of David. In the second vision (Zech 1,18–21 = Heb 2,1–4), the four horns represent the powers from the four corners of the earth. The four smiths were to terrify the four horns, that is, all the powers of the earth who are responsible for the condition of Judah. Here the prophet repeats the message of Hag 2,22. The third vision (Zech 2,1–5 = Heb 2,5–9) depicts a man with a measuring tape on his way to Jerusalem to measure its length and breadth in preparation for its walls. Another angel then appeared, shouting to the one with the prophet to hasten and tell the man with the tape measure that Jerusalem would be inhabited without walls, for the Lord himself would be to her a wall of fire and his glory would be in her midst. This seems to be Zechariah's answer to those who were afraid to invest in the house of God before the construction of a protecting wall. He as much as said to them, "take care of the things of God first and he will be your wall of defense" (see Mt 6,33). To this vision have been added three separate pieces: an exhortation for those in Babylon to flee to Zion because destruction was coming to the former (Zech 2,6–9 = Heb 2,10–13); the announcement that Yahweh would dwell in Jerusalem calls for rejoicing (Zech 2,10 = Heb 2,14); with the Lord's return to Zion, the nations would know, as would the people themselves, that Yahweh was in their midst. Only as the nations join themselves to him can they become his people too (Zech 2,11–12 = Heb 2,15–16). Zech 2,13 (= Heb 2,17) contains a liturgical formula. The fourth vision (Zech 3,1–7), concerning the purification of Joshua, is not the same as the others: It is not identified as a night vision. Its main feature appears to be the reinvestiture of Joshua as high priest of the new community. This does not mean that he was not the high priest before; it means rather that a new condition prevailed, unlike that which existed before deliverance from Babylon. Again there may be more here than meets the eye. There is a sense in which Joshua stands for the community. Hence he was accused by the Satan of his unworthiness—as the community was not worthy of the immense compassion of the Lord. That was why conditions—opposition, failure, indecision—afflicted it. But, as Deutero-Isaiah said, it had endured double for all its sins. Yahweh had forgiven his people and brought them back to the land. So Joshua was to be stripped of his filthy garments because his (the community's) sins had been purged. A clean turban and vestments replaced the old. Henceforth he was to rule the house of the Lord and have charge of his courts so long as he walked in the ways of the Lord and observed his charge. It is difficult to separate Joshua as high priest from Joshua as representative of the community. This vision may well have been in the mind of the author of the book of Hebrews when he wrote of the Great High Priest of our faith. The stone set before Joshua (Zech 3,8–10) is manifestly related to the foregoing. The gem of seven facets ("one stone with seven eyes") may be related to the golden plate fastened on the turban of Aaron (Ex 28,36) bearing the inscription "holy to Yahweh" (seven letters in Hebrew = *qdš l-yhwh*). The stone here is parallel to the crown of Joshua (Zerubbabel) in Zech 6,11. The whole thing symbolizes the position of the high priest, purified, cleansed of guilt, who with his friends and the Branch form the foundation of the new community. The fifth vision (Zech 4,11–14) centers on the golden lampstand and the two olive trees. The interpretation is provided by the angel himself in answer to questions of the prophet. The golden lampstand is the Lord, the seven lamps and seven eyes are those of the Lord, and the two olive trees are the political and cultic heads of the community (Zech 4,11–14). If verse 9 belongs to the vision, the frame of reference is both present and future—that is, after the foundation of the temple had been laid, but before it was finished, for the prediction is that Zerubbabel would finish it. The land might be faced with great difficulty, but before Zerubbabel it would become a plain of achievement.

The interesting thing about the whole section is Yahweh's word to Zerubbabel that the fortunes of the new community will rest upon and

be accomplished by the spirit of the Lord, not by the methods employed by the nations of the world. This is a striking expression of the
philosophy of the prophets and writers of the period. The spirit of
the Lord is at work in the world for the re-establishment of his people,
and all the political forces operative in the four quarters of the world
are under his direction. History is the sphere of his activity directed
toward the consummation of his purpose through his people. The sixth
vision (Zech 5,1-4) has to do with the flying scroll bearing the curse
ranging over the face of the entire land (not the earth here). It appears
to be directed to those who remained in the land during the exile,
those who had appropriated the property of the *golah* in the land that
had been at the mercy of thieves. The vision foresees the removal of
this curse and the consequent solution of the problems of land and
other property. Vision seven (Zech 5,5-11) centers in an ephah measure, with a leaden lid, containing a woman, symbolizing the captivity
of sin in the land held in securely in the measure of guilt. The woman
represents the totality of sin, which could not be removed by any
power of man. It could be removed only by the power provided by
Yahweh. The place to which the measure was to be carried was Shinar
(Babylon), really at the opposite pole from Jerusalem. The eighth
vision (Zech 6,1-8) is noteworthy because of the conception that underlies it. The four chariots again reflect the universal proportion of
the prophet's thought—the four quarters of the earth. The function of
the chariots was to patrol the earth to observe the diaspora wherever
it might be and bring the people to the homeland. Particularly notable
is the statement of the satisfaction of the spirit of Yahweh with those
who went to the north country (= Babylon; see Zech 2,6-7 = Heb
2,10-11) whence returned the *golah*. By Zerubbabel's and Zechariah's
time a significant number of exiles must have returned to Judah, possibly in more than one movement. At least the word of the Lord to the
prophet was commendatory of the response of the people to the decree
of Cyrus extended by Darius—all at the instigation of Yahweh.

The prophecy following the last of the visions (i.e., Zech 6,9-15)
has manifestly been tampered with (see A. Van Hoonacker, *Les Douze
Petits Prophètes* [Paris: Librairie Victor Lecoffre, J. Gabalda & Cie.,
1908], pp. 628-34; K. Elliger, *Das Alte Testament Deutsch*, 25: *Die
Propheten: Nahum, Habakkuk, Zephanja, Haggai, Sacharja, Maleachi*
[Göttingen: Vandenhoeck & Ruprecht, 1950], pp. 119-22). It deals
with the crown for the "Branch," that is, Zerubbabel, but at least in
part has been reapplied to Joshua, the high priest (v. 11). Evidently
the gifts from the authorities and *golah* in Babylon had reached Jeru-

salem (Ezr 7,15ff.). The deputation that bore it, or now had charge of it, was to hand it over to the prophet, who was directed to take it and make of it a crown to be "set upon the head of Joshua" (Van Hoonacker, pp. 631f., has *before* Joshua). It is generally thought that in view of MT *crowns* (vv. 11, 14) the reference to Zerubbabel has fallen out because of his sudden disappearance, after which authority was vested in the high priest—or that the whole frame of reference was shifted from Zerubbabel to Joshua. Be that as it may, two persons were in the mind of the writer because he speaks of the Branch who shall build the temple of the Lord, be invested with majesty (splendor), and sit and rule upon his throne. A priest shall be beside his throne and the counsel of peace shall be between both of them (v. 13). The prophecy thus emphasizes, as it now stands, the dual government reflected in the early chapters of Ezra where Zerubbabel and Joshua are nearly always mentioned together. This passage may be the scriptural background for the two-messiahs conception in the Qumran community. Once again the prophet refers to those in distant lands (Zech 7,15) who will come to help in the reconstruction of the temple if persons now engaged in the work will hearken diligently to the voice of the Lord.

Zech 7 is really a sermon based on a historical episode or text—an embassy sent to Jerusalem in the person of Bethelsharezer and Regemmelech to inquire about fasting. The oracle is dated in the fourth year of Darius (518 B.C.). The inquiry was utilized, at the direction of the Lord, to address "all the people of the land and the priests" (Zech 7,5) on the subject. In reply to the question posed by the Bethelsharezer mission, the word of Yahweh was that obedience was the way to maintain relationship with him. The people were using the ritual ordinances for their own ends. The will of the Lord was to be found in the words of the former prophets spoken in better times (Zech 7,7). Then there is an exhortation reminding us of those former prophets— according to some scholars an insertion of another of Zechariah's oracles. External cult acts have no virtue in themselves, says Zechariah. They must issue in deeds consonant with the faith they proclaim. That is, such deeds as true judgments at the city gate, remembrance of the covenant—such is the import of *ḥesed* (= steadfast love, devotion, loyalty) in v. 9—the practice of brotherly love, assistance for rather than oppression of widows, orphans, strangers, and the poor, and no underhanded scheming of one against another. The discourse on the original question continues, with a sharp reminder of the earlier generation's refusal to obey the injunctions of the prophets because of its stubbornness and hardness of heart. The Lord's spirit through the prophets' word failed to penetrate their adamantine minds, and as a result, the nation was overthrown, the people were scattered, and the pleasant land became desolate. The application of Zechariah's words rings clear: Let the *golah* and the people of the land in 518 B.C. not be like their fathers!

Zech 8 is mostly a concatenation of seven declarations and promises (vv. 1–18), each introduced by the familiar formula, "Thus says Yahweh," to which are added two other short prophecies. The prophet speaks of the Lord's jealousy for Zion; his return to and dwelling in Zion and Jerusalem, the faithful city; the beautiful sight of children playing in its streets and old men leaning each on his staff—evidence of a long period of peace and prosperity; the marvel of it all in the eyes of God and man alike; and the salvation of the Lord's people from east and west now dwelling in Jerusalem as his people in faithfulness and righteousness. Verses 9–13 recall conditions deplored in Hag 1,5–6. Zechariah urges the people to be strong, to listen to the prophets, and to remember how it was with them before they undertook rebuilding the Lord's house. Since they have put themselves to work on it, the Lord will deal with them quite differently from the way he dealt with the fathers. Peace and tranquility will be sown and the productivity of the soil insured by the dews and rains of heaven. Instead of the nation being used as a curse word, it will henceforth be a word of blessing. Verses 14–17 state that as the Lord did evil to Jerusalem and did not relent in the time of the fathers, so now he will do good without relenting, only the people must live by the qualities announced in the covenant—truth, judgment, honesty, and concern for one another. Then the prophet returns to the cultic observances of fasting (vv. 18–19), which will be a time of joy and happiness if the people genuinely love truth and peace. Finally, verses 20–22 contain one of the most universal messages of the Old Testament. It could well come from Zechariah, who must have been struck by the variety of peoples that were present in the land in his time and then obsessed with hope that they might join themselves to the people of the Lord in Jerusalem. That would come about only, however, if they remained truly his people in obedience and covenant loyalty and thus became irresistibly attractive—reminiscent of the declaration of Jesus in Mt 8,11.

It has often been pointed out that the prophecies of Haggai and Zechariah breathe the spirit of Ezekiel, particularly in his conception of cultic responsiveness and in his visions of the new community (Ez

40–48) with its temple-centered organization. Both of our prophets connected the welfare of the people with the progress in temple reconstruction. They believed that the long, hard experiences of adversity were due to neglect of the cult institutions. Their condition could be ameliorated only by resolute action in the direction of making amends by rebuilding the temple. To that end they sought to inspire the *golah* to undertake the work and thus fulfill the vision of Ezekiel. And they did succeed, for their proclamations were heeded, the authorities set to work, and despite all discouragements and opposition, the temple was rebuilt. It was finished in 516 B.C. But in the process somewhere, Zerubbabel disappeared. Just what happened to him is uncertain. He may have been recalled, or he perhaps died. The rearrangement of the oracle on the messianic crown, noted above (Zech 6,9–14), suggests that something out of the ordinary took place. Furthermore, there is no mention by name (though "your governor" occurs in Mal 1,8) of another political governor of Judah until Nehemiah. Did the strong nationalistic preaching of Haggai and Zechariah initiate a movement to make Zerubbabel king? And was that movement then squelched by the Persian authorities? We do not know. We do know that henceforth the ruler or chief official of the community was the high priest (see Albright, *BP* 88).

Further Prophetic Literature of the Period

For some time now it has been recognized that the series of prophetic poems transmitted in the book of Isaiah, chapters 56–66, nearly all come from the period dealt with in this section of our monograph. A few may be older, a few later. Most scholars agree that this portion of Isaiah bears a strong resemblance to Is 40–55. Eissfeldt thinks much of it was written in conscious dependence on the oracles of Deutero-Isaiah. Whereas the only criteria for dates and relationships are internal in character, there appears to be no evidence against some of them coming from Deutero-Isaiah himself. It is not beyond possibility that this prophet, like Haggai and Zechariah, returned with the *golah* and delivered some of these prophecies in the homeland. Haggai and Zechariah were not the only prophets active in the first years of the return (see Zech 1,5; 7,3; 8,9). The same spirit prevails, and some of the same problems are apparent. For example, Is 58 is concerned with the same theme treated in Zech 7—fasting. In Zechariah the discourse concerns the request about the fasting of the people brought to the attention of the prophet by Bethelsharezer and his companions. Is 58 gives us no historical pretext but has the same solution as that offered by Zechariah. The complaint here is that although the people sought the Lord daily and by fasting attempted to show their allegiance to him, he did not respond (v. 3a). The prophet then tells them why the Lord took no pleasure in them—when they fasted it was for their own pleasure. Their cultic ceremonies were not supported by actions consonant therewith. They oppressed their workers, they quarreled, and they resorted to physical violence (vv. 3b–4a). Such performances were not calculated to win the approval of the Lord. The fast pleasing to the Lord was "to loose the bonds of wickedness, to undo the heavy burdens, to let the oppressed go free, and to break every yoke" (v. 6). It was to share bread with the hungry, to lodge the poor and outcast, to clothe the naked, and to make themselves available to their own people. If such were the fast of the nation, the Lord would not withhold his blessing. They would then experience satisfaction even in drought, "be like a watered garden," like a perennial spring, and they shall build up the waste places and "raise up the foundations of many generations" (v. 12). Then, too, many of the thoughts expressed in Is 60–62 parallel those in Zechariah. Compare Is 60,10–16 with Zech 6,15, and Is 61,1–62,12 with Zech 8,1–17.20–22. The underlying conception of Is 57,16–18 seems very much like that of Zech 8,20–22. The main thrust of Haggai is the promise of blessings if the old institutions were rebuilt. To that Zechariah adds the old prophetic demand of covenantal faithfulness as it applies to relationship between Yahweh and the people and to that which must be operative among the covenantal people themselves. The contemporary (if they are so) poems in Isaiah follow closely the preachings of Zechariah but accentuate more the message of "the former prophets." Yet they too are shot through with the promise of Yahweh's blessing upon the redeemed people who are responsive to his call. Whether from Deutero-Isaiah, his disciples, or other prophets, these poems represent preaching in Jerusalem at the time of the rebuilding of the temple and the re-establishment of the cult after 520 B.C.

On the other hand, a number of the pieces in this collection (Is 56–66) clearly bear the stamp of other times. Is 57,1–6, with its emphasis on the detestable practices of foreign cults, could easily be pre-exilic (see Ez 8). So also could Is 57,7–13, which is reminiscent of Ez 16,23. Is 63,7–64,12 (Heb 64,11) sound very much like Lam 3. The oracle against Edom (Is 63,1–6) breathes the spirit of Lam 4,21–

22 and Obadiah. All these may be older, perhaps reworked and reapplied, compositions. Is 66,1–4 is occupied with temple building but may reflect earlier ventures on the part of those remaining in the land after the events of 587 B.C.

The writer has elsewhere (*ZAW* 74, 1962, pp. 177–95) endeavored to show the possibility of the prophecy of Joel coming from the period with which we are concerned here. It has been said that Joel, as it now stands, bears the form of a psalm of lamentation. As such it fits in very well with the situation deplored by Haggai and Zechariah, notably the former, who speaks about lethargy with reference to religion and crop failures. There was a sharp cleavage between the rich and poor—paneled houses and near starvation (Hag 1,4–6; 2,17). Joel, too, attributes the calamity that has befallen the land to the neglect of religion. In both Joel and Haggai, prophecies were attendant upon crop failure. Conditions in the land, the object of popular complaint, called forth prophecy. Despite natural adversities, Joel implies that some were still getting drunk—a telling admission of indifference and apathy amid the most abject poverty (Jl 1,5). Haggai denounces those who dwelt in paneled houses (Hag 1,4).

Yet it was not so much economic disparity that troubled the prophets as the popular unconcern for things that really mattered. Whereas all the prophets call for repentance, there is an urgency in Joel (Jl 2,12ff.), Zechariah (Zech 1,3b) and Haggai (Hag 2,15,18) not so pronounced elsewhere. Haggai (Hag 2,21f.) and Joel (Jl 3,2) envision judgment upon the nations, both, no doubt, eschatologically. Joel calls upon the people to "sanctify a fast" (Jl 2,15) in which all groups are implored to participate. Fasting was one of the preoccupations of Zechariah (Zech 7,3ff.) who stressed the moral as well as the cultic aspects of the ceremony. It is not beyond credibility that economic and social betterment did not become evident at once. Such changes take time. Furthermore, religious leaders like Zechariah and Joel saw that much more than a physical structure was needed to turn the tide. People had to be aroused toward a revitalization of their covenantal obligations under Yahweh. The times demanded sincere repentance. That is why Joel (Jl 2,13) called for a rending of hearts and Zechariah for true judgment (Zech 7,9). Only then could adversities afflicting the land be ameliorated and the promised prosperity ensue. Joel's cult prophecy (Jl 2,19ff.) fits in quite well with the general atmosphere already described. In the immediate post-exilic period, priests and prophets joined in a program of activity aimed at the re-establishment of the Yahweh community under most adverse circumstances. Like Haggai, Joel seems to accentuate the need for cooperation in getting the people to adhere to the Lord amid the turmoil, despair, lethargy, and uncertainty of the time. They saw that only their genuine response to the needs of the hour could avert utter disaster in the Valley of Decision and bring order out of the existent chaos. Joel pleaded for cultic renewal as Haggai and Zechariah demanded the reconstruction of the temple itself. The times called for both, for without the building there could be no real cultus and without cultic observances there could be no real religious mobilization to meet the demands of life enjoined by the old prophets. Carelessness and indifference in these matters would lead to compromise with local cults and ultimate disintegration of Yahwehism. It is still so.

For the present it is best to leave out of consideration the second half of the book of Zechariah (Zech 9–14). There is entirely too much uncertainty about the date of these chapters. There are good arguments for the several general positions that have been taken on it. For instance, Otzen (*Studien über Deuterosacharja* [Copenhagen: Prostant apud Munksgaard, 1964]) regards Zech 9 and 10 as pre-exilic—time of Josiah; Zech 11 just before the Judean exile; Zech 12–13 early exilic period; Zech 14 from late in the post-exilic age. Van Hoonacker (pp. 649–662) holds to the substantial unity of these chapters and dates them toward the end of the reign of Darius I. Eissfeldt thinks of at least two different authors—one for Zech 9–11; the other for Zech 12–14—and dates the material from 300–280 B.C. (*The Jerusalem Bible* [New York: Doubleday & Co., Inc., 1966], p. 1139, dates the material to the last decades of the fourth century B.C.)

There are doubtless other pieces in the Bible coming from the Darius I period that cannot at present be identified. Much of the material is poetic in form, and it is extremely hazardous to date such compositions without specific datable references. Suffice it to say that the *golah* experienced much between 538 B.C. and 485 B.C. Light from the east cast its welcome rays upon the dark period of the Jewish exiles, as well as upon those who remained in the land. The Cyrus decree was implemented under Sheshbazzar and renewed and extended under Zerubbabel and Joshua. With the assistance of the prophets Haggai and Zechariah, the authorities engaged in the most essential public building enterprises. The altar and temple were reconstructed and regular worship services instituted. Sacrifices and feasts were observed, so that by the early fifth century conditions had improved as we shall see in the next chapter. However, the period was not without its troubles and perils. Increasing tensions between the *golah* and the people of the land are made evident in such sources as can be dated. In fact it was not until the time of Nehemiah and Ezra that real progress, religiously speaking, took place. The whole century between Cyrus and Nehemiah was fraught with all sorts of problems. There was both progression and regression but no real stability. It was extremely difficult to learn and apply the lessons of the past in a constructive way—as it always is.

What was being done in Judah and Jerusalem was to be of tremendous significance for the future. Here under the tap-hammer blows of history was to be forged a new community out of which the Savior was later to come. But outside of that immediate community other great things were happening. Cyrus opened up interrelationships in the world of his time that were fraught with enormous consequences. Cambyses carried the lines of empire to Egypt—even to Ethiopia. Darius linked east and west and south by a road system and an interconnection of life and culture hitherto unknown. Interinfluences of culture and civilization were to become easier, more marked and more extensive—thus preparing the way for the coming of the Greeks with still further expansion in all directions. Theologically speaking, it cannot be doubted that God was at work in that world. First he purged his people through exile, then he sent Cyrus, his servant, to liberate them from their bondage to build new institutions patterned on the old so as to conserve the good and relevant deposits of past experience. Then came Darius, whose conquests brought together and intermixed peoples and ideas—not without considerable pain and, sometimes, the gravest dissatisfaction. But through it all the way was being prepared on a magnificent scale, from all sides, for further movements in the economy of God in his dealings with man.

Selected Readings

Bright, J., *A History of Israel,* Chap. IX. Philadelphia: The Westminster Press, 1959.

Ellis, P., *The Men and Message of the Old Testament,* Chap. XII, pp. 1–5. Collegeville, Minn.: The Liturgical Press, 1963.

Heinisch, P., *History of the Old Testament,* Chap. XLIII. Collegeville, Minn.: The Liturgical Press, 1952.

Ricciotti, G., *The History of Israel,* 2nd ed., II, 1–23; 78–79. Milwaukee: Bruce Publishing Company, 1958.

IV

The Reign of Xerxes I

The sudden disappearance of Darius beclouded the skies of the Persian empire, and they cast their shadows upon the Jewish community in Judah and upon the Jews still in Babylon. Just when things began to look better for them, they fell victim to the times in many ways. Once again there is an extreme paucity of information, and what we do possess is frequently subject to error on the part of the interpreter since it cannot be definitively controlled by other evidence. In the first place, Xerxes was chosen to succeed his father not because he was the oldest son but because he was the first son born to Darius after he had assumed the throne and also because he was the son of Atossa, daughter of Cyrus and sister of Cambyses. In preparation for his role as king of Persia, he was made king of Babylon by Darius and was domiciled in the new palace erected in Babylon between 498 and 496 B.C.

Shortly thereafter Xerxes appears on the monuments at Persepolis with his father (see Ghirshman, *Persia*, plates 246, 255). He occupied that position for about ten years before he assumed power as head of the empire. He was a somewhat temperamental person, with no mind of his own, and thus susceptible to influence from those around him—a weakness that was to cost the empire dearly later on. Nevertheless, to judge from the monumental portraits and the description of Herodotus (7:187), Xerxes was an imposing personality, one who did well on state occasions. He might have done much better as a ruler if those around him had been less ambitious.

The Course
of Empire (485–465 B.C.)

Had Xerxes been the man his father was, history might have a far different story to tell. Josephus (*Ant.* 11:5:1) says he inherited the piety toward God exhibited by his father and did the same things for the Jews. In some respects he certainly did follow in the footsteps of Darius, notably, as Josephus informs us, in the direction of religion. He exalted Ahuramazda, proclaimed him the greatest of the gods, and paid homage to him at every opportunity. According to a Persepolis foundation tablet (*ANET* 316f.) composed in Akkadian, Xerxes speaks in almost the same language employed by his father to describe the activity of his god. He (i.e., Ahuramazda) was the god responsible for the earth, the sky, mankind, and the well-being of his devotees, and the one who placed the king on his throne. Everything Xerxes undertook he carried out under the "shadow" of the great god who gave him support until his purpose had been achieved. Significantly, the inscription ends with a kind of hortatory prayer in which he admonishes all who long for prosperity in life and happiness in death to live in harmony with the law of Ahuramazda, to serve him alone and regard with reverence the cosmic order (*arta*). The final sentence voices the profoundest desire of the king—that Ahuramazda guard him and his family and keep the countries over which he rules from evil. Under the inspiration and direction of his god alone was his building done and his conquests carried through successfully. One of the clues to the religious zeal of Xerxes is his destruction of the so-called demon sanctuary and his decree that the demons were no longer to be worshiped. At their sanctuary he set up a shrine of Ahuramazda (X Ph, lines 35–41).

In the same inscription (lines 13–28) Xerxes mentions 29 nations over which he claimed sovereignty (see Ghirshman, *Persia,* plate 211— east staircase of Apadana at Persepolis). At the time of the death of Darius, Egypt was in revolt and that was the first situation the new monarch had to deal with. Xerxes suppressed it in short order and with a harshness not hitherto experienced in Egypt under the Persians. Temple property was seized and the people treated with malevolence. Moreover, the old custom of royal titulary was abandoned, so that the coffin of the Apis bull that died during Xerxes' reign bears no monarchial name—perhaps because the priests deliberately refused to inscribe the name of the king or because they believed there was no one with the official title. Achaemenes, the king's brother, was put in charge of governmental affairs and appears to have ruled with a heavy hand. Babylon seems to have accepted the new king with alacrity. He paid a visit to the city soon after his accession but upon his return to Ecbatana ordered a change in title from simply king of Babylon to king of Parsa and Mada, king of Babylon, king of countries. The officials of Babylon were not slow to catch the significance of the change, and revolt broke out. Zopyrus, the satrap, was slain by would-be usurpers. Xerxes acted swiftly and appointed his brother-in-law, Megabyzus, in his place. In a short time the city was subjugated and subjected to extreme reprisal. The fortifications erected by Nebuchadnezzar were leveled, the temple of Esagila, as well as others, demolished, and the 1800-pound gold statue of Marduk deported to become part of the king's treasure. That must have been an appalling sight to the people of Babylon, because from then on no king could take the hand of the god Marduk on New Year's day as the legitimate ruler. The protesting priest was butchered—a sign that the Persian general meant business. That, too, would settle the perennial problem of any future upstart who might seize the hand of the god and thus legitimate himself as king. That was precisely what Xerxes aimed to do. Along with these public demonstrations of punishment went the confiscation of the property and businesses of merchants and other citizens. Babylon had thus lost its independence as a kingdom under the Persians and had become a satrapy of the empire. So far as we know no imperial inscriptions were erected in either Egypt or Babylon in Xerxes' reign. There are a few ownership inscriptions on seals and vases bearing the simple statement, "Xerxes the great king," and a few of the Elephantine documents are dated in the reign of Xerxes (Cowley, *Aramaic Papyri,* nos. 2, 5, 6). There is also a Saqqarah grave-inscription dated in the fourth year of Xerxes.

Xerxes is perhaps best known for his unsuccessful campaign against the Greeks. After Darius had been worsted in his attempts to conquer the mainland of Greece in 492–490 B.C., he resolved at once to make a later attempt. To that end he gathered his strength and made plans, but before they could be executed he died. No sooner had Xerxes subdued the rebellious provinces of Egypt and Babylon than he was reminded of his father's chief ambition by his own officials. Herodotus says (7:5) that he had at first resolutely set himself against a Grecian campaign. So desperate were his Athenian advisers and to such tactics did they stoop that they hired a disreputable oracle peddler to prey on Xerxes. Even worse, they twisted earlier prophecies to their purpose. Perhaps nowhere does his weakness show up so glaringly as in his senseless attack upon Greece and in the several phases of the war's conduct. Only the barest outline of that struggle can be given here. For a full account the reader is referred to Herodotus (Books 7–9) from which all subsequent accounts are drawn.

Xerxes was not inclined toward the venture; he was much more interested in court life, in the erection of monuments, and in building enterprises. But he was prevailed upon by Athenian exiles and seekers of glory by war in his own retinue to undertake an adventure in which his far more capable father had come to grief. Nevertheless, when his mind was made up, he set himself to the task with assiduity. He organized an army composed of forty-six nations, commanded by twenty-nine officers, all of whom were Persians. Other generals were relegated to subordinate positions—a telling indication of the Persian influence based on a growing distrust of other peoples. Six generals were placed over these officers, and Xerxes himself occupied the position of commander-in-chief. The core of the land-forces of the Persian king was the so-called Ten Thousand Immortals composed mostly of Persians, though in that contingent were Medes and Elamites now thoroughly loyal. They must have been a beautiful spectacle, garbed as they were in colorful uniforms bearing elaborate decorations (*Her.* 7:83), a magnificent instrument for parade purposes that at the same time exhibited inherent weaknesses for actual combat. It was organized on the basis of national contingents, not upon that of weapons—an inexcusable organizational blunder. There were 80,000 horses, besides those used for the chariots. There was also an Arabian camel corps. The huge land army was supported by 1,207 triremes made up of contributions from Phoenicia, Egypt, Cyprus, Cilicia, Pamphylia, Lycia, Dorians from Asia, Caria, Ionia, the various islands, and from the Hellespont. Each fighting ship was accompanied by Persians, Medes, and Sacae—

to prevent defection. In addition there were 3,000 naval transport vessels. This time, Xerxes resolved there would be no rush attack. There would be a slow, deliberate advance of the army supported by the navy. The army was mobilized in Cappadocia whence it proceeded to Sardis, the Persian capital of Asia Minor where it remained until the spring of 480 B.C. The army was led up the western plains and valleys of Asia Minor to Abydos, where two ship-bridges had been thrown across the Hellespont. It took the huge army a whole week, moving day and night, to cross. Once in Europe the way was even more difficult for such a vast horde. Certain troops did have supplies following them, but for the most part they depended on what they could get from the countryside. The greatest problem was water; Herodotus more than once says that the rivers did not have enough water for the army; that must have been the case especially in the summer months. The army and navy met at Therma in Thessalonica, a deliberate plan to create consternation for the Greeks who might be foolhardy enough to resist the progress of Persian advance. It succeeded with some but had precisely the opposite effect on others. The provinces of Thessaly, Locris, and Boeotia sent earth and water so that with few exceptions the way was open as far as the Isthmus of Corinth, where the Spartans had determined to make a stand. When the Persian army finally marched, there was virtually nothing in its way until it reached Thermopylae, where Leonidas and his Spartans held the pass until a hidden way around it betrayed them. Meanwhile the Persian fleet was not faring so well at the hands of Themistocles in the straits of Artemisium. Had it not been for the opening of the Thermopylae pass, which virtually forced the withdrawal of the Greeks the Persians might have lost then and there. As the Persian forces moved on, they ravaged such of the country that had offered resistance. The fleet sailed south to Phalerum, endangering the Greek navy at Salamis. All Xerxes needed to do was to sit tight and let the Greek force become disrupted by internal quarrels. But he was not so minded, preferring to press the battle. He landed some of his troops on the island in the strait to cut off escape of Greek sailors, and then the engagement was on. Had not an Athenian ship forced battle, the Greek navy might have disintegrated. In the ensuing battle the Persians were defeated, and their force on the island was wiped out to a man. Xerxes, angered at his fleet commanders, had the Phoenician commanders executed with the result that both theirs and the Egyptian ships withdrew. The king himself fled to Sardis and left the army in the hands of his seasoned generals, notably Mardonius and Artabazus, the former in charge of direct operations and the latter to guard the supply routes. The Greeks were rent with internal disagreements between the Athenians and Spartans upon which Mardonius attempted to capitalize but without success. The Spartans had in the meantime been convinced that they would have to come out from behind the isthmus and fight. Receiving word of this move, Mardonius again struck at Athens and then withdrew to Boeotia. Full of fight, the Greeks marched through Attica and encamped at Cithaeron opposite the Persian camp. The cavalry skirmishes proved disastrous to the Persians, and before it was over Mardonius was killed as he led his troops on a frontal attack against the Greeks. They followed the Persians into the fortified camp, whence they fled after the death of their general, and slaughtered them without mercy. Thus ended the battle of Plataea with the Greeks winning a glorious victory. Yet the struggle was not over. The final blow was struck at Mycale in Ionia, just opposite the island of Samos. With the Persian defeat there the mainland of Greece was delivered as were all the major islands in the Aegean. The Greeks sailed north and destroyed the pontoon bridges across the Hellespont. Cyprus also was delivered. The formation of the Delian league against Persia, the treachery of Pausanias, and the defeat at the Eurymedon river ended Persian control of Greece and led to defection on the part of many Ionian states; with it was concluded Persian influence in the west.

It is thought that there is some indication of trouble among the Jews of the *golah* and their neighbors in Judah at the beginning of the reign of Xerxes. In Ezr 4,6 is reference to a formal accusation lodged against the *golah* at the beginning of the reign of Xerxes, who is elsewhere in the Bible (e.g., in Esther) known as Ahasuerus. It is certainly possible, even probable, that the enemies of the Jews endeavored to stir up friction in Jerusalem at the time. On other opportune occasions no time was lost in fanning the always smoldering embers of hatred and jealousy as may be seen from the history of the community related in Ezr 4–6, but that there was a full-fledged revolt in Palestine in 485 B.C. is difficult to justify on the basis of present evidence. Professor Julian Morgenstern's theory of a thorough-going destruction of Jerusalem in 485 B.C. (*Hebrew Union College Annual* XXVII [1956], pp. 101–179; XXVIII [1957], pp. 15–47; XXXI [1960], pp. 1–29) brought on by an uprising of the Jews and administered by surrounding peoples such as the Edomites, Moabites, Ammonites, Philistines, Sidonians, Tyrians, and even some Persians is too inferential to carry conviction. Moreover, the book of Malachi hardly supports such a catastrophe. (See below.)

Xerxes, though not very astute as a military leader, was nevertheless somewhat of an organizer and builder. His efforts at greater unification of the empire and the stricter control exercised over the satrapies has already been noted. There was some progress along economic lines as shown by the Persepolis Treasury Tablets, nearly all of which come from the reign of Xerxes (see G. G. Cameron, *The Persepolis Treasury Tablets* [Chicago: University of Chicago Press, 1948]). Wages for workers on the various building projects were paid partly in cash, whereas before they were paid in kind. There is some indication that in the later years of Xerxes there was a reversion to the old method, but the introduction of the new method, probably by royal edict, marks a significant advance in economic history. In all probability it was brought about by the growing stock of precious metal in the king's exchequer but at the same time offered a greater degree of choice to the worker on the basis of individual need or desire. Furthermore, with the increasing use of coinage elsewhere in the empire it became one more boon for the trader and banker. This marks an advancement, if not the beginning, of a money economy still in the process of development. Whereas it is true that the Persepolis documents apply only to a local situation, there is every reason to believe that similar practices were current elsewhere in the great centers of the empire. The banking house of Egibi was active in Babylon between the time of Nebuchadnezzar and Darius; that of Murashu's sons at Nippur reached its height after the time of Xerxes, perhaps assisted by the economic practices and policies instituted in the period of Darius and Xerxes. The tablets themselves exhibit an elaborate system of accounting in which value of goods paid in kind was reckoned on the basis of monetary equivalents. All kinds of skilled and unskilled workmen were employed by the government and paid from the royal treasury. There were masons, sculptors, carpenters, designers in wood and stone, ornament makers, goldsmiths, beer handlers, tax handlers, special handlers of copper receipts, armor makers, boys employed as drivers of asses, boys attached to the royal house, accountants, and even sheepherders. There is the record of a priest being paid for his services (Tablet 11). In a number of instances the nationality of the workers is given: Egyptian masons, Syrian laborers, Ionian column workers, Carian goldsmiths. It may be of some significance that most of these tablets come from the early and late portions of Xerxes' reign, that is, before and after the Greek campaign. Inasmuch as so many of these tablets are devoted to the payment of some type of builder or other, they must be connected with the continued construction at Persepolis begun by Darius.

A brief survey of the construction activity of Xerxes will help to fill in certain details to make more clear both the character of the man and that of the Persian world in the score of years during which he was its master. The treasury tablets noted above testify to what must have been a real building spree in the last years of his reign. That it was more than ordinary work is shown by the type of skilled laborers, artists, mechanics, ironworkers, decorators, and so on, employed. The tremendous complex of buildings at Persepolis represents a colorful display of the plans of Darius, with no less flare for such projects by Xerxes. The archives point not only to the careful business transactions associated with the work but the enormous expenditures and number of personnel required for the work. First of all there was the huge Apadana (= palace) with its elaborate staircases whose sides were covered with sculptured reliefs composed of processions of soldiers, dignitaries, and subject peoples parading before their king at the New Year's festival (see Ghirshman, *Persia*, plates 209–213). Undoubtedly these huge panels represent the climax of Persian art. Then Xerxes made additions to the palace of Darius but at the same time erected a new one for himself to the east of the complex. He also built a harem for his wife Amestris and a new gateway of all lands. He had completed the gateway of Darius, which was the place for the procession to enter the Apadana on the feast day. The north-northwestern section of the complex, which hitherto remained unoccupied, became the site of a new gateway with a gigantic entrance some eighty-two feet long and forty feet high. On each side were massive bull reliefs extending further out than the other relief sculptures (see Ghirshman, *Persia* plate 207, and for a view of the overall plan of the Persepolis buildings, plate 256). Through that gateway entered the heads of other than Median and Persian delegations to the Hall of a Hundred Pillars, which was the throne room. The Medes and Persians seem to have entered through the Darius gateway, then proceeded to the Apadana and on to the west entrance to the throne room. The most amazing characteristic of these buildings is the artistic relief work depicting all sorts of scenes and executed in the most perfect fashion. Every possible wall is covered with these sculptured reliefs. It certainly points up the genius of Xerxes' school of art and the intellectual appreciation and tastes of the king. It reflects the might and power of Persia in his time along other than military lines. There is some indication that Xerxes was responsible for building operations elsewhere, but mostly for the completion of or additions to works already set in progress by Darius— notably at Susa. It was probably Xerxes' love for art that impelled him to rob Greece and other lands of such objects as he could carry away. Arrian (*History of Alexander and Indica,* trans. E. Iliff Robson [Cambridge: Harvard University Press, 1961]) reports that Alexander the Great returned to Athens bronze statues transported to Persia (3:16:7) and gave back to the embassies of other Greek states the works of art and votive offerings Xerxes had taken (7:19:2). (For art of the Achaemenian period see E. Porada, *Ancient Iran* [London: Methuen & Co., Ltd., 1965], pp. 142–78. It includes a large number of colored plates of building details and smaller art objects such as jewelry, pottery, seals, rings, bracelets, etc.)

A word is in order here about the religion of Xerxes. Everywhere in his building is to be found the great sign of Ahuramazda—as, indeed, it is found on the monuments of Darius. That means that in essence he followed the faith of his father. In the Persepolis inscription (XPa) are repeated the statements of Darius (DNa, lines 1–4) to the effect that Ahuramazda is the creator of heaven, earth, sky, man, and the welfare of men, and then the king claims that the "Colonnade of all lands" was built by the favor of this god. Furthermore, he says that whatever good construction may have come from his hand was due to the blessing of Ahuramazda, to whom he then prays for protection for himself, his kingdom, his and his father's buildings. Such statements appear throughout his inscriptions in what appears to be a formulary manner. To Ahuramazda he owes his kingship. The most interesting of all his records is the famous Daiva inscription (X Ph) that lists the countries over which he ruled and how he put down unrest among some of them by the help of his god. Then he goes on to write about his destruction of the shrine of demons and sets down the proclamation that they shall not be worshiped any more. Even the location was fitted out for Ahuramazda devotion. The other business he mentions may also have to do with the practice of religion or the setting right of illicit conduct arising from *daiva* worship. He exhorts those who desire happiness in life and blessedness in death to respect the law of Ahuramazda and worship both Ahuramazda and Arta reverently. Before he crossed the Hellespont, Herodotus (7:53) says, he concluded his address to the Persian nobles "And now let us offer prayers to the gods who watch over the welfare of Persia"—that is, to Ahuramazda and Arta. He is said to have sacrificed a thousand oxen to the Trojan Minerva (*Her.* 7:43). One of the Treasury Tablets (11) records payment of 5¼ sheqels of silver at the equivalent value of one sheep for every three sheqels, paid by Shakka for the services of a haoma priest from the sixth to twelfth months of the second year of Xerxes. The haoma—a narcotic or intoxicating substance—cult was banned by the Zoroastrians because of the excesses involved in the conduct of its rituals. The flourishing of this cult as late as Xerxes demonstrates that the early Achaemenid kings were not Zoroastrians (see also Cameron, *Persepolis Treasury Tables,* pp. 5–8). It is certain also that Magian libation priests operated in the period of Darius, but whether they continued into that of Xerxes is not known. Herodotus (7:54) speaks of Xerxes pouring a libation into the sea from a golden goblet, "praying the while with his face turned to the sun." Yet that is not quite the same as the conduct of a Magian libation ritual. In the Herodotus passage cited above it is said that "the Magians poured libations to the heroes who were slain at Troy" when Xerxes was passing the site on his way to cross the Hellespont. We may be absolutely sure that Xerxes was a fire-worshiper because fire altars were not removed and were still present in the reign of his successors. Reference was made above to Xerxes' removal of the daivas, or demons, which was one aspect of his reforming activity. There is one other aspect of that, namely his veneration of the Arta as shown by the name given to his son Arta-xerxes, which in Persian means "Arta's kingdom" (= justice + kingdom) or "possessing a kingdom of justice." Arta is interpreted by R. G. Kent "as an archangel attending Ahuramazda." Darius wrote about righting the wrongs done to people (DB, 1:67–71); his insistence upon truth (DB, 4:40–45); about how he conducted himself according to righteousness (DB, 4:61–67); enjoined his subjects to follow his law (DNa, 15–30) and the right path (DNa, 56–60); and that right was his desire (DNb, 1–27). Xerxes repeated some of the propositions in his own inscriptions and likewise urged his people to respect the law of Ahuramazda and to worship Arta with reverence. That would insure a happy life and blessedness in death. From this we note a strong accent on the doing of right, which is deified in the term Arta.

Being the type of person he was, Xerxes could be expected to react toward his defeat in Greece the way he did. Most of his building program came after he returned to his capital; he then took care also of his social life. According to Herodotus, the Persian nobles' wives or concubines accompanied them on the Greek campaign. Whether Xerxes was thus accompanied we do not know, though some of his harem was certainly present. On important occasions, he did consult Artemesia, the queen of Halicarnassus, and was thrilled by her conduct in the battle of Salamis. In a Council of War at Phalerum, Artemesia disagreed with the unanimous advice of the sovereigns and ship captains and warned against a sea fight with the Greeks. Xerxes chose to disregard her counsel, though he was pleased with her outspoken opinion (*Her.* 8:68,69). In the ensuing naval battle at Salamis she distinguished herself by ramming one of the ships of her own group to avoid capture by the Athenians (*Her.* 8:87,88) for which she received high praise from Xerxes. Later he entrusted some of his children to her care at Sardis. He himself spent the winter and a portion of the following year there, too, where he fell in love with his brother Masistes' wife. When she resisted his advances he conceived the idea of marrying his brother to another woman. After the betrothal, he returned to Susa where he fell violently in love with his son's bride, the daughter of Masistes—and she responded. This led to harem intrigue, for when Amestris, the first wife of the king, heard about it she resolved to get rid of her brother-in-law's wife whom she blamed for the whole affair. Xerxes and his brother quarreled furiously over the matter while Amestris had her way. She mutilated horribly her sister-in-law. Masistes and his followers hurried away in the direction of Bactria hoping to stir up a revolt against his brother, which might have had serious consequences had not the latter sent a detachment after him and had him slain. Thus was initiated the palace intrigue in which Xerxes lost his life. He was struck down in his own bedchamber by a group of conspirators led by his uncle Artabanus who hoped to succeed his nephew. He was assisted by the royal chamberlain and by Megabyzus, Xerxes' grandson. Xerxes was entombed in the royal sepulchre near that of Darius at Naqš-i-Rustam.

The Story
of Esther

This is not the place to enter into an extended discussion of all the problems connected with the book of Esther; however, something must be said about it because it purports to center on court activities in the reign of Xerxes, who is here called Ahasuerus. Most scholars agree that it is a historical novel, but perhaps the emphasis has fallen too much on the noun rather than on the adjective. The more one reads the book, takes into consideration the names and references to Persian court life, and studies it with the archaeological and linguistic aids that have come to hand, the more he must be impressed with its reflection of the period from which it purports to come. Naturally it was composed from a tendentious point of view, but that does not militate against the basic historicity of many of the aspects around which it is woven (see H. Cazelles, "Note sur la composition du rouleau d'Esther" in *Lex Tua Veritas* [Trier: Paulinus-Verlag, 1961], pp. 17–29). It might be described as a history of salvation as conceived by eastern Jewry.

First of all, in the light of the Susa and other excavations in Persia, it is apparent that the description of the palace complex of buildings fits in quite well with archaeological discoveries. With the above de-scription of Persepolis—Susa was similar in plan though not so elabo-rate—compare the reference here to "the gate of the king" (Est 2,19); the inner (Est 4,11) and outer (Est 6,4) court of the palace; the resi-dence of the queen (Est 1,19; 2,16); the women's quarters (Est 2,9) where there was a court (Est 2,11); and the second women's quarters where the harem was kept (Est 2,14). When Esther went from one to the other she had to cross the court between them where Mordecai could communicate with her. In Est 1,5 we read about a seven-days feast held "in the court of the garden of the *bitan* of the king," which Oppenheim (*JNES* XXIV [1965] 328ff.) has shown here means the "kiosk" of the king and agrees very well with the usage of the term in this period. As he points out, the author of Esther has the king giving a feast for his subjects at Susa "in *the court* of the garden of the 'kiosk' of the king" while the king himself was engaged with his advisers in the pavilion itself. Note also in Est 1,6–7 the description of the ele-gance of the decorations—the white curtains and blue hangings gath-ered by a linen cord to silver rings, the marble pillars, the gold and silver couches on mosaic pavements, the varied golden cups—which is now abundantly illustrated from the remains uncovered by the archae-ologists (see Ghirshman, *Persia*). Herodotus tells us of the inner coun-cil of the king composed of seven counselors (cf. *Her.* 3:31, 83, 118) as affirmed also in Esther (Est 1,14; Ezr 7,14). Boys and girls were brought from subject peoples to the king as tribute (*Her.* 3:97), a near parallel to Est 2,2. The intercession of Esther for her people is much like that of Darius' wife when Intaphernes, one of the seven counselors, and his family were under sentence of death (*Her.* 3:118–119). The secret communication between Otanes and his daughter Phaedima, the wife of Cambyses, to expose the pseudo-Smerdis is similar to that be-twēen Mordecai and Esther after she became the wife of Xerxes (*Her.* 3:68, 69). After the removal of the Magi at the beginning of the reign of Darius—a veritable slaughter of them begun by the execution of the leaders and continued by the Persian mob—the event was celebrated by a commemorative feast (the Megophonia) when no Magian was permitted in sight on pain of death (*Her.* 3:78–79). Compare the feast of Purim among the Jews after the destruction of their enemies. The revenge of Esther (Est 8,11; 9,13) was no less reprehensible than the cruelty of Amestris, wife of Xerxes, who had seven pairs of Persian youths buried alive as a sacrifice (*Her.* 7:114), or the terrible execution of Masistes instigated by Amestris (*Her.* 9:112). Xerxes was indeed ruler from Ethiopia to India, Cambyses having subdued Egypt. The great feast spoken of in Esther (1:3ff.) sounds much like the great New Year's celebration held at Persepolis (Ghirshman, *Persia,* pp. 154ff.). The mention of two eunuchs guarding the threshold (Est 2,21; 6,2) reflects knowledge of Persian customs as depicted on the monuments. The portrait of Darius at the tripylon door shows two guards holding a parasol over the head of the king; another relief shows two guards; and an audience portrait in a treasury relief depicts two guards before the king and two behind him (Ghirshman, *Persia,* plates 242, 255). On the inner stairway of the great Apadana are two rows of guards. Death by impaling (Est 2,23; 5,14; 6,4; 7,9; 8,7; 9,13f.) was the favorite method of execution employed by the Persians (see *Her.* 4:43; 6:30). The reference to royal couriers carrying messages of the king to the farthest reaches of the empire was certainly written by a knowledgeable person (Est 8,13.14 and *Her.* 8:98). The road system and methods of communication established by Darius made the sending of such messages easy. The term *purim* (= feast of lots) appears in various Assyrian texts beginning with the nineteenth century B.C. (see *AfO* XIII [1941] 308b). But perhaps most significant of all, some of the names now appear in contemporary literature. The name Mordecai is found in the Persepolis Treasury Tablets (1:22; 25:9–10; 84:18). So is the name Carcas (22:28), and often in the foundation texts. The name borne by one of the sons of Haman, Parshandatha (Est 9,7) is said to occur on a seal from Achaemenian times, written in Phoenician characters. Dalphon is an Akkadian name. Aspatha was also the name of a eunuch of Cambyses according to Ctesias (*Pers.* 9). Most of the others are good Persian names as has been shown by Rudolph Mayer (*Lex Tua Veritas* [Trier: Paulinus-Verlag, 1961], pp. 130–135) and H. S. Gehman (*JBL* XLIII [1924] 321–28). A number of Persian words also occur throughout the book, which seems to indicate that the date of composition cannot have been too late since the usage of such words disappeared rapidly after the downfall of the Persian empire. In addition, some of the names appear to have old Persian spellings.

Interestingly enough the main theme of the book of Esther occurs in synagogue paintings of Dura-Europos dating from the third century

A.D. Two of the most beautifully executed panels in the whole series are devoted to it (see C. H. Kraeling, *The Excavations at Dura-Europos, Final Report VIII: Part I, The Synagogue* [New Haven, Conn.: Yale University press, 1956]; esp. plates LXIV–LXV and description pp. 151–164). The theme depicted is that of the triumph of Mordecai over Haman. The first panel has to do with the honoring of Mordecai and is illustrative of Est 6,8–10. Mordecai is seated on a white horse led by Haman who had suggested the treatment to be accorded to the one whom the king delights to honor, and who here is made to serve as a stable boy. Behind him stand four well-dressed characters who seem to represent either the court or the public who witness the execution of the order of the king. The second panel portrays a scene in which six persons figure—the central person is, of course, that of the king seated on his throne; directly behind him, on the right of the painting, is Queen Esther sitting on her throne; before the king is an important figure presented in a very active pose holding a document in his hand; and the other three persons are probably royal officials. The panel appears to be an interpretation of the decree of the king referred to in Est 9,11–14, as suggested by Professor Kraeling. Attention has been called to this representation only to focus on the artist's conception of the message of Esther. There seems to be not the slightest hint of Purim, though it is the obvious purpose of our canonical Esther to describe the origin of that festival. Of course, it is possible that the artist reflects the emphasis of the Jews in the east in the Sassanian period (to judge from the dipinti [painted writings] upon the panel, this was the most popular painting in the Dura Synagogue of the Sassanian period), particularly that of the Jews in the earlier Persian empire. So far as the present book of Esther is concerned, one must affirm that it has a historical nucleus (see R. de Vaux, *AI* 515). Cazelles has shown that two documents underlie the book, and it could easily be that one of these stories focused on the delivery of the Jews from some now unknown threat of persecution with some reference to a feast of rejoicing while the other centered about the festival. Both, however, must have come from eastern Jewry.

As it stands, the book of Esther is cast within the same framework as that of the Chronicler. The writer has observed elsewhere that the Chronicler uses history for his purpose (*Anchor Bible: I Chronicles*, pp. XVIIIff.), which was to apply the earlier experiences of Israel to the religious situation of his time. Thus he says he draws upon sources of all kinds—the books of the records of the kings of Judah and Israel, the books of prophets, genealogical lists, and so on—which he reinterprets in line with his objectives. The intelligence report of Mordecai to the king to the effect that his palace guards were conspiring to do away with him was recorded "in the book of the records" (Est 2,23), which were brought in later and read to Xerxes during a night when he suffered from insomnia (Est 6,1). In Est 10,2 is found the same language as so frequently found in Chronicles: The author says that the acts of power and strength of the king and the greatness of Mordecai to which he had been elevated by the king are set down in the records of the kings of Media and Persia. The exact detail of these references cannot be discussed here, but those mentioning the records may be of some importance.

Malachi

One of the most pregnant pieces of writing from the period is the book of Malachi. Most scholars agree that it antedates the period of Ezra-Nehemiah (see the cautious statement of J. Coppens, *Les Douze Petits Prophètes:* [Louvain: Publications Universitaires Louvain, 1950], p. 50) and so elucidates conditions in the land between the completion of the temple and events that transpired in Judah in the reign of Artaxerxes I (465–425 B.C.). It is, in fact, the only appreciably certain datable work of the time coming from a prophet or other writer in the *golah* community—at least the only one that can be detected at present. The title is probably derived from Mal 3,1 but is not a personal name as may be seen from LXX. The term *massa'* (= "burden," "oracle") in Mal 1,1 indicates that its formal character is the same as that of the oracles of Zech 9–14. Perhaps the oracles of Malachi were originally floating material of unknown origin of the same general nature as those attached to the prophecies of Zechariah. However that may be, we see a rather unique form in the composition of the oracles themselves. They all follow the same general pattern. The prophet first announces the proposition he wants to discuss, then points out the objections that have been or might be raised against it. Finally the prophet's reply and interpretation are given. One recalls the pattern of the prophet lawsuit adopted by the earlier spokesmen of the Lord (see H. B. Huffman, "The Covenant Lawsuit in the Prophets," *JBL* LXXVIII [1959], pp. 285–95). Before general conclusions are drawn from these oracles it may be well to look at each one in some detail.

The first prophecy concerns Yahweh's choice of Israel (Mal 1,2–5). The proposition is the prophet's declaration of Yahweh's love for Israel.

It has been shown by scholars that "love" here is a synonym for "choice," "election." But in the light of the untoward experiences of the *golah*, the people have been led to question the Lord's election. If that were really true, would he not have seen to it that they advanced in life? As it is, defeat and frustration confront them at every turn. Then the advocate responds with a comparison between Jacob and Esau, a situation well known in the nation's tradition and recognized by every citizen. Jacob was the chosen one; Esau the rejected one. The usual rendering of the word, *san'e* (= hate), is too strong here. As the antithetical parallelism appears to indicate, it is the equivalent of "not loved" (= "not chosen," "rejected"). But the immediate reply of the people was, "yes, but just look at Edom! How they prospered after the downfall of Jerusalem in 587 B.C.! And at whose expense?" The prophet replies that the turning point has already arrived for Edom. They have indeed built, but their work has all been in vain. Edom was already being pushed out of its fastnesses around Sela (Petra) by a stronger and more virile desert people. So much is clear from the assertion, "Your eyes are about to see it." (See my article on Joel in *ZAW* 74 [1962], esp. pp. 187–188). Note the use of the words Jacob and Israel (see below).

The castigation of priests and people for their inferior sacrifices (Mal 1,6–2,9) once again tells us a great deal about local conditions. The people were guilty of offering polluted materials upon the altar. The animals brought to the Lord for sacrifice were refuse—the blind, the lame, the sick, that is, the blemished animals—so that they were viewed as dung (Mal 2,3). Surely this is a mark of the rising tide of commercialism and the growing emphasis on status. Conditions in the land had improved greatly, at least among the upper classes, all signs of the evident greatness and goodness of the Lord. He was regarded as a great God by other nations (Mal 1,11), and everywhere communities of his people found themselves, incense was offered to his name. Likely the tradition voiced in Deutero-Isaiah about Cyrus as Yahweh's servant and the references to the God of the heavens to whom prayer for the king and his sons is enjoined in the decree of Darius underlies the statement. Or it may simply be a recognition of what Yahweh has done for his people among the nations: He not only preserved them but directed the great kings to release them from captivity and provide for their rehabilitation. Yahweh was in charge of history and by its movements was carrying out his purpose in the world. Such a majestic God demands attention and regard on the part of those who have been chosen as his instruments. If he is a Great King, as they claim, where is the honor that should be accorded him? The covenant with Levi (Mal 2,4) deserves special comment. The priests are subsumed under the general tribe of Levi, and no distinction is drawn between priests and Levites. Hence the Deuteronomic conception is still in vogue and the injunctions of the P code not yet applied in Judah. The same high regard for Levites prevails also in the writings of the Chronicler. One function of the Levitical priests was instruction, stressed here (Mal 2,6) and in Chronicles (2 Chr 17,8f; 15,3; 35,3; Neh 8,7.9; see my article, "The Kerygma of the Chronicler" in *Interpretation* 20 [1966], pp. 259–273).

The section on the condemnation of divorce (Mal 2,10–16, with the possible exception of 11b–13a) has wider ramifications than those usually associated with it. Assuredly the whole moral problem of divorce is dealt with, but all prophets were against it. The vehemence with which Malachi speaks here is due to the particular outrage that characterized it. The prophetic complaint is a bitter one. The very altar of the Lord was covered with tears of weeping wives, lamenting over their sad plight. Observe it was the wives of their youth whom they played false, even though they had been faithful all their lives in every way (Mal 2,13b–14). Surely these divorces were not ordinary affairs attributed to normal breakdowns so often prevalent then as now. These divorces were incurred by preference. The perpetrators did so for the sake of personal advantage. One must understand the economic and social conditions in the land at the time to comprehend the reason for such monstrous evils. Moreover, it was not so much the rank and file of the people who were involved; it was rather the upper classes (see names of the guilty in Ezr 10), who should have known better and had more respect for the family institution in Israel—a very important, basic institution in the moral outlook of the nation. E. Würtwein (*Der 'amm ha'arez im Alten Testament* [Stuttgart: Kohlhammer, 1936]) has shown that these upper classes were technically known as "the people of the land" (= *'amm ha-'arez*), that is, the landholding classes.

When Judah was exiled, Samarian landholding groups infiltrated to fill in the vacuum, later to be joined by others (Neh 13,23). These upper classes apparently entered into marriage with comparable parties of the *golah* who soon learned that it was easier, perhaps more practical, to win back their former territorial rights and possessions by intermarriage than by other, more drastic means. In order to contract these marriages they had to renounce earlier ones, that is, divorce the wives of their youth. The prophet's denunciation of these unions of convenience and profit must have had little effect since the problem persisted down to the time of Nehemiah and Ezra. Possibly that was the only way they could redeem their heritage until there was enough power and authority in the community to deal with the problem otherwise. Nevertheless Malachi saw clearly that a stable and worthy cultic order could not be built on foundations that contravened the basic commandments of the Lord who is against divorce (Mal 2,16, though the text is not clear here). In any event, the prophet urges his fellows to take heed of their spirits so as to remain faithful (to the wives of their youth).

A cynical complaint of the people about delayed and unfair retribution is the subject of the next oracle (Mal 2,17–3,5). The form is the same as before—first appears the statement about the Lord's weariness with words and actions of the people. Naturally the latter respond with the query as to how they thus try the Lord's patience. The prophet replies in detail with the charge of the Lord—it is because they accuse him of failure to do justice, with the argument that he is dilatory in the execution of judgment. In fact, the very ones who do evil appear to be favored by him. This and the preceding oracle are closely related, especially if consideration is accorded to the attitude and practices of the landed gentry who are doing quite well, at least momentarily, in their conspiracy with their counterparts among the people of the land. Such duplicity naturally led to carelessness in the performance of religious obligations that in turn incurred the displeasure of the Lord. How could he be considerate with those who remained so glaringly indifferent to him? Malachi's observation is based on history—as judgment was decreed in days of Jehosaphat, Joash, Hezekiah, and Josiah, so would it again be done. And that swiftly and surely. When the community is purified as "in the days of yore, as in former years" (Mal 3,4b), then will its devotion be pleasing in Yahweh's sight. Only then could there be effective judgment in the land. But as things now stand it is difficult to see any striking difference between the community of Judah and their enemies (v. 5). The Lord is is a just judge; he will come to render a decision, but the application must begin with the sons of Levi (v. 3). In his time, Yahweh's judgment is certain and relentless.

Discourse five (Mal 3,6–12) takes up the theme already dealt with by both Haggai and Zechariah a generation or so earlier. Conditions in Judah had not changed materially, as may be inferred from the preceding sermons of Malachi. But this one is sharper and more pointed. Although circumstances were far from satisfactory, the sons of Jacob were not annihilated. The fathers had rebelled against the Lord and failed to follow his statutes, but they were never completely wiped out, not even by the tragic events of 721 B.C. or 587 B.C. There was always a remnant as Isaiah had affirmed, but that was not enough. God would not be content until the whole of the people returned to him. Then he could turn unto them. That was the prophet's topic now. He summoned the nation to repentance and amendment of life and worship. In agreement with all the post-exilic prophets and in line with the demands of the hour, Malachi called for sincerity of renewal in worship. Just as he earlier reproved priests and people for their shabby sacrifices, so he here reproaches the nation for its dereliction in the matter of tithes. The torah was explicit on tithes (Dt 14,28f; 26,12–15; Nm 18,21–32), and penalties for nonpayment were severe. The tithe was largely devoted to the regular support of institutional religion in Israel. Hence it was natural to conclude from the careless and sporadic worship of the time that required contributions were not forthcoming. The identical problem had to be solved by Nehemiah later on (Neh 13,10–13). Evidently Malachi's oracle was called forth by the persistent complaint of food shortages (v. 11). The Lord's word through his prophet was that the windows of heaven would be opened and abundant blessings poured out upon the people if they recognized the time-honored principle of the tithe. History has shown that he was right; whenever a people is faithful to its worship obligations in the widest sense, its blessings are unmistakable.

The final homily of our prophet returns to the question of the Lord's judgment (Mal 3,13–4,3 = Heb 3,13–21). This time the topic is the people's harsh words against the Lord. What is the use in serving him when the proponents of evil are prosperous and thrive on their wickedness, they complain. "They put God to the test, and get away with it" (Mal 3,15b), so that the arrogant were counted fortunate and evildoers prosperous—at least so it appeared. That was the common subject of conversation among the God-fearers of the day. Their whisperings did not escape the ear of the Lord, declared the prophet. In his time God would visit judgment upon them. A book of remembrance—the first such reference in the Bible—was in the process of compilation. In it were recorded the deeds of the evil as well as those of the pious. At the proper moment the distinction between them would become evident (Mal 3,18), and the fate of both would be sealed. The evildoers would be burnt up, while those who revere the Lord's name will have an advocate who will usher them into a period of joy and happiness. The "sun of righteousness with healing in his wings" is doubtless based on the prominent symbol of Ahuramazda that appeared everywhere in the Persian empire. Yet the figure is not to be taken too literally, since Yahweh could not be portrayed. Rather the prophet seems to have appropriated it with an entirely different meaning. After the storm of judgment bound to fall upon all, there rises, in the prophetic vision, the sun of right whose rays will reveal the devastation wrought upon the wicked so that they will be as dust under the feet of the righteous but at the same time will provide light and healing to the doers of right. "Only with their eyes will the latter behold the end of the wicked." Freed from the impediments and obstruction of the wicked they will leap and dance like calves released from the pen (Mal 4,2). The book of remembrance and the use of the future (imperfect tense throughout in Hebrew) indicates that the prophet did not expect an immediate retribution. He was setting forth a principle that would be brought into play in the outworking of the divine economy. Recall Jesus' discourse on Jerusalem in Mt 24; Mk 13; Lk 21 with its accent on "the time will come"—the certainty of judgment, even the judgments of history.

Mal 4,4–6 (= 3,22–24 in Heb) represents later additions. Verse 4 is the work of an advocate of the torah of Moses and is in the spirit and terminology of the Deuteronomist as the reference to "Horeb" and "statutes and judgments" shows. Verses 5–6 take up the theme of Mal 3,1ff., perhaps an expansion upon those passages or a comment in the light of later beliefs and observations. In a sense these last words of Malachi, and the Book of the Twelve Prophets, are prophetic indeed. They remind us of our Lord's words in the parable of the rich man and Lazarus—they have Moses and the Prophets (Lk 16)—and the personalities who appeared on the mount of transfiguration (Mk 9 and parallels). When these commentary supplements became a part of the book is uncertain, but they do reflect the spirit of post-exilic Judaism and project the hope for reconciliation, which was to be fulfilled in Christ.

In summary, let us reflect on the religion and history of the period from which the book stems. Malachi follows closely the prophetic pattern characteristic of Haggai and Zechariah—more so the latter—in accentuating the righteousness of cult and life. The two phases of worship and life are inseparably connected. If anything there is a bit more emphasis on judgment in Malachi, particularly in Mal 3,1–5, which recalls the *dies irae* of Zephaniah. Such a passage as Mal 1,14, which calls for honesty and humility in cultic obligations, points to some improvement in economic conditions in the land. There was a governor in the land (Mal 1,8) who must have succeeded Zerubbabel; the temple was in operation (Mal 1,10; 3,1.10) with a functioning cult. There is also the clear impression that Deuteronomy was still the authoritative code (Mal 1,8; 2,11; 3,8ff.); yet the bringing of the full tithe to the storehouse of the Lord appears nearer to P than to D, which required its payment to the Levites. But that can easily be explained by the fact that the early post-exilic community was small and compact, most groups residing in the vicinity of Jerusalem. There is thus some anticipation of the law of P. It is also significant that Malachi employs the cultic term Israel, which occurs three times, whereas Judah occurs only once. The Chronicler persisted in its use to emphasize the true cultic community representing all Israel. Note that the expression "all Israel" appears also in Mal 4,4 (=3,22 in Heb).

Selected Readings

Bright, J., *A History of Israel*, Chap. IX. Philadelphia: The Westminster Press, 1959.

Josephus, *Jewish Antiquities*, Book XI.

Olmstead, A. T., *History of the Persian Empire*, Chaps. 17–20. Chicago: University of Chicago Press, 1948.

V

Artaxerxes I

The murderer of Xerxes, Artabanus, hoped by his act to claim the throne for himself. Vacancy of the throne nearly always produced a struggle for the prize, and it did so now. The successor was Artaxerxes I (465–425 B.C.), the third son of Xerxes. Darius, his older son, had also fallen victim to foul play, and the second son, Hystaspes, was satrap of Bactria, where he raised the standard of revolt in the belief that he could easily overcome his young, inexperienced brother. Artaxerxes lost no time in rising to the occasion and in two bloody battles succeeded in putting down the revolt. Having worsted Artabanus and then his brother, he demonstrated himself master of his father's domain—but not without challenges elsewhere. It was noted how differently Xerxes had dealt with the provinces of his empire than had Darius I. The defeat of the former's ambitious Grecian campaign was not calculated to help matters, especially in places where there was

the slightest possibility of successfully shaking off the yoke of the
master. So in Egypt we see Inaros, a Lybian dynast, engaged in a foray
outside his territory and into the delta regions of the Nile, somewhere
around 463–462 B.C. He aimed to take the fortress at Mareia. The
satrap Achaemenes met him in battle at Papremus where the Persians
were defeated and the satrap himself slain. The remnants of the Persian army fled to Memphis (the so-called White Wall) where they
made their stand. But despite defeat of the Persians in two battles,
Inaros failed to rally the Egyptians behind him. Many of the latter
fought on the Persian side. In the end, most of lower Egypt fell into
the hands of the rebels whereas Memphis and all of upper Egypt remained under Persian control. Meanwhile, Inaros could expect swift
and drastic reprisal at the hands of the Persians as soon as word
reached the court, and so he sought to strengthen his hand by calling
upon Athens, which had lately shown itself superior to the Persian
forces in Ionia and elsewhere. The Athenians were about to embark
on a campaign of expansion of their own and had gathered a fleet of
some 200 vessels to attack Cyprus. The only hope for Egypt would be
an alliance with Athens, which, if it could be maintained, might rout
the Persians as they had been frustrated in Greece. The Athenians
responded favorably to the embassy of Inaros and sailed from Cyprus
to the Nile delta where they were eminently successful in taking most
of the waterways. That year (459 B.C.) the Graeco-Lybian alliance
won a large part of the city of Memphis—except the White Wall,
which stubbornly refused to yield. Whether they could hold out until
help came must have been a vexing question asked daily. There was
an attempt to encourage the Spartans to invade Athens and thus re-
lieve the Persian position in Egypt, but the plan failed (Thucydides,
1:109–110). By 456 B.C., Megabazos with a great force of both land
and naval units arrived on the scene. There is no agreement among the
historians as to whether the Lybian and Athenian allies withdrew as
the Persians approached or whether they were defeated in battle. In
any event the siege of the White Wall was lifted, and the besiegers
were bottled up on the island of Prosopotis where they maintained
themselves for a time. In the early summer of 454 B.C. Megabazos
drained the surrounding canals and took the island. Few Athenians
escaped. Fifty Greek galleys who had come to support them were destroyed too. The Egyptian revolt was ended.

Inaros was betrayed into the hands of his enemies and executed.
There were still some dissidents in the swamplands, since a force of
60 triremes of Athens went in search of Amyrtaeus a few years later
(450 B.C.). The larger force of 140 galleys under Cimon attacked

Cyprus but later withdrew and were joined by the other 60 in the return to Athens. At the same time the so-called peace of Callias was concluded between Athens and Persia, and Egypt was safe once more for the Persians. But there remained close contact between the Libyans and Athens, for the former sent to the latter a large quantity of grain in the year 445–444 B.C. As a result of activities in Egypt, heavy taxes were levied upon the satrapy. They took the form of outright levies plus income from fisheries and a specified amount of grain for the support of garrisons at the White Wall and at Elephantine. Ethiopia contributed its allotment triennially. Artaxerxes appears in Egyptian texts of the time with the title "King of the South and North," which is qualified by the adjective "great." There are no monumental records attributed to him nor is he listed as having made contributions to any of the religious orders or temples. It was during this reign that the Halicarnassian historian, Herodotus, visited the country to gather materials for his work. The documents from Elephantine indicate a relatively undisturbed community. They have to do with normal cases that might come up in any local community—we have a case of burglary (Cowley, *Aramaic Papyri* no. 7, in 461 B.C.); deeds of conveyance (no. 8, 460 B.C.; no. 13, 447 B.C., which attests the capability of women to hold property); property rights (no. 9, 460 B.C.); loan contracts (no. 10, 456 B.C.; no. 11, 455 B.C.); marriage contracts (no. 15, 441 B.C.; no. 18, 425 B.C. also containing provisions for division of property in case of divorce); assignment of property after divorce has taken place (no. 14, 441 B.C.); and court appeals (no. 16, 435 B.C.). Nothing is found in these documents that exhibits any of the unsettled conditions in lower Egypt in the early period of the reign of Artaxerxes I.

Babylonia

There was no revolt in Babylon this time, perhaps because Xerxes had done such a thorough job of crushing the political spirit of the city that the people were unwilling to risk further violence. Artaxerxes continued the policies of his father and retained his title as simply "king of lands." He does appear to have relented a bit in his dealings with the priesthood. He restored some of the lands to them and reinvested them with their office. At the same time the Magian cult took on new life and was henceforth to exercise an increasing influence. Nevertheless, Babylon did not escape the heavy taxation levied against all satrapies of the empire—it may have had to bear a proportionately heavier burden because of its proximity to Susa. When Susa suffered heavy damage by conflagration (F. H. Weissbach, *Die Keilinschriften der Achämeniden* [Leipzig: J. C. Hinrischs'sche Buchhandlung, 1911], pp. 122–25), Artaxerxes moved to Babylon with his royal entourage, though he never lost his love for the city of his fathers. During the reign of Artaxerxes and Darius II business activities flourished at Babylon—which may be another reason for the comparative quiet at the time. Most of the economic tablets of Murashu's sons at Nippur date from the latter part of this reign and the first part of that of Darius II. The situation at Babylon and its outlying districts is best seen from the cosmopolitan character of the population since the reorganization of Xerxes. All kinds of names now appear in the business documents.

Lands
to the East

What conditions were like in that part of the Persian imperial world may be seen from Herodotus' tribute list (3:89–96), which he informs us was set up by Darius I but was maintained through successive reigns. After all it was always the unbearable burdens of taxation that led to discontent and ultimate rebellion. Such lists are the best sources of economic knowledge and indicators of the progress or regression of people. Whether Herodotus is correct or not in the amounts assessed, they must certainly have been exorbitant; tribute was a means of keeping subject peoples in line. Persian strength exhibited in the reorganization of Xerxes was sapped by increasing tribute burdens, said to have amounted to a total of 2,280 talents. The fact that the numerous satrapies had to be combined for tax-collection purposes and that some of the peoples are missing from the lists points to growing difficulty in collection. Discontent must have shown itself mostly among the peripheral peoples, although the Indians are listed as loyal subjects and conscripts in the army down to the end of the fifth century. The abortive move of the Bactrians under Hystaspes may have been responsible for the more watchful eye of the authorities and hence both an increase in taxes and more effective control exercised over the region during the reign of Artaxerxes.

The Western Satrapies

The five western satrapies (including Asia Minor and Syria) paid a total of 2,110 talents in the time of Darius I. Some of these satrapies may have reduced their payments after the campaign of Xerxes, though probably not by much. A slightly different system of government existed in some of the provinces. For example, Cilicia was governed by a native prince from whom 500 talents were collected but 140 retained by him for the support of the defense forces. But because certain other satrapies periodically contributed additional goods such as maidens or youths, this one contributed a white horse for each day of the year. It is interesting that the fifth satrapy, which included Phoenicia, all of Palestine and Syria, and Cyprus, was assessed only 350 talents—the smallest amount of any of the western satrapies. This would have embraced all the western provinces of the satrapy Across the River—among them Samaria, Judah, Ammon, and Ashdod. The revealing complaint of some people from Judah at this time expresses the feeling of many of the peoples of the empire: "We must borrow money to pay the royal tax (levied) against our fields and our vineyards" (Neh 5,4). The satrapy of Arabia was not taxed, as was the case with certain other peoples for various reasons (see *Her.* 3:97). Possibly like others who learned that Arabia, composed of many tribes, could not be effectively controlled, the Persians resolved to rely on other means of getting what amounted to tribute. Certainly it was not because of the fantastic tales told by Herodotus. The Arabian principalities are said to have supplied the king with spices for which they were famous. If the thousand talents of frankincense reported by Herodotus is perhaps exaggerated, it nonetheless shows the wealth of these people; they alone knew how to produce or acquire the spices required in religious observances, and that may be the reason for the lack of control exercised over them.

It has been estimated that no less than the equivalent of 20 million dollars in taxes found their way into the royal treasury. In terms of present-day values it would have had a vastly greater purchasing power. When it is remembered that precious little of this amount was ever invested in the local areas from which it was gathered, it is easy to understand the economic straits of the people. Most of the gold and silver was made into bullion. Some coinage was employed, but it was used for the purchase of services that were really unproducitve—for uses in war or diplomacy. A great deal of Persian gold was used to foster the internecine warfare between the Greek states to the profit of the empire in the west. The above-noted complaint of the people of Judah, representative of discontent everywhere except in the home province of Persia itself, was bound to lead to trouble unless the people were mollified in one way or another. One example of the serious consequences of overtaxation was the unrest created in the satrapy Across the River, which was under the leadership of Megabazus who had done such an effective job in reducing Egypt. Not too much is known about his revolt, but it seems that he was aided by his two sons. It was countered by an Egyptian, Usiris, and ended in a draw because the inevitable duel fought by the two generals produced a personal friendship between them. So a second force had to be sent under the king's nephew, Menostanes, who lost the duel. Megabazus' honor having been satisfied, he professed willingness to submit on condition that he retain his position. Supported by powerful forces at the court, he was finally pardoned and perhaps restored. Later he once more forfeited the royal favor by committing the unpardonable error of slaying a lion in the presence of the king. Again he was pardoned by the intervention of his friends. The whole business of the Megabazus affair creates the impression of indecision on the part of the king and an easy susceptibility to influence by others. Somewhat like his father, he was easy prey to those around him.

Judah
and the Persians

Just how much support Megabazus had from the provinces of his satrapy is not known. The records are silent about the composition of forces of his supporters or what effect his actions had upon the districts involved. The first dependable information on Judah and Jerusalem after the dated prophecies of Haggai and Zechariah, and the story of events associated with the first returns, occurs in the book of Nehemiah (Neh 1–7), repeated with some amplification in Josephus (*Ant.* 11:5: 6–8). The story begins in the citadel at Susa in December of the twentieth year of Artaxerxes (i.e., December of 445 B.C.) where a delegation of Jews had arrived, possibly with a special appeal to the king. Professor Olmstead (*History of the Persian Empire*, p. 314) thinks that it was a private embassy sent under the aegis of the Jerusalem authorities carrying to the court a reply to the accusation made against them by Rehum and his secretary, Shimshai, to which response had earlier been made by the king (Ezr 4,18–22). He argues that the reaction of the Jews could not have been expressed through official channels because the local governor had already taken his stand against them, as his warning to Artaxerxes indicates. Since it was not prudent for the Jews' defense to pass through openly hostile hands, this committee carried a document bearing the official notice of the king's predecessors permitting the Jews to resettle and conduct such building operations as were designated in their edicts. The attitude of Nehemiah seems to hint that the messengers were on some mission that concerned the state of affairs in Judah. Perhaps the Jerusalem officials were attempting to purge themselves of certain false accusations or impressions that had arisen in connection with the unrest in the west attendant upon the Egyptian rebellion or in connection with the Megabazus uprising in Syria. Some scholars are of the opinion that the Jews were somehow involved in subversive moves in the west in the reign of Xerxes when Jerusalem was destroyed by the armies of the Persian king. That was hardly the case since nowhere is there the slightest indication that the temple had suffered at any time. There is no reference to any rebuilding of the temple as such in the time of Nehemiah and Ezra; there is a reference in Neh 2,8 to the "citadel guarding the house" (omitted by *LXX*) but not to "the house" itself. Josephus does speak of completing the temple (*Ant.* 11:5:6), probably a reference to the Nehemiah notice. Had the Jerusalemites been involved in any rebellious activity, their temple would doubtless have suffered the same fate as did that of Esagila in Babylon. It is not impossible that the Jews became apprehensive amid all the hostility around them and for that reason took action to protect themselves—not simply from local prowlers. A. Gelin (*La Sainte Bible: Esdras et Néhémie* [Paris: Les éditions du Cerf, 1960], p. 65, n.f.) believes there were several such attempts to secure permission from the Persian authorities to reconstruct the walls —Ezr 4,6, in the time of Xerxes; Ezr 4,12.13.16, in the time of Artaxerxes—but that favorable action on their petition was taken only after the Egyptian revolt in 448 B.C. The words, "the Jews who came from you to us, have come to Jerusalem" (Ezr 4,12) points to a substantial migration from Babylon to Judah in the time of Artaxerxes. The speedy implementation of the order of the king (Ezr 4,23), especially the reference to "force of arms" by which the local officials took action, could possibly indicate that some kind of physical destruction took place. But that appears unlikely; the show of armed force was largely for psychological purposes. In any case, Nehemiah inquired from the delegation about conditions in Jerusalem and the welfare of the people. Just what the expression "those who survived from the captivity" signifies is not clear. Does it mean those who remained in the land during the exile or does it refer to those who escaped, that is, returned, from the Babylonian exile? The reply of the delegation says, "the survivors who remained there in the province after the captivity" were in deplorable circumstances, in a disgraceful condition, with the walls of Jerusalem still in ruins. The hostility manifested toward the Jews by their neighbors prevented any effort to rebuild the walls, and fallen walls fostered lack of zeal for any serious undertaking for the progress of the community. Naturally the Jewish authorities did not want to overstep the bounds of the edict granted them or still further provoke their jealous and resentful neighbors. They had always been on the best of terms with the Persians, and if they were to serve them now, possibly as a kind of buffer state between Persia and Egypt, their situation could not remain in the compromising position in which it had existed from the days of Darius. It is not beyond comprehension that the Jewish representatives had come both to clear themselves of complicity in any plot against their overlord and at the same time to explain the assistance a strong Judah could render the empire because of its location. They may have hoped, in this way, to repay in some measure the favors extended to the *golah* by the great king Cyrus and his successors and to bolster the sagging morale of the Jerusalem community.

The position of Nehemiah at the Persian court demonstrates the respect in which the Jews were held there. He was the royal cupbearer, an extremely important official in the royal household (see *Her.* 3:34). Inasmuch as he served in the presence of the Queen (Neh 2:6) he must have been a eunuch, which explains his actions later on in connection with the temple (Neh 6:10f.). From Tobit (Tb 1,22) we learn that Ahiqar, the cupbearer of Esarhaddon, was next to the king. That tradition, like many others, was taken over from the Assyrians by the Persians. Cupbearers and eunuchs were among the servants of kings given special instruction, which indicates their significance in the royal administration. Thus Nehemiah takes his place with the other Jews who, according to tradition, occupied positions of importance and authority in both Babylonia and Persia. The reaction of this lay Jew to the report of his brethren concerning Judah and Jerusalem is indicative of his sensitive and devout nature. His prayer and fast "before the God of the heavens" betrays more than ordinary concern for the fortune and well-being of his people. It betokens a sense of divine summons to be of assistance to them in their struggle against adversities that convulsed them for a century and a half.

Nehemiah's interview with the king was delayed for several months after the conference with his brother Hanani. The time was April, 445 B.C.—apparently the dates in Neh 1, 2 are based on the autumnal year, that is, the beginning of the year falling in the autumn—possibly at the great New Year's festival celebrated so lavishly by the Persians

(see Olmstead, *History of the Persian Empire,* Chap. XX). So much of
the interval was doubtless spent in meditation and fasting that the
weight of troubled thoughts left their mark upon him. The king could
not help noticing the difference in his outward appearance from that
of the others around him and from his usual happy mien. In view of
the nature of the man and the troubles that beset him, his conduct can
hardly be interpreted as a clever device to gain the attention of the
king. The latter's inquiry frightened him, for he had no way of know-
ing how the king would react to his petition, which required an explanation that would recall the disconcerting events that transpired so
recently in the satrapy Across the River. Note the careful wording of
the explication of his appearance—"Why should I not be depressed
when the city, the site of the graves of my fathers, lies in ruins with
its gates destroyed by fire" (Neh 2,3). The reference to "the graves of
my fathers" was a master stroke in view of the care that the Persian
kings bestowed on the sepulchres of their fathers. The personal appeal
of Nehemiah was a master stroke of diplomacy because it removed the
negotiations from the realm of political expediency. Jerusalem is nowhere mentioned in the petition of the cupbearer, though it was in
his mind and was the surest indication to him that the harassing tactics
of the Samaritans and their supporters had succeeded in hampering
the efforts of the *golah* to discharge the edicts of Cyrus and Darius.
Nehemiah was both alarmed and pleased by the king's reply, "What
then do you want?" He must have thought through carefully the procedure he now followed. He asked, prayerfully, that he be sent to "the
city of my fathers' sepulchres" to rebuild it. As was the way of Hebrew
storytellers, we are left to fill in imaginatively the details of the remaining conversation, being told only that the king granted his request after
he had given him a time-limit for his absence from court. To be absolutely certain that his mission was understood and would have some
promise of success, he solicited directives for the governors of Across
the River to permit transit across their territory and an order to the
imperial forester for timber to be used in the reconstruction of "the
citadel guarding the house, for the wall of the city, and for his own
house." The king was responsive to his request because "the good hand
of my God" was with him. To make doubly sure that his orders would
be carried out, the king provided an army escort.

These negotiations and preparations were protracted over a period of
years. The first overtures took place early in 445 B.C., but according to
Josephus (*Ant.* 11:5:7), Nehemiah did not arrive in Jerusalem until
five years later—which is probably correct although the name of the

king is not. The governors of Across the River must have regarded Nehemiah's adventure with disfavor, but his careful calculations and preparations were designed to forfend any trouble he might encounter. They were overawed by the escort and the official documents he presented to them. Sanballat, the Persian governor of Samaria, and Tobiah, the Ammonite governor, were greatly displeased but could do nothing overtly to counter the plans of the new governor of Judah. Opposition was due in some measure to a fear of encroachment upon their authority. Both Sanballat and Tobiah were Yahwehists. The two sons of the former bore Yahweh names—Delaiah and Shelemiah (see Cowley, *Aramaic Papyri,* letter 30, line 29)—and Tobiah took up residence in the Temple during Nehemiah's absence (Neh 13,4–9), a sure indication that he, too, considered himself a Yahwehist. Behind it may also have been no small degree of jealousy precipitated by the prominence into which the province of Judah had been catapulted by the attention devoted to it by Artaxerxes. In Neh 2,10.19 we get the first information on the organization of the Palestinian section of the satrapy Across the River. Sanballat, who bears a Babylonian name, was the successor of Mithredath (Ezr 4,7) and Rehum (Ezr 4,8). In theory he had no jurisdiction over the province of Judah, since the Persians had earlier appointed Jewish governors—Sheshbezzar, Zerubbabel. Who succeeded the latter is not known, though there may have been one or more before Nehemiah (see Mal 1,8). However, the Samaritan commissar acted on the basis of the old Babylonian arrangement whereby Jerusalem and part of Judah were annexed to Samaria (see Alt, *KS* II 327ff.), a de facto situation the *golah* did not accept (Neh 2,20b), especially since Nehemiah claimed to be the legitimate governor. It took quite a time for Sanballat to realize that the times had wrought a change. Nevertheless, what these outsiders could not achieve legally they endeavored to accomplish in other ways. Besides Sanballat and his district of Samaria, Tobiah of Ammon and Geshem (Gashmu) of Arabia were operating under the Across the River satrap. Tobiah was not an Ammonite as his name shows; he was governor of the territory of Ammon in Transjordan, and the scion of an old and prominent family (B. Mazar, "The Tobiads" in *IEJ* 7 [1957], pp. 137–45 and C. C. McCown, "The 'Araq el-Emir and the Tobiads," in *BA* XX [September, 1957] 63–76). The third member of the triumvirate conspiring against Nehemiah and his associates was Geshem, who was the father of Qain, the king of Qedar. Some 40 years later Qain was to unite the tribes of North Arabia into a huge confederation spread over the vast area found east of the Dead Sea to the Nile delta (I. Rabinowitz, "Aramaic Inscriptions of the Fifth Century B.C.E. from a North-Arab Shrine in Egypt," in *JNES* XV [1956] 1–9). This Geshem could have been no ordinary tribal chief; he was a powerful intertribal leader who had the support of the Persians, who, as observed above, laid no tribute upon the province of Arabia, though it was reckoned with the fifth satrapy. Arabians were said to have assisted Cambyses in the conquest of Egypt. The Persians were keen-eyed enough to see that to maintain control of Egypt they required the support of the Arabs, who could keep open or closed the land routes to the valley of the Nile. Perhaps Nehemiah was *urged*— let alone permitted—to go to Jerusalem to rebuild the walls as part of the king's further plan to secure his obstreperous subject satrapy in Egypt. A walled Jerusalem with a strong Arab kingdom could be of tremendous help to imperial interests in the southwest. The opponents of Nehemiah were thus more than local tribal heads. It is not impossible that Hanani (Neh 1,2f) and his committee were sent to Judah in the first place either by the Jewish community of Babylon or Susa, or by the royal authorities, to investigate conditions there. If they were sent by the latter, their mission might have had something to do with the strengthening of Judah, which, together with Samaria, Ammon and Geshem's province, could have been viewed as having considerable potentialities for the maintenance of imperial interests in the southwest. In that case the concerns of the Jews and Persians would have coincided although each had his own aim or purpose. God was using the Persians now, as he had Cyrus earlier, to further his plans for his people.

Whereas Nehemiah was summoned by the Lord to perform a significant service for the *golah* by securing their position, he also contributed materially to the Persian cause. But his chief interest centered on the preservation and advancement of the Jewish religious community, and to that end he laid his plans. He was careful not to exceed his authority, but neither did he lose sight of his God-given task. There was bound to be conflict between him and the other governors of the three provinces of Across the River, since both parties looked at the matter from different viewpoints. That Nehemiah had no thought of interfering with the jurisdictions of his neighbors is shown by the fact that he set his mind and hand to the work he had come to do. He took a minimum of time to survey the situation (Neh 2,11–16) after which he called together the community and its leaders to apprize them of his findings. He then revealed publicly, for the first time, the purpose of his coming—"to restore the wall of Jerusalem that we may be held in derision no longer" (Neh 2,17). The context of the passage reflects a much more extended explanation of Nehemiah's mission (see Neh 2,18). Certainly the resolution of the assembly—"we will set to work building"—could have been adopted only after a thorough briefing on the evidence of divine guidance thus far. The comment of the writer: "And they supported the good work," speaks volumes. How the project was viewed and understood by the other governors is apparent from their comment: "What is this thing you are doing? Are you going to rebel against the king?" (Neh 2,19). The reply of Nehemiah to the effect that the Jews were under divine mandate and protection and that Sanballat, Tobiah, and Geshem "have no share or right or memorial in Jerusalem" set the record straight. What the Jews were about to do was serious religious business in which they could not share because they had no real interest in it. They were compromisers and opportunists and sought Yahweh only when it suited their convenience. As a matter of fact, the very survival of Judaism was at stake, and any deviation from Nehemiah's plans by permitting them to share in the work would have jeopardized the whole purpose he had in mind. The exact details of Nehemiah's firman from the king are not disclosed, but it must have been specific in the statement of rights; hence Nehemiah could clearly affirm that other peoples had no claim in his plans or their execution. Nor did they have any memorial in Jerusalem; it was solely the city of Nehemiah's fathers—not those of Sanballat, Tobiah, or Geshem whose center of ancestral activity lay elsewhere. It is rather striking that Nehemiah confronted his detractors by a declaration of faith in the Lord—the God of the heavens—who, he believed, would crown his work with success. He probably could have appealed to his royal commission or threatened them with the forces that had escorted him and presumably remained with him at least for a time.

The job Nehemiah and the *golah* were to undertake was formidable indeed. The method of procedure was well worked out and exhibits the organizing genius of the man in command. Neh 2,13–15 and 3,1–32 are the best descriptions of the city of Jerusalem in the Bible. Furthermore, the second reference records the wide and general participation of the various groups in the building operations. Representatives from localities reckoned to Judah; the various heads of families, the high priest, other priests, Levites, temple slaves, officials of all types, and members of various guilds were assigned to construct specific sections of the wall, the local residents to areas adjoining or near to their homes. It seems apparent that construction work consisted largely of filling in breaches, in some cases large ones, made by the destroyers.

According to Neh 6,15 the task was completed in fifty-two days. Josephus (*Ant.* 11:5:8) says it took two years and four months to do it; he states that it was finished in the twenty-eighth year of Xerxes (= Artaxerxes), that is, in 438–37 B.C. Unfortunately no regnal year is given in Nehemiah, but if the first audience with the king occurred in the twentieth year (Neh 2,1), eight years would have elapsed between then and the filling in of the breaches of the wall—perhaps just about right for the time required for the latter (see Albright, *BP* 53, 63 and notes 126, 127; and J. Bright, *A History of Israel,* p. 365), if one takes into account all the delays suffered by the builders.

There was some secrecy surrounding Nehemiah's plans that did not become clear until the work was under way, so that whereas Sanballat was aware of something afoot, he was not quite sure what it was. When he was informed that reconstruction was already in progress, he became furious. His first tactic of interference was ridicule, in which Tobiah joined (Neh 4,3). Fortified by prayer and the willing hands of those who were inspired by his zeal, the brave leader forged ahead until the breaches were filled in to half the height of the wall. When ridicule failed to disenchant the workers, the opponents resorted to stronger measures. Here for the first time (Neh 4,7) the four hostile provinces are named—Sanballat (the Samaritans), Tobiah (Ammonites), the Arabians, and the Ashdodites. In other words, Judah was surrounded by obstructionists—the Samaritans to the north, the Ammonites to the east, the Arabians to the south, and the Ashdodites on the west. Accordingly the Arabians were reckoned as the immediate southern neighbors. The author of the verse follows the Chronicler's conception, which placed them between Beersheba and Gerar. Curiously enough there is no mention of Edom or Edomites, an indication that the region later occupied by the Idumeans was regarded as part of the province of Arabia.

The next step the foes took was to spread threats among the workmen among whom their partisans lived. They circulated a rumor that they would fall upon the builders by a surprise move and kill them. Josephus says they actually did kill some of Nehemiah's men (*Ant.* 11:5:8) and planned to have Nehemiah himself removed by paid assassins. When these rumors persisted (Neh 4,16) and alarmed the workers, Nehemiah was forced to take countermeasures. He had not exceeded his authority and was certain of divine protection, but he had to act for the sake of morale. He set up a system of guards for the protection of the builders and then addressed them with words designed to allay their fears and inspire them with confidence (Neh 4,14). In the end, enemy harassments had the opposite effect than that for which they were intended. Everyone concerned was moved to work all the harder for the consummation of the objective. They worked from dawn until the stars appeared. Those who lived outside the city were directed to remain there and not to return to their homes for the night—both for personal protection and for purposes of guarding the construction work from possible sabotage. Before the doors of the gates were hung, one last effort was made to frustrate the plans of Nehemiah. Sanballat and his cohorts resolved to lure him into a trap in the guise of reaching some accommodation with him in a personal conference. The first reaction of Nehemiah was that he was too busy to attend such a meeting (Neh 6,2–4). Four times communications passed from one party to the other. Finally a courier from Sanballat arrived with a very disturbing message with the charge that the Jews were planning rebellion and proposed to make Nehemiah king, that he had even hired prophets to go around proclaiming "There is a king in Judah" (Neh 6,7). Such false reports were circulated among the surrounding provinces and were confirmed by Geshem, who was the most powerful of Nehemiah's opponents as recent studies have shown. They threatened to transmit this complaint to the king of Persia unless Nehemiah appeared at the proposed conference. The curt answer of Nehemiah called their bluff, and they knew it. Nevertheless, annoyance did not cease, for feelings ran deep. When the conference plot proved unsuccessful, false prophets instigated by Tobiah and Sanballat endeavored to snare him into the temple to put him in contempt of his own followers, for he was a eunuch. But that did not work out either; Nehemiah refused to be drawn into the scheme. Meanwhile, Tobiah sought to put pressure on him through his relatives and those who were bound to him by oath. Tobiah was one of the people of the land who was deeply involved with prominent families of Judah by marriage. The correspondence that took place between him and his highly placed relatives was a perfect set-up for misunderstanding and for setting family heads at variance with Nehemiah. The intervening passage (vv. 15–16) is out of place here, and the Tobiah episode belongs immediately after Neh 6,14. All measures aimed to distract the builders and terrorize their chief failed. The enemies of Nehemiah found their self-esteem considerably diminished when they were finally faced with a fait accompli.

Such performances were enough to wear down the patience of any man. But Nehemiah had to contend with a host of other problems (Neh 5) not connected directly with external resistance, though some of them may have been inspired by it. Some of Nehemiah's drastic measures to cope with increasing pressures exerted upon him from all sides, particularly the one requiring those workers who lived outside of Jerusalem to reside in the city, may have been responsible for creating certain economic hardships. The seriousness of the situation within the little community itself is illustrated by the wives joining their husbands in demanding that some action be taken to ameliorate their conditions. The complaint voiced by these people was that characteristically raised in any community under severe stress and strain—lack of food, many debts, and excessive tax levies. We have seen above how some of these outcries may have been caused by imperial imposts. In fact, the economic and social climate revealed here sounds very much like that reflected in Malachi (Mal 3,5–15). It is not difficult to understand the perennial food problems in the unpropitious land of what was then Judah, accentuated by local regulations necessitated by the hostile environment. To meet the barest needs for food, many families were compelled to pledge what little possessions they had. Some were forced to sell their children into slavery. What made such transactions so odious was that foreclosure often came at the most inappropriate times when they were unable to redeem them. Taxes took no small amount of their yearly produce.

Note that complaints were raised against "their Jewish brothers" (Neh 5,1), not against the imperial authorities. That such accusations should be hurled against members of the *golah* community by their brethren offers a telling impression of internal covenant conditions. The less successful or fortunate Jews were at the mercy of the more affluent and unscrupulous ones. The latter came by their position and possessions by illicit acts and dealings and relationships with the people of the land. And those who were unfaithful to the religious obligations of the covenant had no compunction against taking advantage of their covenant brothers. Their misconduct was not in lending and receiving pledges—the law permitted it (Ex 22,25–27; Dt 24,10–13), even the selling of oneself or members of the family (Ex 21,7; Lv 25,39–40) —but rather in taking advantage of the abject necessities of their brothers to their own aggrandizement. The emergency in which the community found itself demanded a firm hand to deal with these outlandish practices. So long as the poorer classes had no further obligations than to keep themselves alive they could possibly tolerate the situation. But now that double duty was laid upon them and all Jews were involved in the project of rebuilding the walls to the equal protection and relief of all concerned, they could not understand why their more well-to-do brothers were so prosperous while they languished

in dire poverty. It was, in all probability, the breakup of families enslaved by necessity that precipitated their bitter outcry.

Nehemiah's reaction is related in Neh 5,6–13. Engaged too busily
with actual construction plans and work and distracted by the enemies
of the *golah,* he was not conscious of difficulties that should not have
existed in the first place. Apprized of the duplicity of some of the
more opulent Jews, he was profoundly disturbed and considered the
problems very carefully, which was another facet of his character—he
never acted on the spur of the moment. He first "reprimanded the
nobles and officials" (Neh 5,7) for charging interest, which was itself
a violation of the law (Ex 22,25; Lv 25,36f.; Dt 23,19). The appeal
seems to have fallen on deaf ears since he was constrained to convoke
an assembly of the people to bring all possible pressure to bear on a
speedy solution of the problem. He began his address by reminding
them that they had redeemed from enslavement to outsiders all the
Jews their economic circumstances permitted, only to have them re-
enslaved by their brothers. What they were doing was not good. "Ought
you not to walk in the fear of our God?" (v. 9), he asked. How could
they carry on as they were doing without incurring the reproach of
their enemies and at the same time maintain the strength and solidarity
of their resistance? Then he revealed to the assembled brethren his
own attitude and actions. He and his retainers had lent money and
grain to many. On that basis he appealed once more to the offenders
to desist from their claims, to return fields, vineyards, olive groves, and
houses, so that famine, starvation and the further rupture of families
might be averted. The guilty ones finally agreed to accept his advice.
That was not enough. He required a stringent religious oath from
them, made them swear to fulfill the promise they had made orally.
The added imprecation reflects the degradation of some of the community.

The administration of Nehemiah (Neh 5,14–19) could well be the
model for those in authority in any age—at least for such as can afford
to do so. Though he had a legitimate claim on the public treasury,
neither he nor his brothers ever drew upon it. That would eventually
have meant a further increase of taxes and added materially to the
already overburdened community. The contrast between his attitude
and the practices of former governors is glaring. Nehemiah's posture
was dictated by his "fear of God." He acquired no real estate; he participated in the work, as did his attendants. Moreover, he provided
daily rations not only for himself and his servants but for other Jews
and for those of the surrounding nations who cast in their lot with the

struggling community—all out of his own pocket so as not to burden the people (see 2 Thes 3,8). He could surely ask God to remember his good deeds on behalf of the people. That prayer ought to be interpreted in the context of the times (see *ANET* 307, col. 2; 316, col. 2; 317, col. 1). Nehemiah's overriding concern for the duty he had been sent to perform (Neh 7,1–3) is further demonstrated by the appointment of various overseers and caretakers. No sooner had the last stone been laid and the doors of the gates hung than he proceeded to appoint gate-keepers and make plans for dedication. Because of the unstable conditions referred to above, he selected the best and most reliable man available as commander of the citadel, with his brother Hanani, who was a devoutly interested Jew, as custodians of Jerusalem. Their function was to see that the city was protected at all times. Strict orders were given that the gates be secured not only at night but also during the heat of the day, that is, at siesta time (But see now G. R. Driver, *ZAW* 78 (1966), p. 4b for a different rendering). Moreover, not a single house was to be left unguarded. To carry out the command of Nehemiah they were to appoint the head of each household to serve as sentry in front of his own house—a master stroke of diplomacy.

When the *golah* returned from Babylon they gravitated to their ancestral towns around Jerusalem and in outlying sections of Judah. Several times in the lists (the *golah* list in Ezr 2,70; the builder list in Neh 7,73; the introduction to the population list in Neh 11,1ff.) it is stated that the Israelites remained or lived in their cities. They would naturally have preferred to live there, especially in view of conditions in and around the capital. Now that the walls were rebuilt and a good measure of security established, matters took on a different shape. Remember that the chief purpose of the returning *golah*—all the groups since the days of Cyrus, except those under Nehemiah—was to rehabilitate the institutions of religion in Jerusalem. The temple and altar were rebuilt two generations earlier, but even these could offer little stability in a community infiltrated with all kinds of compromisers. The result was little or no effort on the part of the better people of Judah to form a strong religious center at Jerusalem. Simply because Nehemiah came to rebuild the walls of Jerusalem does not imply that he was not concerned about the religious institutions. In fact, he came to strengthen them. He knew very well that there could be no vigorous religious community without people who were capable, devoted, and close to the locale of their function. Otherwise worship would remain desultory and half-hearted. So the first thing he did after restoring the walls and setting up security measures was to put on a campaign to repopulate the city. The goal set was to bring one tenth of the people of Judah (Neh 11,1) into the city. Both Josephus (*Ant.* 11:5:8) and Sirach (49:13) attribute to Nehemiah the building of new houses and the restoration of old ones; the former mentions especially his provision for priests' and Levites' housing out of his own resources. The cult could not function or the community become healthy without the services of more people and officials. The list recorded in Neh 11,3–24 is probably an adaptation of an archival document but with a few later additions represents substantially the period of Nehemiah. The list of towns (Neh 11,25–36) emphasizes the concern of the authorities to have representatives from every local town of Judah in the capital, despite the reluctance of some of them to give up their homes, friends, and farms.

According to the present arrangement of the book of Nehemiah, the service of dedication of the walls did not take place until after the repopulation of the city. Perhaps Gelin (*La Sainte Bible: Esdras et Néhémie*, p. 111, note a.) is right in suggesting that Neh 12,27–43 originally followed Neh 6,15. As it now stands, Neh 12,1–26 appears to be an insertion, for Neh 12,27ff. logically joins clearly with Neh 11,36, of which it is a continuation. The dedication ceremony must have been a colorful affair consisting of procession and sacrifice. The former consisted of two groups each composed of a choir, an official, the family heads, priests with trumpets, and Levites with musical instruments. From the starting point—which is not stated—one group proceeded toward the right, the other toward the left. The topography of the wall is given in connection with the movement of each group. This was an extraordinary circumambulation whose purpose was the ritual purification of the wall assuring the removal of any contamination and endowing the wall itself with a sort of sanctified power of protection. When the respective processions reached the temple area colossal sacrifices were offered so that its precincts rang with shouts of joy on the part of the participants, including women and children. In Neh 12,43 the writer has succeeded in capturing some of the enthusiasm generated by the occasion by using the term joy, rejoice (*śāmaḥ*) five times. With this accomplishment appears a slight break in the clouds that had hung over the land since shortly after the dedication of the second temple.

When the time specified in his firman had expired, Nehemiah returned to the Persian court. That was in the thirty-second year of Artaxerxes, that is, in 433–32 B.C. If he began his first term as governor in the twentieth year of Artaxerxes (445–44 B.C.), then his period of service lasted twelve years. The "some time later" (Neh 13,6) when he requested another leave of absence is quite indefinite. Certainly travel between Jerusalem and Susa, or even Babylon, might require upward of six months both ways. Considerable time was doubtless spent in making reports—it is altogether possible that the so-called memoirs of Nehemiah were reports to the royal officials—and getting further instructions from the king. For example, we know that Arsames, the governor of Egypt, was absent from his post for about three years (see Cowley, *Aramaic Papyri*, Letters 27:2; 30:4; 32:2–7). Upon returning to Jerusalem he found many things distasteful to him. Eliashib —either the high priest, or another priest of the same name—had gone so far as to provide spacious quarters for Tobiah in the temple chambers. When he was confronted with his actions, his only defense was that Tobiah was somehow related to him. This is the first time Nehemiah is portrayed as taking a direct hand in cultic affairs—a practice not uncommon in the Persian period as we know from Cambyses' reformation of the Neith cult at Sais in Egypt, the Darius I reforms in Egypt, and the famous Passover letter of Darius II. In any event, Tobiah and his belongings were thrown out, the defiled rooms cleansed, and the temple utensils and provisions replaced. Moreover, he found the house of God neglected and abandoned, the reason being that the Levites who were responsible for many of the services had returned to their homes. They had been left unsupported and hence had to fend for themselves. Nehemiah took immediate steps to bring them back to their posts and saw to it that the tithe for their support was reinstituted. Alert as he was, he observed flagrant violations of the Sabbath both by Jews and Phoenician merchants. To end illicit traffic on that day he instituted rigorous measures, threatening to arrest every violator of his regulations. He must have been aware that Jeremiah (Jer 17,19–27) and Ezekiel (Ez 20, 12–24) had traced the misfortunes of Judah to Sabbath violation—and he desired to avoid anything that might militate against the city and community he had labored so assiduously to preserve.

The problem of intermarriage was one of the most stubborn and persistent problems to face the *golah*. Earlier conditions in the land were somewhat mitigated thereby, but Malachi had already protested the practice. Nehemiah's attention was first directed to it when he noticed the mixed speech of children of such marriages. The languages of Moab and Ammon varied from the Hebrew only dialectically. Just what that of Ashdod was is not certain. The new community in process of formation required purity in both family and language if it was not to vanish in a series of compromises. It is not accidental that Jewish communities in exile gradually disintegrated—for example, the one at Elephantine. The *golah* had now reached its most critical stage. It had a temple, an altar and a fortified city, but more than material structures were needed to maintain it. A pure cult with a pure people conducting their religious and domestic affairs in a pure language was essential. Otherwise it would lose its national identity, and with it would go the religion of the fathers. So serious was the infraction that Nehemiah had to resort to drastic action to purge the little community of its misdeeds. He argued with them, cursed them, beat some of them, and plucked out the hair of others. Finally he made them "swear by God" to refrain from intermarriage. Once more let it be noted that this was not simply a misdemeanor of the poorer, uneducated classes. One of the grandsons of Eliashib, the high priest, was a son-in-law of Sanballat —Nehemiah chased him out. The reform measures of Nehemiah exhibit not only his zeal for the well-being of the *golah* but also his profound devotion to the cult of the Lord. His farsightedness was a guarantee that the Lord was active in the affairs of his people and would not let them go.

If Neh 10 is to be placed after Neh 13—it may owe its present position to the Ezra section immediately preceding it—it represents the legal document drawn up by Nehemiah to remedy conditions dealt with in Chapter XIII, or if not a formal document, a list of legal stipulations formally agreed upon in a ceremony publicly subscribed to by members of the community. To the present writer it appears as a legal document (see Neh 10,1) with all the marks of such a memorandum— names of religious and other officials—and bearing the official seal. A comparison between this chapter and chapter 13 suggests that the two are related in some such manner (see my *Ezra-Nehemiah, Anchor Bible,* XIV 175).

Before proceeding further with our story, let us pause for a short summary of the world and work of one of the greatest laymen in the time of the *golah*. Nehemiah came to Jerusalem, ostensibly on a community mission, in a response to a report on the tragic state of the city of the graves of his fathers. His first term as governor began in 445–44 B.C. and continued until 433–32 B.C.—a period of twelve years. Some of that time, perhaps as much as five years, was devoted to preparations and negotiations of various kinds. He conceived his function to be the establishment and consolidation of the *golah* community center at Jerusalem. This he achieved by reconstructing the walls of the city and thus providing for the community a secure center as a base for life and cultic operations. From the vantage point of the Persians there may have been another purpose in Nehemiah's mission, that is, to create a strong Jewish buffer state in the midst of an unstable political situation in Palestine and Egypt. It is a matter of record that the Jews were always on excellent terms with the Persians, which the latter used on more than one occasion for their own purposes. Nehemiah was a high-ranking member of the Persian court—a eunuch and the cupbearer of the king—and hence carried more than ordinary prestige. Only a person of superior standing could have handled the Jewish problem in the west at the time. There was the rivalry between the local provinces, which were, however, submerged in a common hostility toward the members of the *golah* attempting to rehabilitate themselves in their homeland. Customs and practices developed over more than a century were bound to collide with the plans and designs of the Jews endeavoring to realize the privileges conferred upon them by the series of royal decrees from Cyrus, Darius I, and Artaxerxes I. The new governor dealt astutely and effectively with the other provincial governors and in spite of endless harassments ultimately brought his mandate to a successful conclusion. He did it without creating further difficulty for the Persian authorities. But he did much more than rebuild the walls of Jerusalem. He reorganized the Jewish community by giving it a base of operation; he brought representatives from all the outlying towns and villages to Jerusalem; and he made Jerusalem once more into a viable cult center—something absolutely essential if the cult of the Lord was to be preserved for the future. The province of Judah was organized into five districts (*plk*)—(1) Jerusalem, divided in two subdistricts (Neh 3,9.12); (2) Bethhaccherem (Neh 3,14); (3) Mizpah (Neh 3,15); (4) Bethzur, also divided into two subdistricts though only one is recorded as having participated in the reconstruction of the walls (Neh 3,16); and (5) Keilah, divided into two subdistricts (Neh 3,17.18). We also learn from the same list of the residence and functioning of guilds of skilled artisans—goldsmiths (Neh 3,8.31.32), ointment mixers (Neh 3,8) and other craftsmen from Benjamin (Neh 11,35). Truly the hand of God was operative in all this. The cult-reforms instituted during his second period of residence demonstrate as much. There can be no doubt of the need for and effectiveness of the work of Nehemiah. Still, more than he was prepared to do was essential if his work was to be of lasting significance and fulfill the dreams he obviously cherished for the land and people of the fathers. (For further observations on Nehemiah see Albright, *BA* IX [1946] 10–13.)

**Other Evidences of Persian and Greek Activity
in Fifth Century B.C. Palestine and Syria**

There is now an abundance of archaeological evidence for activity in
Palestine and Syria in the Persian period. Life was not at a standstill,
though it must have been somewhat hazardous in many places. The
Phoenicians were engaged in sea commerce all through the period as
may be seen in the pottery discoveries off the coast of Israel at three
points—in the vicinity of Ashkelon and Ashdod, of Caesarea and Dor,
and of Achzib (see article by D. Barag, in *IEJ* XIII [1963], pp. 13–19).
Almost every excavation in the region has its Persian level. At Gerar
and Gaza pottery from the period appears. At the latter place Sir
Flinders Petrie uncovered a Persian dagger and a clay sealing from á
papyrus with the image of a Persian fire worshiper (*Ancient Gaza III*
[London: The British School of Egyptian Archaeology, 1933], pp. 1,4),
also Persian weights (*Ancient Gaza IV*, pp. 13–14), and art work of
granular gold whose design may come from Persia (*Ancient Gaza V*,
p. 10f.). Lachish, which was destroyed by the Babylonians, was reoccupied from the last half of the fifth century into the fourth. An excellent residency of the period was found there with tile drains and other
amenities, together with fine Attic sherds (*Lachish III: The Iron Age*
[London: Oxford University Press, 1953], p. 133). An Aramaic inscription was found there that may date from the Elephantine age (*ibid.*,
pp. 358f.). There was evidently a Greek colony at Ashdod where numerous imported Greek sherds were found as well as an excellent gold
ibex-shaped earring from the Achaemenian age and an ostracon with
Aramaic script from the Nehemiah-Ezra period (*ILN*, Dec. 7, 1963,
p. 944; *BA* XXVI [1963] 139). Meanwhile an Ashkelon sherd was
found at Athens (*QDAP* 4 (1935), pp. 179–180). Farther up the
coast at Stratos Tower Persian pottery was discovered (*RB* LX [1963],
583). There was a large building at Tell Qasile on the Yarkon river
near Tell Aviv which was probably used for administrative purposes
and dates from the Persian period (*IEJ* 1 (1950/51), p. 212; *BA* XIV
49). At Achzib there is indication of imports at the same time (*RB*
LXII [1965] 546). As Albright has remarked, during the Persian period
the whole eastern Mediterranean coast from Egypt to Syria was dotted
with trading posts (*AP* [1960] 142). But there are also innumerable
signs of activity farther inland that must not be overlooked. To begin
with the far north, at Hazor a building in Area B, stratum II, and the
reconstruction of the citadel in stratum III are assigned to the Persian

period (*Hazor I* [Jerusalem: The Magnes Press, 1958], pp. 54–65). At nearby Ayyelet Hashshahar were uncovered the ruins of a large residence constructed of heavy terre pisée walls with a large well-drained courtyard (S. Yeivin, *A Decade of Archaeology in Israel* [Istanbul: Nederlands Historisch–Archaeologisch Instituut in het Nabije Oosten, 1960], p. 29), and in the mountains of central Galilee—Tell Harashim —were unearthed an abundance of sherds (*ibid.*, p. 27). There is some evidence of Persian influence at Megiddo. Samaria presents numerous remains from the Persian period, such as good Greek pottery, a building complex that appears to have been that of an official, an Achaemenian cup (Crowfoot and Kenyon, *The Objects from Samaria* [London: Palestine Exploration Fund, 1957], pp. 3, 216) and Persian seal impressions. A pit of pure Persian pottery was found at Taanach. Gibeah (IV A) also has a level of the period, but the instability of local conditions in the area at the time is reflected by the crudely constructed remains at Bethel. The situation at Shechem is somewhat confused. Stratum V appears to have been destroyed somewhere near the beginning of the reign of Xerxes (485 B.C.), perhaps 480 B.C. (see G. E. Wright, *Shechem* [New York: McGraw-Hill Book Co., 1965], p. 167). Seal impressions and jar-handles of the period were found, notably a Persian seal impression depicting a hunting king (a well-known motif from Persian coins) and perhaps a stylized winged symbol of Ahuramazda. The fact that similar situations occur at Bethel, Gibeah, Gibeon, and now Shechem may be of some importance. Was there a general destruction in the area at the time or are other unknown factors involved that cannot yet be accounted for? There was a Phoenician trade colony at Tell Makmish in the Persian period, and at Tell Sukas commerce was vigorously pursued all during the Persian wars and after. Jar-handles stamped with the word *mosah* appeared at Gibeon, which shows that there was some kind of occupation though it could not have been extensive. There was no building at Ramat Rahel in the period of the second temple. The place served as a kind of dump where a number of objects from that age were found. Among them was a host of *yahud* stamps that show the position occupied by the Jews at the time (see Y. Aharoni, *Excavations at Ramat Rahel, Seasons 1959 and 1960* [Rome: Università degli studi, Centro di Studi Semitici, 1962], pp. 27–35). Perhaps the most interesting finds of the period have come from Tell Goren at Engedi, which seem to show that the place was resettled soon after the beginning of the return from exile. Its most flourishing state was reached in the time of Artaxerxes I—age of Nehemiah-Ezra—and of Darius II. It declined rapidly after about 400 B.C. apparently as a result of the changing political climate in southern Judah (*IEJ* 14 (1964), p. 126). It is not yet clear what the exact character of stratum V at Tell Arad is, but it appears to belong to the period from the early return to that of Nehemiah. The sherds from the Persian period (such as Attic ware) may prove a settlement to have been there at that time. An inscribed Aramaic ostracon dates, by script, from the Elephantine period. A very important observation has been made by the excavators (*ibid.*, pp. 125f. n.8) to the effect that Tell Arad suffered a rapid deterioration toward the end of the fifth century B.C., because of their being overrun by nomadic invaders from the desert who intruded through Edom as far as the Negeb and southern Judah. In their wake cities were destroyed and the countryside ravished. Such movements were not yet apparent in the time of Nehemiah as the place names in Neh 11,25–35 prove. Hopefully further publication of results at Engedi and Tell Arad will fill in many of the gaps in our knowledge of the late fifth and early fourth centuries. It has been reported recently (*ILN* [July 2, 1966], pp. 26–27) that the finest building excavated to date at Zarethan in Trans-Jordan is a palace of the late Persian period. It was discovered immediately below the Hellenistic building. It was some 71 feet square with a paved courtyard surrounded by rooms. The open court was drained by a canal. The walls of the building were of mud brick laid on a stone foundation and it may have had a tile roof. In the same level was discovered a small incense altar with geometric designs with the figure of a horse and man painted red and black. The inscription on it is in Hebrew and reads *lyknw* (= "to Jakinu"). Professor Pritchard thinks both palace and altar belonged to the man named in the inscription. Once more we have evidence of rather stable conditions in the area around Zarethan in the fourth century. The most impressive picture painted by archaeological discoveries in western Asia in the Persian period is that of ferment, trade, and intercommunication, which accentuates at once the dangers confronting the Jewish community in Palestine and at the same time heralds the preparation of the world for the realization of the hopes and dreams of Deutero-Isaiah (Is 49,6).

Greece
and Anatolia

The political events involving Greeks and Persians in the reign of Artaxerxes I are exceedingly complicated. It has been said above that after the fiasco under Xerxes, the Persians never again invaded Europe in force. Henceforth it was to be a kind of war of nerves and wealth. The Greek cities of Ionia had freed themselves of Persian rule and paid their corporate tribute to Athens while the local farmers and business men were still required to pay rent to Persian estate owners. Frequently the Persians employed their gold in diplomacy and thus held off the day of reckoning for more than a century. The successive political and diplomatic moves under Artaxerxes can be studied with the help of any history of Persia. Here it is our purpose to call attention—no more, and often without explanation or detail—to other movements taking place in the western world at the time. The fifth century B.C. was probably one of the most eventful and momentous in history. It was then that Herodotus, the father of history, went on his travels in preparation for his great work. The very year that Nehemiah had his first interview about Judah with the Persian king, Herodotus recited his history at Athens. Aeschylus (525–456 B.C.) had just died and Sophocles (495–406 B.C.) and Euripides (480–406 B.C.) were at the height of their work. Under the direction of Pericles, who was the greatest statesman Athens produced, Phidias was commissioned as director of art and himself built the Propylaea on the Acropolis. He also constructed the magnificent temple of Athena (the famous Parthenon) and a statue of the goddess that was dedicated in 438 B.C., when Nehemiah was building the wall of Jerusalem. It was also the age of Socrates, who was born about 469 B.C.

Although Athens had learned much from her experience with Persia and had developed, eventually, into *the* center of culture and thought, she had not yet shaken off altogether her past attitudes. She did pass from tyranny to democracy in politics and from magic to philosophy in the sphere of thought. The Persian wars forced upon her considerations of human relationships and upon her intellectual giants the probing of the mind as it came to grips with reality. While Anaximenes set up a Babylonian sundial (*Her.* 2:109) in Sparta, his pupil, Anaxagoras, was compelled to flee from Athens because of the unwelcome reception of his astronomy. Around 459 B.C. when the Athenians came to the aid of the Egyptians in their revolt against Persia, a disciple of Pythagoras, Oenopides of Chios, took advantage of the situation to visit Egypt where he studied the "scientific" advances of the country and observed the Nile inundation with the Egyptian system of calendration. Upon his return he worked out a calendar reform on the basis of a compromise between the Pythagorean and Egyptian calculations and inscribed it on a bronze tablet set up at the scene of the Olympian games. It must not be forgotten that the early philosophers came from Asia Minor or were the descendants of Ionic immigrants to Thrace where they came in contact with thought from the Orient to a much wider extent than did those of the mainland. One of the first great systematicians, Democritus, wrote about Asia Minor in his "Phrygian Treatise." He is said to have studied with Egyptian priests (*Diodorus Siculus* 1:96) and must have traveled far up the Nile since he wrote a tract on the people of Meroë, which was then the capital of Ethiopia. After the peace of Callais (c. 449 B.C.) Democritus made an extended journey through portions of the Persian empire, notably Babylonia, because he composed several essays on "Chaldean" subjects. Clement of Alexandria says that on his visit to Babylon Democritus saw a stele of Ahiqar (*Stromata* 1:15), some of whose writings he incorporated in his own. (For the list of Ahiqar quotations and references, see R. H. Charles, *The Apocrypha and Pseudepigrapha of the Old Testament*, II [Oxford: Oxford University Press, 1913], pp. 716f.). From Babylonia he continued on his travels to Persia where he gathered material to write about the religion of the Magians. The influence especially of Babylonia on his mind may be seen from his writings in mathematics and astronomy, the latter of which can be explained only on the basis of those contacts (see Olmstead, *History of the Persian Empire*, pp. 333–341). But the man from Abdera found no welcome at Athens. Hippocrates was born on the island of Cos, off the southwestern coast of Asia Minor, in 460 B.C. In fact the so-called Hippocratic Corpus found its beginnings in this period in the practices of the Asclepiads in Cos and at Cnidus. Ionian thinkers were active almost everywhere, and it must not be forgotten that the Persian court physician Ctesias, who served for seventeen years under Artaxerxes II, was born at Cos early in the latter half of the fifth century.

Archaeology has not yet presented more than an outline of the Persian occupation of Asia Minor. There was such an occupation at Gordion, southwest of present Ankara, which was put out of action in the middle of the fifth century. Persian remains have turned up at Sardis, notably in tombs; otherwise little of the remains of that period have been uncovered to date (*BASOR*, CLXXXII [April, 1966] 15).

It was perhaps during Nehemiah's second term as governor of Judah that the Peloponnesian war broke out (431 B.C.) and Thucydides began his great history of that war. It is doubtful whether Persia had any part in precipitating the conflict, but it was greatly to her interest. In the thirty-year peace treaty they had promised exactly the opposite to the Spartans and the Athenians, and when war actually broke out they supported the Spartan navy. In the course of the struggle Artaxerxes must have been delighted to observe the negotiations of the two principals for allies from among their compatriots. He did nothing against piracy of the Phoenician ships carrying cargo to Athens. He smiled at the refusal of the Lycians and Carians when they withheld Athenian tribute. As time wore on the Persian king lost all interest in the civil conflict, and the slaying of two Athenian tax agents by the Lycians didn't raise a ripple in Persian diplomatic waters. The wresting of control of Notium from the Athenians in 430 B.C. and its regain by them three years later went unnoticed, for it was presently to return to Persian hegemony. There was, of course, nothing he could do when Aristophanes referred to a chorus of slaves as *Babylonians* or when Euripides shouted that Asia served Europe as a slave. By 425 B.C. cities in Pontus, on the north coast of Asia Minor, were lost with only a feeble attempt to retrieve them. The mental powers of the king were weakened by his physical debility—he was already dying—when he sent his ambassador Artaphernes to Sparta for clarification of their requests. Intercepted on the way, his documents were decoded and he was sent back home in the company of Athenians. But at Ephesus they were informed of the death of Artaxerxes and Damaspia, his wife, on the same day. That ended Athenian hopes and portended victory for Sparta.

Art
Contributions

To judge from archaeological reports, there are few remains of consequence. It is known that Artaxerxes built the southeast entrance to the hall of Xerxes at Persepolis and part of the great relief processions of the tripylon was completed under him. It was mentioned above that the palace of Darius at Susa was destroyed by fire, and since Artaxerxes had neither money nor ability to rebuild it he constructed a much smaller one at the southern edge of the city. In addition he erected a small hypostyle temple in his later capital. He built a tomb for himself at Naqš-i-Rustam beside those of his father and grandfather. There is a relief at Persepolis depicting the king on his throne (Ghirshman, *Persia*, fig. 248). Although there was nothing new in monumental art after his day, there is evidence of the refinement and humanity of its forms—due in all probability to contact with the Greeks. (See H. Frankfort, *The Art and Architecture of the Ancient Orient* [Baltimore: Penguin Books, Inc., 1955], Chap. XII.) Ivory from Egypt, Syria, and

Greece was introduced. Gold and silver vessels of the Achaemenian period have been found at numerous areas from the shores of the Black Sea, Asia Minor, Syria, and, of course, in Persia proper. In one of his inscriptions Artaxerxes I speaks of a silver dish or saucer made in his house. The famous motif of the long-horned wild goats appears on a beautiful golden bowl from Hamadan (Ecbatana). Even the stone vases with their horizontal grooved rings have it. The Achaemenians also continued the use of cylinder seals (H. Frankfort, *Cylinder Seals* [London: The Macmillan, Company, 1939], plate XXXVII). Ghirshman calls attention to the diffusion of Achaemenian-Persian art from India to Siberia. It seemed to win acceptance in the outlying countries at the very time the dynasty was weakening and was on the way out. (For Achaemenian art influence in Anatolia see E. Akurgal, *Die Kunst Anatoliens von Homer bis Alexander* [Berlin: W. de Gruyter, 1961], pp. 167–81.)

Selected Readings

Bright, J., *A History of Israel*, Chap. IX. Philadelphia: The Westminster Press, 1959.

Josephus, *Jewish Antiquities*, Book XI.

Olmstead, A. T., *History of the Persian Empire*, Chaps. XVII–XX. Chicago: University of Chicago Press, 1948.

VI

The Work of Ezra

It would be superfluous to reargue the case for the date of Ezra. Most scholars today place him after Nehemiah, and that is the position taken here. There are, of course, good arguments for the traditional date—the seventh year of Artaxerxes (Ezr 7,7–8)—that is, 458 B.C. if the king is Artaxerxes I. Virtually all those who hold the position that Ezra followed Nehemiah locate his activity in the reign of Artaxerxes II (405–359 B.C.), that is, beginning in 398 B.C. It should not be overlooked that Josephus (*Ant.* 11:5) places both Ezra and Nehemiah, in that order, in the reign of Xerxes (= Artaxerxes) by whom is clearly meant Artaxerxes I. It may be well to list here some points to be kept in mind in connection with the date of Ezra: (1) The post-exilic Davidic family register ends with the sons of Elioenai whose last son was hardly born after 405 B.C.; (2) The last high priest to actually officiate was Jehohanan (Ezr 10,6) (while the

131

Nehemiah list [Neh 12,10–11.22] contains the name of Jaddua, his son and successor, there is no indication that he had yet assumed office); (3) Darius II (424–405 B.C.) is the last Persian king to be mentioned (Neh 12,22) unless the Artaxerxes, noted above, is the second king to bear that name, in which case the reference would be to Darius III (336–333 B.C.)—too late for any consideration here; (4) The name of Bigwai, the governor of Judah in 408 B.C., does not appear in either Ezra or Nehemiah; (5) Difficulties with the Samaritans virtually disappeared or were deliberately played down, since they are not mentioned in Ezra, not even in the list of foreign women who intermarried with the Jews, except in Neh 13,28, which tells us that Joiada's son married Sanballat's daughter; and (6) Sanballat was no longer functioning in 408 B.C. since the appeal from the Elephantine Jews was made to Delaiah and Shelemiah, the sons of Sanballat (Cowley, *Aramaic Papyri*, no. 30). It appears that the Samaritan problem for the moment had been pretty well overcome by the measures taken by Nehemiah, and after the reconstruction of the wall of Jerusalem the efforts of the leaders of the Jewish community were focused upon other matters.

It is possible that Nehemiah recognized his limitations as leader or governor—after all he was a eunuch and could perform no religious functions—and when he had gone as far as he could, resolved to commit the internal affairs of the *golah* to more capable hands. His work was centered on provision for the external security of the Jews in Jerusalem. When that was achieved he realized that the success of the people of God demanded cultic reorientation that he could not direct by virtue of his limitations as a layman. He must have been in touch with the Jewish colonies in Babylon during the time of his absence from Jerusalem and may have made a proposal to them to furnish the necessary cultic leadership. In any case, considerable time would have been required to implement any conclusion to which the Jewish authorities might have agreed. Albright (*BP* 93, and note 193, 112f.) has suggested that "the seventh year of Artaxerxes" (Ezr 7,7–8) should perhaps read "the thirty-seventh year," the term for thirty having dropped out of the text by haplography (see further J. Bright, "The Date of Ezra's Mission to Jerusalem" in *Yehezkel Kaufmann Jubilee Volume* [Jerusalem: The Magnes Press, 1960], pp. 70–87 of the English section. For arguments against this reading see A. Emerton, "Did Ezra Go to Jerusalem in 428 B.C.?" in *JTS* XVII [1966], 1–12). Such a date would fit best into the scheme of events as now known from the Bible and other sources, although one cannot be absolutely certain about it. There are problems of correspondence with known facts that bedevil any view on the matter of date; the one followed here seems to leave the fewest unresolved problems. Proceeding, therefore, on that basis, Ezra must have been inspired to undertake his mission directly or indirectly at the behest of Nehemiah. It is not beyond the realm of possibility that when he found cultic chaos upon his return to Jerusalem, Nehemiah sent to Babylon for help, and the Ezra expedition was dispatched in response.

Whatever may have been the impetus behind the Ezra movement, it was a legitimate one, authorized by the king, even encouraged by him. We are told (Ezr 7) that the scribe organized a small group of Israelites, priests, Levites, singers, gatekeepers, and temple slaves that he proposed to lead to Judah. By permission of the king who provided everything he requested and because the hand of Yahweh his God was with him (i.e., Ezra), the contingent left Babylon on the first day of the first month and arrived at Jerusalem exactly four months later. But before outlining the official document under whose authority Ezra proceeded, it is necessary to inquire who this man really was. Our sources affirm that he was both scribe and priest. He was reckoned to the Aaron-Zadokite descendants (Ezr 7,2) by the Chronicler (see also 1 Chr 6,3–15) or someone who was responsible for the genealogy, which is here considerably curtailed. The purpose of the writer of this chapter was either to attribute to the great lawgiver priestly prerogatives or to present only enough of the genealogy to prove his identity as a legitimate priest. Certainly his interest in the torah and in cultic matters is enough to demonstrate that he was more than an ordinary layman with ordinary or superficial concern for such arrangements. Just what is meant by his position as scribe is far from certain. Does it mean that he held a special office at the court or in the governing circles domiciled at Babylon, or has it something to do with his activity among the Jews? H. H. Schaeder thought Ezra was a kind of secretary for Jewish affairs in the government (*Esra der Schreiber* [Tübingen: Mohr, 1930], pp. 39–59; see also E. Meyer, *Geschichte des Altertums* [Darmstadt: Wissenschaftliche Buchgemeinschaft, 1954], vol. 4, pt. 1, 42f.). However that may be, he could have been no ordinary Jew. To be charged by the king with responsibility for an important mission meant that he was at least a well-known and competent person. Moreover, he was entrusted with political (Ezr 7, 25.26) as well as religious responsibilities. That the Persians often employed gifted and trusted foreigners in the service of the court is beyond dispute. In the time of Darius I a fleet commander by the name of Udjeharresne was given the portfolio as chief physician, companion, and director of the palace. He apparently was a sort of go-between for the king between Sais, the seat of Neith, the mother of Re, and himself. He seems to have been in charge of religious affairs for the temple at Sais and as such informed the king of conditions there, in fact petitioned him for a redress of grievances. He requested that foreigners be expelled from the temple and that the temple itself be restored to its pristine splendor. Darius ordered forthwith that the foreigners who had taken up residence there be thrown out together with their belongings, that the temple be cleansed, and that those who rightfully belonged there be reinstated. He further ordered that certain emoluments be given to Neith and the other gods and that the regular cult festivals and procession be reinstituted. This the king did, says Udjeharresne, because he apprized him of the greatness of Sais, the city of the gods. What is more, the order of Darius was inscribed on a statue now in the Vatican and is the only inscription of its kind to come from the Persian period (G. Posener, *La Première Domination Perse en Égypte* [Cairo: Bibliothèque d'étude, 1936], pp. 166ff. For further remarks on other Egyptian documents of the period with the same intent see Meyer, *KS* II [1924] 91–100). That is a striking parallel to the position and activity of Ezra, whose certification was not inscribed on stone but probably on some other writing material, a copy of which found its way into the temple archives from which the writer of Ezr 7 quoted. Not much is known about the religious concerns of Artaxerxes. Berossus says he had Anahita temples in the provincial capitals, and his inscriptions tell of his invocation of that god and Mithra. If that is so he may have responded to Ezra's request in much the same way as Darius did to that of Udjeharresne. And we have contemporary testimony to the effect that Darius II in 419 B.C. intervened in fixing the date for the Passover and Unleavened Bread festivals for the Jewish garrison at Elephantine (Cowley, *Aramaic Papyri*, no. 21). A century and a half later Antiochus Soter (280–262/61 B.C.) rebuilt the great temples of Esagila and Ezida at Babylon where he offered prayers for the welfare of his kingdom (*ANET* 317). In view of these documented cases of Persian and Seleucid interest in the religion of other peoples, there can hardly be a doubt that on this occasion Artaxerxes acted precisely as the Chronicler says he did. Nehemiah's intercession on behalf of his brethren in all probability convinced the king that the Jews were not hostile toward the empire, in fact were an asset to it, especially after he learned from his cupbearer the true state of affairs in the involved provinces of the satrapy Across the River. Just what relation existed between Nehemiah and Hanani and Ezra is obscure. There may have been some misunderstanding at times among them.

That Ezra's mission was undertaken at his own request is apparent from Ezr 7,6b. The official edict of the king (Ezr 7,12–26) was issued in the diplomatic language of the time—Aramaic. Several items in it are to be noted. First of all the qualifications of the king's emissary are stressed. Three times Ezra is mentioned by name. He is twice referred to as "the priest, student of the law of the God of the heavens" (vv. 12, 21). He is said to be possessed of "the wisdom of your God" (v. 25). Next comes reference to the formal document granting the request of Ezra and spelling out his authority to direct "an investigation about Judah and Jerusalem" as prescribed in "the law of your God." In addition the decree included a proclamation of license enabling all who were willing to do so to accompany him. Behind the edict lies the sanction of the king and his seven counselors (see Est 1,14 and Xenophon, *Anabasis* 1:64f). Besides the scrutiny of the religious situation in Jerusalem (see H. Schneider, *Die Bücher Esra und Nehemia* [Bonn: Hanstein, 1959] pp. 132f., and Josephus, *Ant.* 11:5:1), Ezra was delegated to bear to Jerusalem the contributions of the government and the Jews still in Babylon for the amelioration of conditions in the house of God and for the sacrifices to be offered upon its altar. He was to have a free hand in the distribution of those contributions and in consultation with his brethren, the disposal of the surplus. If needs of the house of God required it, he was given authority to draw upon the local treasury of the empire. The order on the local fiscal agents (vv. 21–22) sounds very much like the Persepolis Treasury Tablets in some respects, although they were receipts of payments or requisitions for such to individuals or groups of workers on imperial projects. Once more the religious requisites are stressed (v. 23). Moreover, the religious functionaries were to be exempted from any tax or other impost. Such exemptions are not unknown from other sources. Herodotus (3:91) says the whole district of Arabia in the fifth satrapy was not taxed by Darius Hystaspes. The final directive of the decree is more difficult to reconcile with the supposed jurisdiction of the local governor, whether Nehemiah, Hanani, or their successors—that is, the appointment of magistrates and judges whose duty would be to handle all cases in accordance with "the law of your God and the law of the king" (v. 26). It may be that the reference is to cultic matters, though that would be somewhat doubtful in view of the meaning of the Aramaic terminology. Perhaps the Chronicler has stretched the decree a bit here by attributing to the priest an authority he was to possess only later (see 1 Chr 26, 29f. where David is said to have appointed such functionaries, and Jehoshaphat's designation of priests and Levites to handle civil cases, 2 Chr 19,8ff.). The codicil decreeing the sentence to be meted out to those who are disobedient to the law (*data'* = "the public law") of God or that of the king is meant to accentuate the fact that Ezra was invested with the authority of the Persian administration in every-thing he did. From the standpoint of the Chronicler, the Persian kings were viewed as successors of David (see Is 44,28a; 45,1) and although they may not have been aware of it, they were the Lord's agents execut-ing his plans and purposes. Artaxerxes thus did what Hezekiah and Josiah had done earlier—decreed cleansing and then beautification of the temple and cultic reformation in line with the law of God. Deeply devoted to the mission upon which he was to embark, Ezra voiced his thanks to Yahweh, to whom he attributed the king's motivation to enhance the temple, and expressed gratitude for the choice of himself as the one to carry out the royal decree.

According to the list in Ezr 8,1–14, exactly 1,500 persons signified their readiness to undertake the mission (*LXX*–1,510; 1 Esd 8–1,794), besides 38 Levites and 220 temple slaves. That number does not in-clude women and children, so that there must have been a sizable con-tingent that accompanied Ezra to Jerusalem. Gathering them at the point of embarkation for preparation and inspection (Ezr 8,15–20), Ezra observed the absence of Levites—perhaps another indication that many of the Jews, especially the more capable ones, were well satisfied with their lot in Babylon and hence were loathe to jeopardize their own and their family interests. After considerable searching, he finally found a total of thirty-eight Levites—eighteen of the family of Mahli and twenty of that of Merari—willing to accompany his group. Since he had informed the king that "the hand of our God favors all those who seek him but his fierce wrath falls upon all who forsake him" (v. 22), he was ashamed to ask for a cavalry escort. So he decided to place himself and his companions under the protection of God. In the farewell service of intercession they were assured of the Lord's safe conduct across the dangerous wastes they would have to traverse. To guard against possible contingencies on the journey, he took special precautions with the vessels for the temple services and the gold and silver that had been contributed by the king and by their own brethren. Preparations took twelve days (Ezr 7,9; 8,31) so that this wave of *golah* departed on the twelfth day of the first month. The journey of just under four months (Ezr 7,9) was apparently uneventful. The hand of their God had preserved them from enemies and waylayers (Ezr 8,31). A short time after their arrival at Jerusalem they delivered their treasures to the proper authorities. On the way they also delivered the official documents of the king to his satrap(s) and governors of Across the River, who were duly impressed and lent their support to the objectives of the mission.

But now the question is what is the sequence of events after the initial ceremony of the transfer of the contributions? The most realistic approach to the problem at present is that of A. Gelin (*Le Livre de Esdras et Néhémie*, 2nd ed. [Paris: Les éditions du Cerf, 1960], p. 14) who thinks the clue to bringing possible order out of the confused materials now deposited in the books of Ezra and Nehemiah is the several references to days and months in the relevant chapters. These are as follows:

(a) Ezr 7,9—the first day of the first month (beginning of movement in Babylon).

(b) Ezr 8,31—the twelfth day of the first month (embarkation on journey).

(c) Ezr 7,8–9—the first day of the fifth month (arrival at destination at Jerusalem).

(d) Neh 7,73–Neh 8,2.18—from the first day of the seventh month to the eighth day of the same month (reading and exposition of the torah during the Feast of Tabernacles).

(e) Ezr 10,9—the twentieth day of the ninth month (the Jerusalem assembly).

(f) Ezr 10,16—from the first day of the tenth month to the first day of the first month (presumably of the second year) (period required for consideration of cases of mixed marriages).

(g) Neh 9,1—the twenty-fourth day of "this month," that is, the first month of the second year (a service of fasting and confession).

Hence the order of the Ezra-Nehemiah chapters would be:

(a) Ezr 7–8—proceedings attendant upon Ezra's return to Jerusalem.

(b) Neh 7,73–8,18—ceremonies connected with the reading and interpretation of the torah.

(c) Ezr 9–10—the subject of mixed marriages and how it was handled.

(d) Neh 9—the penitential service.

If that is the proper sequence of events, it means that Ezra proceeded with his work quickly. As he saw it the chief purpose of his coming was to harmonize the cultic community of the *golah* with the law of the Lord. The first order of business then was to inform the people of that law. It may be of some interest here to call attention once more to the Dura-Europas Synagogue paintings (C. H. Kraeling, *The Ex-*

cavations at Dura-Europas, pp. 232–35 and plate LXXVII), panel III of which is believed to represent Ezra reading from the scroll of the law. The background for the panel is Neh 8. With the three other panels the series depicts a remarkable conception of the covenant—panel I showing Moses summoned to deliver Israel from Egypt; panel II, Moses on Mt. Sinai receiving the tables of the law; panel III, Ezra reading the law to a reconstituted people; and panel IV, Abraham's reception of the divine promise. And in the whole of post-exilic Judaism, we must not forget the place of the torah, which is so powerfully portrayed here in Nehemiah. The emphasis on Moses and the torah in the work of the Chronicler is striking—the former occurs some thirty-one times, the latter forty times. The torah as a book is referred to nine times, eight times as a written document. It is denominated fourteen times as the torah of the Lord, of God, or of the Lord God. That is presumably what Ezra brought along from Babylon, that of which he was the skilled interpreter, and that which he was sent to impart to the people for their guidance in community cultic service and life.

If the above outline of time sequence is correct, it was only two months after the arrival in Judah that the stage was set for the great ceremony of the reading of the torah. It is very fully and picturesquely described in Neh 8 and took place in the seventh month. That was the month when the Feast of Tabernacles, which Josephus (*Ant.* 8:4:1) describes as "a most holy and most eminent feast of the Hebrews" was celebrated. The background upon which Neh 8 is constructed is Lev 23,33–43, which provides for a solemn assembly on the first and eighth days of the feast (for a detailed discussion of the origin, significance, and ritual of the Feast of Tabernacles see R. de Vaux, *AI* 495–502). It was primarily a feast of rejoicing because it was connected with the season of ingathering in the autumn. That is why the people assembled for the celebration were admonished to refrain from weeping and mourning (Neh 8,9–10). It has been said that Ezra's first public ceremony marks the beginning of Judaism. That may be true if qualified to mean that it signifies the initiation of Judaism on Jewish soil. In fact Ezra was apparently shifting to Jerusalem a phenomenon that had been pursued among the Jews in exile for many years. The only way they had then to express their faithfulness and devotion to Yahweh was the study of the torah and the celebration of such family or community rites as did not involve the temple cult. It is significant that the service described in Neh 8 did not occur in the court of the temple but "at the plaza before the Water Gate."

The main purpose of the assembly was to listen to the reading from "the book of the law of Moses" (Neh 8,1), which Ezra had brought with him from Babylon (Ezr 7,14). It was doubtless the latest edition of the Pentateuch. The external arrangements are impressive indeed. Ezra brought the law before the assembly in such a way that all who were gathered could see the scroll. Moreover he stood on a podium—a kind of pulpit—in plain view of the assembled congregation. He was flanked on the right and left by six priests. When he opened the scroll "in the sight of all the people," all arose—possibly the origin of the modern Christian liturgical practice of the congregation standing for the reading of the Gospel—because it was a most solemn occasion. The service began with an invocation by Ezra to which the people responded with a ringing "Amen." He then began to read from the "book of the torah of the Lord." Meanwhile the people remained standing, quietly and reverently listening as the designated Levites explained what was being read by Ezra. "They read from the book of the law of God in translation in order to make it intelligible and so helped them to comprehend the reading" (Neh 8,8). The meaning seems to be that while Ezra read from the Hebrew text, the Levites translated what was being read into Aramaic, the language of the people at the time. The hearing of the torah had precisely the effect the leaders envisioned. In their lifetime the assembly had never heard the word of God so clearly and cogently expounded. Ezra must have selected his lessons carefully—he could not have read the whole Pentateuch from dawn until midday—since the people were informed of their failure to conform to the requisites of the torah. The curses and threats against nonobservance struck home, for the hearers realized the grave peril in which they stood, "for all the people wept when they heard the words of the torah" (Neh 8,9). Then it was that they were reminded of the feast that was set for the seventh month—Tabernacles—which was a time for joy and thanksgiving. The Levites went about urging the people to "be calm, for the day is holy, and you must not be dejected" (Neh 8,11). That led to a spectacular observance of the feast such as had not taken place since the days of Joshua (Neh 8,17), and there was great rejoicing as the season demanded and the torah commanded. Apparently the law-reading rite set into motion a wave of concern because after the dismissal of the congregation the family heads, priests, and Levites returned the next day for further study of the torah. For then it was that they discovered the real import of the Feast of Tabernacles that they celebrated in the fashion noted above. But that was not all they found written in the scroll of the torah of the Lord as they continued

their quest through the seven days of the feast during which Ezra read
from the scroll "from the first day until the last day" of the festival
(Neh 8,18).

To see the first result of that study of the torah we must return to
the book of Ezra (Ezr 9–10). From the seventh month until the ninth
month there is no specific information as to what went on in the
community, though it is not difficult to imagine that the events connected with the first reading of the torah kindled the zeal of leaders
and people to inquire further about its teaching. Whether Ezra had
purposely selected his studies and readings in view of the persistent
problem that so disturbed the *golah* is not disclosed, but it could not
have been far from his thoughts, especially if he had been informed
by Nehemiah of conditions in the land. Something of the embarrass-
ment caused by mixed marriages has already been mentioned, but it
appears to have been a protracted affair because of the poverty afflicting
the *golah*. To Ezra it must have been quite serious since it involved
a contamination of the "holy seed" (Ezr 9,2), which was an exceedingly important consideration under present conditions. In any case,
it was the officials who approached Ezra with what he doubtless already knew: "The people of Israel, the priests and the Levites have
not kept themselves separate from the peoples of the lands with their
abominations . . . because their sons have married some of their
daughters" (Ezr 9,1–2). What must have been the hardest blow of all
to Ezra was the specific accusation leveled against the officials and
chiefs as being the prime offenders "in this breach of loyalty." Ezra's
immediate reaction was one of chagrin and mortification. No doubt he
got just what he wanted—some kind of popular recognition of guilt—
but he was hardly prepared for the widespread practice of mixed marriages after Nehemiah's brush with it (Neh 13,23–27). Yet he acted
like a good priest or pastor in humbling himself before God in the sight
of all those who had gathered that day before him. His self-identification with the people is clearly evident in the confessional prayer he
offered at the evening oblation—note especially the frequent appearance of the pronouns "we" and "our" and "us," which occur throughout (vv. 6–15). And it can hardly be the editorial use of the first-
person plural; it was rather a genuine, heartfelt sympathy with the
sinners. The quotation from "thy servants the prophets" is a patchwork
of references, mostly from the Deuteronomic sources (see my *Ezra-
Nehemiah, Anchor Bible*, p. 79), which betrays a wide knowledge of
the torah. Why was the scribe so deeply moved by intermarriage? Did
not Moses himself marry a Kenite woman, later a Cushite, Joseph an
Egyptian, and Mahlon and Chilion Moabite wives? First, such prac-

tices were a violation of Dt 7,1–4, upon which passage the catalogue of Ezr 9,1 is based—with the exception that in the former neither Moabites nor Ammonites are included. It is rather striking that nowhere here do we find reference to Samaritans, though they may be subsumed under the general term "the peoples of the lands." This was not exactly a racial matter since a number of those named are Semites. What was uppermost in the mind of Ezra was the absolute necessity for the maintenance of Jewish identity if the covenant was to be preserved in the midst of rapidly changing world events and the interplay of peoples in the Persian empire. The Babylonian Jews were scarcely in a position to carry on a full program of religion, and those who had returned since the days of Sheshbazzar and Zerubbabel had made little progress until Nehemiah came and attacked the lethargic situation with a vigorous hand. But there was a point beyond which he could not go. It was Ezra's mission to breathe new life and spirit into the *golah* by injecting the provisions of the torah. Nehemiah gave them a body; Ezra was destined to provide them with a soul.

News of Ezra's self-humiliation spread rapidly throughout the city, for while he was still in the act of praying and confessing the corporate sin of the people "a very large congregation of men, women and children of Israel assembled themselves around him" (Ezr 10,1). Through his attitude they became more conscious of the fact that his mortification was the outgrowth of their misdemeanors, not his own. Hence the profusion of tears. Then one of those who had returned earlier, Shecaniah—note that he was of the clan of Elam—spoke to Ezra on behalf of his brethren, making full confession of this violation of the torah. He must have become aware of the fact that the whole community was in grave peril of being wiped out in syncretism with their stronger and better-endowed neighbors. His response was tantamount to a concession to Ezra, whose pronouncements were taken as authoritative. Shecaniah is not named in the list below, though some of his family are, yet he too included himself by self-identification with the guilty. The course of action suggested by him (Ezr 10,3) is significant inasmuch as it calls for the making of a covenant with God to put away all foreign wives with their offspring and a pledge of the whole community to support whatever demand Ezra might make. "Arise! for it is your duty; we are with you. Act with resolution" (Ezr 10,4). And so he did. At last there was cooperation from within the community itself —a quite different situation from that experienced by Nehemiah. But there was also a basically different approach. Not much can be achieved with a noncooperative people! So, with the encouragement of the officials voiced by Shecaniah, Ezra acted decisively. He could not be sure of the sincerity of this wholesome reaction to the demands of the torah until he had sworn them to abide by the terms of their own proposal. Having completed the swearing ceremony, he returned to his quarters in the chamber of Jehohanan (either a priest or the high priest) where he continued to fast and meditate. No time was lost in further pursuit of the matter. A proclamation was issued summoning all the *golah* to report at Jerusalem without delay. The order was delivered orally by official couriers to the residents of Judah and Benjamin (here probably a geographical designation) commanding them to appear within three days. Failure to obey the summons would incur severe penalties. It must be remembered that Ezra had behind him the authority of the Persian king whom he represented, as well as that of the local officials who had sworn to carry out their own proposal.

The proclamation had its effect, for "all the men of Judah and Benjamin" responded and came to Jerusalem within the specified time, which was "the twentieth day of the ninth month" (Ezr 10,9). That was the time of the winter rain. The gravity of the problem is reflected in the widespread response at the most unpropitious season of the year. Weather conditions and serious concern combined to produce an emotionally charged situation, for the meeting was held in the open plaza in front of the temple with torrents of rain pelting the unhappy assembly. The address of Ezra was short and to the point—he used almost the same words employed by Shecaniah earlier. He made three points: (a) they were unfaithful to the Lord in that they married foreign women and thus added to Israel's guilt; (b) they must now confess their guilt before God; and (c) they must henceforth conform to his will and as a sign of their willingness to do so separate themselves from the peoples of the lands and their foreign wives. The congregation responded with firmness, thus accepting the authority of Ezra, but they pleaded with him to make haste slowly. The severity of the weather and the condition of the people would but make for confusion, perhaps rebellion, if they pressed for immediate decisions under such unfavorable external circumstances. They were ready to commit the matter to the hands of officials who would take up each case separately and locally. Ezra agreed, despite some opposition, and appointed the family heads to investigate those in their charge and report back when they had completed their task. Three months later they filed their report with Ezra. The list of violators was drawn up and apparently then submitted to another assembly. The list was divided into three sections, one dealing with the offending priests, another with the Levites, and a third with laymen. As it now stands in the MT, the list contains the names of 27 of the clergy and 84 of the laymen, or a total of 111 persons in a community numbering perhaps less than 30,000—not a very large number but composed mostly of high-ranking individuals, and hardly enough to justify the excitement the problem of mixed marriages seems to have created. Three possible interpretations present themselves: (a) the whole thing was far less serious than surface considerations warrant; (b) only a partial list of the guilty ones has been transmitted here; and (c) the reformation was a failure. It appears unrealistic to suppose that the matter was not a serious one. Otherwise it would hardly have attracted so much attention and that in writers other than the Chronicler (e.g., Malachi). To claim that the reform was unsuccessful contradicts the fact that, so far as we can check, the problem seems to have disappeared. It is far more likely that we have a curtailed list of transgressors. A comparison of other lists of the Chronicler with those from other sources, or even those of the versions, reveals that he often presents less (sometimes more) names. Rudolph (*Esra und Nehemia* [Tübingen: Mohr, 1949], p. 97) suggests that a complete list might have been embarrassing to the Chronicler. But the Chronicler does not minimize guilt or spare offenders elsewhere, no matter how prominent they were in the community. Moreover, would not the appearance of the names of persons of repute have been equally embarrassing? The Chronicler was vitally concerned about the cultic status of the *golah* and did everything he could to bring it into harmony with the legal requirements set forth in the book of the torah of the Lord. To that intent he endeavored to convict the guilty and have them purge themselves of sin so that they would not bring the community under the judgment of God. It is not impossible that the list may contain only the names of representative persons; for example, the 84 or more laymen is a multiple of twelve, which was a favorite number of the Chronicler. But if there was schematization of the list of laity, why not for the clergy?

The success of the movement to divest the community of guilt brought satisfaction to the people as may be seen from the service of praise participated in by the assembled Israelites "on the twenty-fourth day of this month" (Neh 9,1)—that is, of the first month—or twenty-three days after the report of the investigators was submitted (Ezr 10,17). It must have been an auspicious occasion. The people appeared in fasting attire and in a state of penitence. Those who had been proven guilty of marrying foreign women "stood up and confessed their sins" (Neh 9,2) according to a definite ritual pattern. They had already purged themselves of culpability, for they had "severed relations with all foreigners," but their guilt had to be removed by a formal declaration of absolution. Once more a reading from "the book of the torah of Yahweh" figures in the service. Since it lasted for half a day, half of that time was devoted to the reading, the other half to worship and confession. Whether the two aspects of the service—reading of the torah and confession—alternated at specific shorter intervals is uncertain; it is possible that the torah was read as a kind of accusational exhortation to which the congregation responded in the way described in Neh 8,5–6. If so, then we have here an excellent illustration of the place that was accorded to the torah in the special—as well as regular —services of worship by the *golah* community. The penitential psalm sung by the Levites exhibits one of the favorite methods of instruction and exhortation employed by the Chronicler. Some sort of confessional prayer with petitions was doubtless part of the ritual conducted by Ezra on this occasion. But whether it was this one is uncertain. As it now stands the psalm is composite; it contains quotations and reminiscences of many Biblical passages (see *Ezra-Nehemiah, Anchor Bible,* pp. 167–169, for details) and like Pss 78 and 105–106 manifests a profound feeling for the historical experiences of the people of God. The influence of the Deuteronomist is apparent in almost every verse. The psalm concludes with an acknowledgment of transgressions issuing in consequent hardships and adversities. A spirit of pious hope that Yahweh will accept the confession and grant forgiveness pervades the whole of it.

So far as direct evidence goes, this marks the end of Ezra's work. But there is strong circumstantial evidence that he did far more than lead back to Jerusalem a *golah* contingent and settle the problem of intermarriage with foreigners. The fact that tradition has ascribed to him writings other than the canonical book that bears his name—see the four books attributed to him by the Vulgate and *LXX*—has implications. Even though Ezra's name does not appear in the New Testament, the Christians composed a treatise known as the *Revelation of Ezra* in imitation of IV Ezra. Josephus and the Talmud accord him a prominent role, the former referring to him as "the first priest of the people" (*Ant.* 11:5:1), an expert in the law of Moses, and a personal friend of king Xerxes (= Artaxerxes). Some Targum manuscripts attribute to him authorship of Malachi. The tractate *Baba Bathra* (16a) ascribes Chronicles to him. Origen believed "Ezra, who was exceedingly learned in the law and could repeat orally the entire Old Testament, wrote the law and some other things that occurred and were revealed." It can now be demonstrated linguistically that the man who was responsible for the so-called Ezra memoirs (Ezr 7–10) was also the composer of Chronicles. Both are pervaded by the same style, literary mannerisms, and religious concerns. He was a man well acquainted with the history and experiences of his people, conversant with their religious traditions, and a man who knew how to organize with a purpose. He was an eminent ecclesiastic of superlative insight, courage, wisdom, skill, and resolution, who could inspire the people to follow his leadership in the most critical period of their history. To the present writer the Chronicler could have been none other than Ezra the scribe. But there is yet another contribution of this great and self-effacing man. It was emphasized above, as indeed in the whole story of Ezra, that he was the custodian of the book of the torah of the Lord. The firman of Artaxerxes speaks of him as one "learned in the law of the God of the heavens" and charged by the king to deal with Jerusalem and Judah according to "the wisdom of your God which you possess." Thus he must have been well-known for his work with the torah while still in Babylon, indeed so well-known that his fame came to the attention of the king. We know that the Pentateuch was substantially complete before the Chronicler produced his work because he used it, although it was not yet promulgated in its final standardized recension. Such being the case, it could well be that we owe the Pentateuch as it now exists to Ezra. (For the period of Ezra, see Albright, *BA* IX (1946) 13–16.)

The World of Darius II (424–405 B.C.)

The reign of Darius II did not begin very auspiciously. As has already been stated, Artaxerxes and his wife are said to have died on the same day. They had an only son who succeeded to the throne under the name of Xerxes II. After only a month and a half he was murdered during a drunken spree by his half-brother, who then attempted to take over the empire. Meanwhile Ochus, another son by a Babylonian concubine, married to his half-sister, Parysatis, and made satrap of Hyrcania from which he later moved to Babylon, was busy gathering support for himself. Stalling off a summons to return to Susa, he gradually succeeded in having himself recognized as king by the cavalry, the satrap of Egypt, and the royal eunuch. Business men and bankers hastened to make their peace with him before he departed for the capital to settle accounts with Secydianus, the son of Artaxerxes and a Babylonian concubine, and murderer of Xerxes. Things turned out well for him because the army no longer supported the usurper because of his murder of the rightful heir to the throne. Ochus soon had the situation well in hand and did away with him. But only after considerably more intrigue and murder was the new king firmly enthroned under the name of Darius. Whether it was through the scheming mind of the queen or the ruthlessness with which he dealt with his opponents, the king soon grasped tightly the helm of state. Persian gold once more became the diplomat and warrior in the perennial contest with the Greeks. Some time in the first year of his reign peace was again established with Athens on the basis of that made earlier by Callias. Two years later the war between Athens and Sparta was temporarily halted by the peace of Nicias in 421 B.C. (Thucydides, *History*, 5:17–20), which might ultimately have spelled trouble for Darius if it had not been for the stupidity of Greek politicians. About 413 B.C. the Peloponnesian war was resumed, sparked by an Athenian expedition against Sicily that exhausted the aggressors and encouraged rebellion among her tributaries in western Anatolia, notably Sardis. That brought to the scene the capable Persian diplomat and military genius Tissaphernes who was placed in charge over the whole area. Tribute formerly paid to Athens was now directed to the east. One by one the Athenian subject territories revolted or were subdued. A treaty between the Lacedemonians and Tissaphernes sealed the doom of Athens. Nevertheless the restless Greeks were not minded to succumb and, as before, bided their time until a new opportunity arose.

Meanwhile matters were not going well elsewhere. Xenophon (*Hellenica* 1:2:19) informs us of a revolt in Media that was nipped in the bud but reflects natural unrest in a vast empire beset by all sorts of difficulties in the higher realms of authority. The eunuch who helped to put Darius on the throne schemed to make himself king and lost his life in the move. Family troubles kept the court in turmoil and eventually led to severe strains in the governing circles. Phoenicia was imperiled by Arab and Egyptian menace. Rebellion raised its head in Cyprus. The political pot was once more boiling over in Asia Minor, aided and abetted by intrigues in the palace at Susa and fanned by ambitious officials on the scene. The two sons of Darius II, Arsaces and Cyrus, were being pitted against each other by the wily Parysatis, the mother of both. The former was the older of the two, born before Darius assumed the throne, and was the natural successor to his father. But the mother had other ideas. Her favorite son was Cyrus—named after the great founder of the Achaemenid line—whom she endeavored to promote, probably in harmony with an older Persian custom that dictated that the first son born *after* the accession of the father should be the legitimate heir. To this end Parysatis had Cyrus appointed satrap of Lydia, Phrygia, and Cappadocia while the unscrupulous Tissaphernes was demoted to satrap of Caria. This she did in the hope of putting him in the position where he could raise an army that might assist him in ultimately worsting his brother. Though only about sixteen years of age at the time, he was made commander-in-chief of the imperial forces in all of Anatolia. Now the Greeks applied to the Persians the strategy that had worked so well against them—of pitting one side against the other. Spartan representations against Tissaphernes fell on open ears at Sardis where once more Persian gold became the decisive factor. The Spartans were placated with it in the hope of checking the by now successful ventures of the Athenians. When Tissaphernes urged upon Cyrus the old policy, he was ignored, and the stage was set for the resumption of hostilities between the Peloponnesians and Athenians, which ended in the second reduction of Athens in 404 B.C. The Persians had won again, but the noose was tightening around their necks. The rebound of the Greeks was finally to be too much for them—but the time was not quite at hand.

Darius
and the Jewish Colony at Elephantine

The name of Darius II occurs only once in the Old Testament (Neh 12,22) in connection with the list of high priests as family heads—Eliashib, Joiada, Johanan, and Jaddua—which purports to carry the known names as far as Darius the Persian. Otherwise there is no discernible reference to this king in the Bible. But we do have a considerable body of material in the Elephantine Papyri that depicts conditions in the Jewish colony and on several occasions shows the attitude of Darius toward the Jews in Egypt. Although one must beware of applying the principle of analogy indiscriminately, Darius seems to take the same position with reference to the Jews at Elephantine that Artaxerxes took with reference to the *golah* in Judah and Jerusalem.

But first a look at this Egyptian colony of Jews and its fortunes in the time of Darius. (On the possible origin of the Jewish community in Egypt see Chapter I.) The papyri dating from the reign of Artaxerxes I reflect a rather peaceful and prosperous situation quite in contrast to that obtaining in the period under discussion. The turbulent events transpiring elsewhere in the empire had their effect in Egypt too, as may be seen from the documents of the period. The most unsettled years in Egypt coincided with rebellions in Anatolia and Media at the beginning of the last decade of the fifth century B.C. From the first half of the reign of Darius we have documents dealing with marriage contracts, transfer of property, claim settlements, grain accounts, and so on. One of the most interesting of the papyri is the famous Passover letter (Cowley, *Aramaic Papyri,* no. 21) of Hananiah to Jedoniah, the head of the Jewish colony, in the fifth year of Darius' reign (i.e., 419 B.C.). Who this Hananiah was is not known. Some have conjectured that he was Nehemiah's brother (Neh 1,2) or the commander of the citadel at Jerusalem (Neh 7,2), but that is doubtful. The name was a common one as may be seen from the onomasticon of the period compiled from many sources. But that he came from outside Egypt is almost certainly the case, having been sent from either Palestine or Babylon to investigate the religious situation of the colonists. His influence on them may have been salutary for their religion, but it meant increasing difficulties for them with their neighbors. That he endeavored to bring them into line with the more orthodox practices of Jerusalem may be seen from the letter itself. What is of particular significance for us is that the letter is based on a royal firman like the one carried by Ezra to Jerusalem. Only here we have an indirect reference to the command of the king, which was delivered through the satrap Arsames and then embodied in Hananiah's written order to Jedoniah. The letter specified the time and manner of the celebration of the Passover and the Feast of Unleavened Bread, or so it is believed by many scholars. The text is too broken for absolute certainty. The clear parts set forth the following points: the letter was sent by Hananiah to Jedoniah; it greeted the Jews at Elephantine as "my brothers" who compose the Jewish garrison; it was sent in the fifth year of Darius to Arsames at the direction of the king; whatever the festival was, they were to count fourteen days and from the fifteenth to the twenty-first day of Nisan they were to "be clean and take heed" and do no work, nor to drink . . . anything with leaven; from sunset until the twenty-first day of Nisan "bring [it not] into your dwellings but seal it up during . . . days"; and the conclusion repeats the salutation. As can be seen from this description, the names of the festivals are broken out of the papyrus and can be restored only by conjecture. Professor Emil Kraeling (*BMAP,* pp. 92ff.) thinks the injunction had to do only with the Feast of Unleavened Bread, which was celebrated by the exclusion of leaven. It does not, he suggests, permit the Passover, which, according to Deuteronomy (Dt 16,7), was to be sacrificed only at the sanctuary chosen by the Lord (i.e., Jerusalem). Since the order came from the king, it must have had extraordinary significance, perhaps marking the departure from a common practice of the colony. The term for Passover (*psh*) occurs several times in other Elephantine documents where its interpretation is obscure, but it does suggest that it was celebrated there (for further and thorough discussion of the problem, see A. Vincent, *La Religion des Judéo-Araméens d'Eléphantine* [Paris: Geuthner, 1937], Chap. V). The requisite for such high authority for the religious decree reflects unusual circumstances of some kind that demanded more than local backing. The Jews at Elephantine had a syncretistic type of religion all along, but this attempt to bring it into line with more orthodox practices seems to have accentuated the hostility of the Egyptians toward the Jews. It is possible that royal authority was invoked in the first place as a protective measure and that when troubles broke out at other places in the empire requiring the attention of the Persian authorities, the Egyptians took matters into their own hands. The letter of Hananiah appears to have had a good effect according to another papyrus (Cowley, *Aramaic Papyri*, no. 22), which is a list of contributions by the members of the Jewish garrison to the God Yahu. The papyrus is dated in the fifth year but whose reign it was is not stated. The probability, however, is that it was the fifth year of Darius. (On paleographical grounds, F. M. Cross, Jr. dates this letter in the fifth year of Amyrtaeus [404–399 B.C.] [Wright, *BANE* 193, note 34] suggesting that the name of the king was omitted because of the uncertainty as to the claims of control at the time of Artaxerxes II and the Egyptian upstart whose initial signal years were the same. Cross's date would make the papyrus about twenty years later.) If that can be taken as fairly certain, it would be the same year as that of the letter of Hananiah. The contributions must have been for the regular support of the religious institution and not for some special project such as building, for the amounts are too small.

Column vii of this list (Cowley, *Aramaic Papyri*, no. 22) contains a summary of the contributions, which designates specific amounts to be given to Yahu, Eshembethel, and Anatbethel. This at once raises the question as to the character of the religion of the Jewish colony at Elephantine. Albright has referred to it as "a symbiosis between heretical Yahwism and a syncretistic Aramaean cult, rather than a fusion between the two" (*BASOR* 90 [1943] 40). The papyrus affirms that the money was received by Jedoniah, probably the head priest, and then paid out to the other deities' representatives proportionately. The names of other gods, Herembethel and Anatyahu, occur in Cowley, no. 7 and no. 44 respectively. These four divine names were therefore cultic in significance and represented an Aramaean combination that arose among Jews under pagan pressures sometime in the seventh century. Vincent (*La Religion*, p. 360) thinks that the Jewish garrison at Elephantine came pretty largely from around Bethel in the territory of Ephraim, where there was a cult center after the Assyrian conquest of Israel (2 Kgs 17,28). Just how active it was is uncertain, but it may be assumed that the Assyrian governors kept it going as strongly as possible for precisely the same reasons Jeroboam established it in the first place (1 Kgs 12,27–28). Josiah destroyed it (2 Kgs 23,15), but once more it seems to have been revived when the Babylonians removed the district in which it was located from Judah. Bethel was not destroyed in the Babylonian conquest of 587 B.C. but was leveled sometime later, around 500 B.C. It may have been refugees from that holocaust who escaped to Egypt who formed part of the garrison at Elephantine. They regarded themselves as Yahwehists though they developed a pantheon with the above-named hypostatizations of Yahweh (see Albright, *From the Stone Age to Christianity,* 2nd ed. [Baltimore: Johns Hopkins Press, 1946], p. 286).

The next thing we hear about the Elephantine community is a letter of complaint (Cowley, *Aramaic Papyri,* no. 27) to an official about the troubles suffered by the Jews at the hands of the priests of Khnub. The substance of the document is an effort of the Jews to clear themselves of any blame for the turn of events. The officials are reminded of the loyalty of the Jews to the Persians at an earlier time, possibly at the beginning of the reign of Darius, when the Egyptians rebelled. Now the priests apparently bribed the local governor, Waidrang, and with his assistance had demolished a part of the king's property. Moreover, they had erected a wall segregating the two groups and stopped up a well that furnished water for the Jewish colony. The Jews further complained that they were no longer able to provide proper sacrifices to Yahu. So they were requesting not only an investigation of the situation but were also asking for a restoration of property. All this happened while the satrap Arsames was absent on a mission to the Persian court in the fourteenth year of Darius (i.e., 411 B.C.). Two possible reasons suggest themselves for the harassing acts of the Egyptians. One is the resentment created by the loyalty of the Jews who must therefore have helped to quell the rebellion of the Egyptians. The other is the offense created by the Jews' animal sacrifices. As a matter of fact both may have been involved. In a spirited appeal to Bigwai, the governor of Judah (Cowley, *Aramaic Papyri,* no. 30), we learn that during the same year the same group of conspirators burned the Jewish colony's temple, which had stood since the days before Cambyses' invasion of Egypt when Egyptian temples were destroyed but theirs was not. Because of this serious misfortune they sent an urgent appeal to Bigwai, to Johanan the high priest and his colleagues, to Ostanes the brother of Anani, and to the other important Jews at Jerusalem "at the time when this evil was done to us." None of these persons responded to the appeal since Jedoniah now wrote again, three years afterward (in the seventeenth year of Darius), to the governor of Judah requesting him to order their temple to be rebuilt. The local authorities were adamant in their refusal to permit it. If Bigwai would respond favorably, Jedoniah promised that sacrifices would be offered and prayers said for him by the Jews at Elephantine. At the same time, a similar request with explanation had been sent to Delaiah and Shelemiah, the sons of Sanballat, the governor of Samaria. This message brought a response from Bigwai and Delaiah (Cowley, *Aramaic Papyri*, no. 32) with the order directed to Arsames that the temple be rebuilt "as it was before" and in the same place so that the cereal-offering and incense-offering might again be offered upon its altar. Negotiations were protracted, to judge from Cowley, *Aramaic Papyri*, no. 33. Five property-holders, including Jedoniah, the head of the community, pledged contributions for the work of rebuilding if permission to do so was granted. They accepted the directive that burnt-offerings were not to be offered and declared their readiness to abide by the injunction to offer only cereal and incense offerings. The temple of Yahu was apparently rebuilt sometime between about 407 B.C.—the date of Cowley, *Aramaic Papyri*, no. 33—and 401 B.C.—the date of a deed of property-transfer in which it is stated that Yahu, the God, resides in the fortress of Yeb, and that the property in question borders on the Temple of Yahu (Kraeling, *BMAP*, Papyrus 12).

This correspondence tells us something of the conduct of affairs in Jerusalem toward the end of the reign of Darius. Bigwai was the governor of Judah, probably the successor of Nehemiah. Sanballat, though probably too old to function since his son Delaiah is named as joining with Bigvai in the order conveyed to Arsames, was still governer of Samaria. The authority over the Jewish garrison—at least so far as religious matters were concerned—was vested in the governors of Judah and Samaria, who outranked Arsames in that respect. Inasmuch as the reply of Bigwai and Delaiah is a joint one, there now seems to have been some kind of modus vivendi between the two provincial governors. Although Jedoniah had requested permission for three types of offerings—as may have been the practice originally at Elephantine—the official order authorizes specifically only two, as noted in the preceding paragraph. As Kraeling observes (*BMAP*, p. 107), the religious officials must have been consulted, and they demanded the privilege of retaining exclusive rights for burnt-offerings for the Jerusalem temple. Most scholars believe, however, that burnt-offerings are not mentioned here as a concession to the Egyptians who were offended by such animal sacrifices. Johanan was still high priest, having succeeded his grandfather Eliashib (Josephus speaks of Joiada, the son of Eliashib and father of Johanan, having occupied that office, *Ant.* 11:7:1, but if so it could not have been for long). According to Josephus, Johanan and Bigwai could not have been on very good terms. In the first place he was not favored for the office of high priest, his brother Jesua being the candidate supported by the governor. The relationship was still further strained when Johanan murdered his brother in the temple for which the whole community suffered indemnity for seven years, which consisted of the payment of a specified sum for each sacrifice offered on the temple altar. We do not know how long Johanan lasted after that, presumably not long. Josephus says Jaddua became high-priest in the reign of Darius (*Ant.* 11:7:2) who, in the light of the suggested succession of governors of Samaria in recently discovered Samaria papyri (F. M. Cross, "The Discovery of the Samaria Papyri" in *BA* XXVI [1963] 110–121), must be the second rather than the third Persian king by that name. All this means that Jaddua entered upon his office before 405 B.C. when Darius II died, perhaps soon after the date of 408 B.C. when Cowley, *Aramaic Papyri,* no. 30 was written.

One of the most tantalizing problems of the Persian period is that of the relationship between the Jewish community and the Samaritans. Relations reflected in the Elephantine papyri appear to have been at least tolerable and thus in conflict with such biblical evidence as we possess. Of course we do not know precisely what political or other pressures may have been exerted upon the respective parties at the time nor the extent of the authority of Bigvai. Did he, for example, exercise the same control over the religious affairs of the Samaritans as he did over those of Elephantine and the Jews at Jerusalem? If so his consultation with Delaiah, with whom he issued a joint directive with reference to building operations at Elephantine, must have been diplomatic and a matter of courtesy rather than compulsive. On the other hand there must have been two distinct centers of political authority, otherwise Jedoniah would not have appealed to both on what appear to be equal terms. It was remarked above that in the time of Ezra there is no mention of a Samaritan problem—it may have been played down somewhat by him. Samaritans are not included in the lists of foreigners who had intermarried with Jews (Ezr 9,1; Neh 13,23–24). Nehemiah's violent reaction against Eliashib's son who had married Sanballat's daughter could have been due to other reasons, for example, Nehemiah's intense antipathy toward Sanballat because of the latter's reprehensible conduct, or to the extension of the prohibition against the high priest marrying a foreigner (Lv 21,14). It is not improbable that bad feelings between officials of Samaria and Judah reflected in Ezra-Nehemiah were, in large measure, due to what the former considered as encroachments on their rights and vested interests and not to religion as such. Yet the profound concern of Ezra for religious purity cannot be brushed aside lightly. There is no objection, so far as the records go, by the Samaritans to Ezra's cult reforms per se. That they should have done so can hardly be expected in view of their syncretistic tendencies. We can be fairly certain that the break between Jews and Samaritans did not come until sometime later on. In the light of the archaeological history of Shechem, it appears that the Josephus story (*Ant.* 11:7:2; 11:8:2,4) regarding the sequence of events that led to the building of a temple on Mt. Gerizim is correct despite some confusion of the names of the Persian kings. It is possible that the building project was actually begun under Darius III whom the Samaritans expected to defeat Alexander. But when that surmise proved wrong, they quickly shifted their allegiance to Alexander, whom they may then have begged to confirm what they had already undertaken. (See G. E. Wright, "The Samaritans at Shechem" in *HTR* LV [1962], 357–66, for a discussion of the whole problem.)

Summary
of the Period of Darius

So far as the Egyptian scene is concerned, some kind of order seems to have been restored toward the end of the reign of Darius. We have noted that the satrap Arsames was absent from 411/410 to 408 B.C. when Waidrang, who was governor of the Elephantine district, in conspiracy with the priests, rebelled. The rebellion was speedily put down with the aid of the Jewish garrsion, but the temple lay in ruins. But by the end of Darius' reign it was either rebuilt or well on the way to being rebuilt. We possess a series of documents from and to Arsames during his absence (see G. R. Driver, *Aramaic Documents of the Fifth Century B.C.* [Oxford: Oxford University Press, 1954] dealing with administrative matters pertaining to his estates in Egypt. They reflect no political difficulties that would indicate that serious unrest in Egypt was very widespread. They do indicate the extensive power to deal with internal matters wielded by the satrap; there is no reference to referral to higher authority. It is rather striking that none of the Brooklyn Museum Papyri (see Kraeling, *BMAP*) date from the period of the Jewish disorders or that of the Arsames correspondence. There is a gap between 416 B.C. and 404 B.C.

Not much in the way of artistic achievements can be dated definitely to the age of Darius II. He must have constructed his tomb at Naqš-i-Rustam, for his is the last burial at that place, where three of his greater predecessors were entombed. We know that either he or Artaxerxes I was responsible for a small palace at Susa after the fire that destroyed it, built at the southern extremity of the site. There was also a small hypostyle hall built in place of the Apadana together with a reception hall alongside of the living apartments. The cache of small ivory fragments, mentioned above, found in a well of the little palace at Susa, dates in part from the period. We do have a mass of coins struck by Darius (Babelon, *Les Perses Achéménides* [Paris: Chez C. Rollin & Feuardent, 1893], pp. xv, 8–11) and the satraps, notably Tissaphernes and Pharnabazus (Babelon, pp. 23–25).

Nothing more can be said at present than has been outlined above about the Jews in Palestine. That some measure of stability was achieved may be seen from the correspondence between Jedoniah of Elephantine and the officials of Judah—Bigwai, Johanan, and the sons of Sanballat. The Jews were apparently consolidating their forces and putting into effect the cultic reforms of Ezra. The "Passover" directive of Darius to the Egyptian colonists proves as much. But we cannot be sure of specifics; our evidence does not permit us to draw any but the most general conclusions. Yet, once more, and from a prophetic point of view, it is not difficult to see the hand of the Eternal One at work, slowly but surely, re-establishing his people for still greater service for the world in the centuries ahead.

Selected Readings

Albright, W. F., *The Biblical World from Abraham to Ezra,* Chap. IX. New York: Harper & Row, Publishers (Harper Torchbooks), 1963.

Bright, J., *A History of Israel,* Chap. X. Philadelphia: The Westminster Press, 1959.

Ellis, P., *The Men and Message of the Old Testament,* Chap. XI, pp. 6–7. Collegeville, Minn.: The Liturgical Press, 1952.

Heinisch, P., *History of the Old Testament,* Chap. XLIV. Collegeville, Minn.: The Liturgical Press, 1963.

Myers, J. M., *The Anchor Bible: Ezra-Nehemiah.* New York: Doubleday & Co., Inc., 1965.

Ricciotti, G., *The History of Israel,* 2nd ed., II, 98–168. Milwaukee: Bruce Publishing Company, 1958.

VII

Artaxerxes II

Only at the end of his reign did
Darius II emerge to lead personally
a campaign against the revolting
Cadusians in Media. Before it could
be concluded, the king fell ill and
had to be removed to Babylon, where
he died in March, 404 B.C. At his
bedside were two of his sons, Cyrus
and Arsaces, the latter destined to
succeed his father. He assumed the
name of his grandfather Artaxerxes
and thus became the second Persian
king of that name. His mother,
Parysatis, had hoped to make Cyrus
the successor of his father by
giving him that honored name, and
she may have been behind the plot
to poison Artaxerxes on the day of
his coronation. The plot and the
suspect were discovered, but through
the plea of his mother, Cyrus was
allowed to return to the satrapy
occupied under his father, thus
awaiting another day—which was to
be soon. Immediately upon his
arrival in Asia Minor, Cyrus set in
motion forces that were to serve him

in the battle for the throne now held by his brother. The Greeks were maneuvered into supporting him. Alcibiades, the Athenian who after the Peloponnesian war joined forces with the Phrygian satrap, Pharnabazus, at once saw through the schemes of Cyrus when the latter hired unemployed Greek soldiers. Lysander, the Spartan leader, gave away the case when he ostensibly met the provisions of the treaty of peace with Persia by paying tribute to the adventurer. Alcibiades, attempting to inform the king of the turn of events, was slain, and Artaxerxes remained ignorant of the plot. After two years' preparation Cyrus was finally ready to execute his challenge (401 B.C.). Naturally there were defections to the would-be king along the way, the most serious being the withdrawal of the army of the Syrian satrap, Abrocomas, who was preparing to reconquer Egypt for the king. Cyrus met with little opposition, except with certain suspicion in the minds of his mercenaries, and proceeded down the Euphrates valley to Cunaxa, some sixty miles north of Babylon. There he was accosted by the army of Artaxerxes, and the two forces engaged in a decisive battle on September 3, 401 B.C. Cyrus might have won the day had he not imprudently pressed forward in person to deal the death-blow to his brother, whom he succeeded in wounding but in the act lost his own life. At the request of his mother, he was finally given an honorable burial at Susa. Xenophon led the retreating Greeks back to Asia Minor in the famous March of the Ten Thousand.

Course of Events
in Asia Minor

Meanwhile affairs were far from settled at the Persian court, which reflects on the weakness of the king himself because he appears to have been susceptible to the influence of others rather than having a mind of his own. His queen, Stateira, was poisoned by Artaxerxes' mother in the wake of the executions that followed the defeat of Cyrus. Parysatis fell from favor temporarily, but because of the vacillating character of the king, she soon regained her voice at the court. The courage of the retreating Greeks inspired their brethren again to take up arms to free their cities from Persian hegemony. Tissaphernes was restored to his old post as viceroy of Anatolia, and Ariaeus was made satrap of Phrygia. When the former demanded a new oath of allegiance from the Ionian cities, they refused it and requested help from Sparta. Thibron, appointed leader by the Spartans, gathered a huge army augmented by the seasoned Greek mercenaries who had fought with Cyrus and met Tissaphernes as an equal. Because Thibron had permitted his troops to plunder, he was superseded by Dercylidas, who decided to play the old Persian game of divide and conquer. He made a truce with Tissaphernes and attacked Pharnabazus, who, confronted with the possible loss of his property, also accepted a truce with the Greek general. At the same time, the Greek cities of Asia Minor petitioned Sparta to open hostilities against the headquarters of Tissaphernes in Caria in the hope of gaining their release from Persian hegemony. This brought an alliance between the two Persian satraps, Tissaphernes and Pharnabazus, who frightened the Greeks into a year's truce. In 397–396 B.C. further machinations by the Spartans forced the Persians into a fresh diplomatic effort supported by gold in an attempt to stave off Agesilaus, the Spartan king, who appeared in Asia Minor. The result, after some further jockeying, was that Tissaphernes was outwitted in a battle in the Hermus valley. At the Persian court, Parysatis, the queen mother, used the occasion to undermine the king's confidence in the viceroy and contrived his death. Despite the death of one of the most astute Persian leaders, the situation in Anatolia continued its see-saw course throughout the reign of Artaxerxes II. There were a number of peace arrangements over the years, each one broken at an opportune moment. In 386 B.C. the king forced upon the Greek delegates assembled at Sardis what has been called the "King's Peace," which must have been rather humiliating to them but which they accepted under threats of serious reprisal should they refuse (see Xenophon, *Hellenica,* 5:1:31). Artaxerxes seemed to have achieved what Darius I and Xerxes could not. Still another peace was concluded in 374 B.C., this time with Dionysius of Syracuse. The treaty of 371 B.C. ran afoul of the Thebans, who had recently won laurels by putting Sparta out of action and so assumed leadership over the continental Greeks. Later on they were to become pro-Persian in their rivalry with Athens (367 B.C.). In 370 B.C. Pharnabazus died and was succeeded by Datames, who had hoped to undertake a campaign against Egypt, which had cut itself loose from Persia, but was prevented from doing so by a succession of uprisings in his own bailiwick. Between 367 B.C. and 362 B.C. virtually all the satraps in the area were in revolt. Datames, himself under suspicion at the court, finally joined the anti-Persian movement and became their leader. The whole turn· of events says a great deal about the morale of both sides. Intrigue became the order of the day, fostered by petty jealousies and the infiltration of all kinds of people into the centers where decisions were made. Xenophon in 355

B.C. referred to Athens as swarming with aliens—Lydians, Phrygians, Syrians, and all sorts of barbarians. We know of a Phoenician colony at Piraeus, where they left inscriptions in their native language and Greek. Most of these people were commercial adventurers of one kind or another seeking profits for themselves with no concern for the best interests of the community.

The Egyptian Problem
and Cyprus

The most consequential and stubborn problem faced by the new king was the successful rebellion of Egypt. Already in 405 B.C., before the death of Darius II, the Delta region revolted under Amyrtaeus, who was regarded as the only king of the twenty-eighth dynasty. His rule lasted but five years. The revolt must ultimately have involved all of Egypt since the last of the Elephantine papyri is dated in the fifth year of his reign. It is a loan contract which mentions the Greek stater as the equivalent of two shekels, the amount of indemnity if the loan is not paid within the specified time. Otherwise we know nothing about conditions or activities of the pharaoh or how he passed from the scene. The papyrus does reflect the growing Greek influence in Egypt. What the lot of the Jewish garrison, always pro-Persian, was we can only guess. Doubtless it was not a very happy one in view of its stand against Waidrang and his supporters who had destroyed their temple.

The change of dynasty occurred while Artaxerxes II was occupied with the defense of his throne against the pretensions of Cyrus. Amyrtaeus was succeeded by a man from Mendes by the name of Nepherites, who became the founder of the twenty-ninth dynasty, which had four kings in nineteen years (399–380 B.C.). The same year that Cyrus marched east to contest the imperial throne, the Syrian satrap had amassed a large army meant to regain Egypt (Xenophon, *Anabasis*, 1:3,5) but when Cyrus approached, some of Abrocomos' Greek mercenaries defected to Cyrus, and the satrap was forced to call off the campaign. After the defeat of Cyrus, some advisers of Artaxerxes urged mobilization against Egypt but were opposed by Tissaphernes, possibly in anticipation of the coming involvements in Anatolia. The result was that Egypt was let alone for some time. At about 400 B.C. Cyrus' admiral Tamos, an Egyptian, defected with his fleet and treasure to his homeland where he hoped to win recognition. Instead, he was slain as a traitor and his fleet and treasure confiscated.

Soon after, Nepherites took over. He was not an exceptionally strong ruler, although he left some 13 minor monuments, including 2 steles at the Serapeum in connection with Apis rites. Henceforth Egypt was on the side of Persia's opponents. She supported Sparta against the king in 396 B.C. When Agesilaus proposed an alliance with Nepherites, he sent no troops but supplied riggings for 100 triremes and half a million bushels of grain (*Dio. Sic.*, 14:79:4). The grain was seized by the Athenian admiral Conon, who was on the Persian side, when the transports put in at Rhodes in 395 B.C. Two years later Nepherites died and was succeeded by his son Muthes, who, according to the Demotic Chronicle (3:21; 4:6) was deposed after a short time because he violated the laws of the land. A usurper by the name of Psammuthis lasted little more than a year, when he was overthrown by Hacoris who erased his name from the small temple at Karnak and replaced it with his own. These rapid successions reflect anything but stability in Egypt where doubtless many people remained wary of too enthusiastic acceptance of independence for fear of the Persians, evidently recognized as still a formidable power. With Hacoris began a really new period in Egypt. He reigned for 13 years and during that period was responsible for no less than 35 monuments. He erected buildings at the great sites—Karnak, Luxor, Medinet Habu, and El Kab in the far south. A host of steles were set up in the Delta region. He enlisted Greek mercenaries in his cause and gathered a sizable fleet. Egypt declined to be drawn into the whirl of Anatolian politics and internecine conflict except where it touched upon Cyprus, which was much closer and therefore of more significance. The naval victory of Conon at Cnidus in 394 B.C. was due in part to the support of Evagoras of Salamis, who was the king of Cyprus. His aim had been to establish a Hellenic Cyprus, but when affairs in Asia Minor turned against Conon and he was compelled to flee to Cyprus, events took another turn. In the meantime Evagoras had brought all the island under his control except Soli, Amathus, and Cition, who instead appealed to the great king for help, reminding him of the escapades of the Salamis king. He ordered the satraps of Lydia and Caria to collect ships and men for an invasion of Cyprus. Evagoras requested help from his Athenian friends, but because of the war with Sparta, they sent only ten vessels, which were intercepted by the Spartans. Egypt now took a hand since it was to her interest to hold the island for the enemies of Persia. As a result Evagoras formed an alliance with Hacoris, who already had reached an agreement with the Athenians. Hacoris agents were actively sowing seeds of discord in Asia Minor while he occupied himself with the support of the religious shrine of Amon at Siwah, which enhanced his standing among the Greeks. The Persian satraps attacked only half-heartedly because of the secret understanding and payoff between them and Evagoras. When the Athenian general Chabrias was recalled by the king's peace in 386 B.C., Evagoras and Hacoris stood alone, but the general went to Egypt as a privateer. Artaxerxes now had to decide which of the two rebels to pick off first. He chose Egypt, for with her gone, Cyprus wouldn't stand a chance. By the spring of 385 B.C. a huge Persian host under the Syrian satrap Abrocomas, Pharnabazus from Asia Minor, and Tithraustes began the march against Egypt, which was defended by one of the great military geniuses of the day. Nothing is known of episodes of the war that continued for three years (385–382 B.C.). The result was a collapse of the Persian effort. It is possible that Hacoris pressed his fortune to invade Syria, since Evagoras controlled the sea lanes, and then ravaged the hostile coastal areas. Hacoris even conquered Tyre. The entire eastern Mediterranean was now ruled by Egypt and Cyprus, and Artaxerxes was not able to carry out another expedition against Egypt. The next best move was an attempted conquest of Cyprus, where Evagoras received full support from Egypt. But the Greek fleet was too much for him; he was defeated at Citium. He also lost the war on the land since Hacoris cut down or shut off further assistance. Then Evagoras resolved to bargain with the enemy, whose terms might have been acceptable had they not included submission to the great king as "a slave to his master" (*Dio. Sic.* 15:8:1–3). Once more intrigues at the court involving Tiribazus, the satrap, who handled negotiations with Evagoras, came to the rescue. The new diplomat Orontes, satrap of Armenia, whose jealousy of Tiribazus was responsible for the latter's removal, came to terms with Evagoras by modification of the offensive clause in the treaty of Tiribazus. The Cyprian war was now at an end, with considerable loss of prestige for the Persians. Isocrates, in his Olympian *Panegyric* delivered in 380 B.C., rubbed salt in the wounds with Greek oratory. Nevertheless Evagoras maintained his side of the treaty for the remainder of his life.

While the Cypro-Persian struggle was yet in progress, Hacoris, "who fulfilled the time of his rule because he was benevolent to the temples" (*Demotic Chronicle*, 4:9–12), died without having secured the succession to the throne. His son, Nepherites II, held the office only a short time when Egypt was taken over by Nectanebo of Sebennytus, the founder of the thirtieth dynasty. He reigned for seventeen years (380–363 B.C.) during which Egypt gained steadily in power and influence. He was supported by the clever Chabrias, who was soon recalled to Athens on order of Artaxerxes when the Persians began preparations for another attempt at conquest of Egypt. After six years, the expedition under the direction of Pharnabazus and Iphicrates was finally ready to proceed from its mustering place at Acco on the Palestinian coast. The new Pharaoh used the respite to good advantage by fortifying the Delta region still further. When the Persian army and navy arrived, it was at first successful in avoiding the fortifications at Pelusium and thus splitting the Egyptian defenses. Old rivalries between the commanders broke out anew and delayed the movement of their forces, which delay the Egyptians used to good advantage. With their age-old ally, the Nile in flood, they forced the enemy to withdraw in disorder—a signal victory contrived by an Egypt without allies. There were further plans of the Persians to reduce the recalcitrant rebels but they came to nothing. Now it was Egypt's turn to become the aggressor with assistance to now one, now another of the parties opposing the empire. Before he died, Pharaoh Nectanebo (for the monuments of this ruler see F. K. Kienitz, *Die politische Geschichte Ägyptens vom 7. bis zum 4. Jahrhundert vor der Zeitwende* [Berlin: Academie Verlag, 1953], pp. 199–212—he lists 107 of them) seems to have established a coregency with his son Tachos, who undertook a campaign of his own in Palestine and Syria. He, assisted by Greek mercenaries and Agesilaus of Sparta and Chabaris, struck in the spring of 360 B.C. There is no record of any major resistance, and soon the whole of the coastal areas of Palestine and Syria had fallen into the hands of the invaders. But Tachos lost his position in the undertaking when his son Nectanebo II usurped it. Tachos fled to Artaxerxes, confessed his errors, was forgiven and made commander of any Persian attempt to regain Egypt. That was in 359/358 B.C., the year the great king died. It was only by the help of the Spartan Agesilaus that Nectanebo survived an attempt by a descendant of the previous dynasty to usurp the throne. Because of events elsewhere in the empire, he remained solidly entrenched for the remainder of his life—a period of eighten years—which was devoted to internal developments. He undertook no campaigns and even appeared unconcerned when Cyprus and Phoenicia were attacked by the Persians.

Other Areas

The excavations at Taxila in India (John Marshall, *A Guide to Taxila* [Calcutta: Superintendent of Government Printing, India, 1918] give evidence of continuing relationships with Persia. The silver coins delivered to Alexander the Great show Persian influence both in form and weight. The somewhat later inscription of the Buddhist Asoka (274–237/6 B.C.), composed in Aramaic script, still abounds in formulas and expressions characteristic of the Persian Chancery. Though there were no campaigns to the east nor are there any records of direct control, relations must somehow have been maintained as may be seen from the patterns of art that persisted after the fall of the Persian empire.

In 379/8 B.C., Artaxerxes was faced with a serious uprising of the Cadusians, on the border of the Caspian sea, which the king undertook to suppress personally. The region was so unpropitious that his army suffered great hardships and might have been wiped out had it not been for the clever diplomacy of the old satrap Tiribazus, who arranged for a separate accommodation between the two Cadusian kings and Artaxerxes. The army, and the king himself, retreated on foot, and in order to avoid any misconstruction the latter resorted to a ruthless purge of those suspected of treachery. That had repercussions to be felt long afterward in the politics of Asia Minor.

Restlessness in Phoenicia has been hinted at above. Hacoris may have tried to invade Tyre in 383 B.C. In any case the whole eastern coast of the Mediterranean was subject to Egyptian-Cyprian control at the time. Syria and the coastal areas of Palestine more than once became the mustering points for Persian arms in their attempts against Egypt. Both the Persian army and navy gathered at Acco under Pharnabazus in 373 B.C. The whole of the west was lost to Artaxerxes between 363–361 B.C. Orontes assembled his forces in Syria for an attack on the Persians. In the spring of 360 B.C. Nectanebo marched into Palestine without opposition, and his soldiers used Phoenicia as a jumping-off place on an expedition against the cities of Syria (*Dio. Sic.,* 15:92:4). There must have been some cooperation between the kings of Phoenicia and Syria—either forcibly or willingly—since Straton I (370–358 B.C.) joined the revolt of the satraps (see *Dio. Sic.,* 15:90). He sent images from Tyre and Sidon to the Delian Apollo, which reflects his devotion to Greek culture and his contacts with the western world. Byblos construction went on all during the Persian period, even though the kingdom was a vassal of the great king. A stone slab with the name of Nepherites was found by Macalister at Gezer (*The Excavation of Gezer* II [London: John Murray Publishers, Ltd., 1912], 313). Coins of the period are present at Byblos of three kings—Elpa'al, Adramelek, and Azba'al. From Sidon there are numerous ones from Straton I (Abdastart). Some have also turned up at Tyre, Gaza, and Ashdod but are not identifiable as to king or ruler.

Palestine and Syria breathe the same air that pervaded Asia Minor and Egypt, but the kings and principalities were neither so wealthy nor so capable financially and otherwise to carry on such a persistent program of intrigue and rebellion. There may have been other reasons why there was not success in this region as there was in the others. Just what the position of Judah was in this period is obscure unless we are to date the coming of Ezra in "the seventh year of Artaxerxes" II (Ezr 7,7). In that case the events described in the preceding chapter would have to be placed here. It may be surmised, however, that the Jews, as well as other neighboring peoples, were aware of the situation but could do little about it. They were nearly always pro-Persian and would hardly have done much, if anything, to hinder or oppose their great benefactor. Hence they must have been busy developing their religious interests and applying themselves to the stabilization of their community from within (see R. Kittel, *Geschichte des Volkes Israel,* 1st and 2nd ed., III [Stuttgart: Kohlhammer, 1929], 676). They could never have been far removed from the momentous events of the time played out so near to them, but, so far as we know, they never did anything to offend seriously either Egypt or Persia.

Building and Art
of Artaxerxes II

In spite of all the troubles that beset the empire of Artaxerxes II—the increasingly heavy burdens of taxation upon those who would pay and the heavy burdens laid upon the provinces that led them to rebel again and again—the king did improve buildings in the homeland. He restored the palace of Darius I at Susa that had been burned in the preceding reign, though the materials and workmanship were less elegant. He also repaired the fortifications. These restorations he says he undertook by the favor of Ahuramazda, Anihita, and Mithra (A²Sa) and as a pleasant retreat (A²Sd). He also provided a new apadana with sculptures at Ecbatana (Hamadan). He claims to have erected there a palace with stone columns (A²Hb). Interestingly enough, on an inscription at Persepolis from either Artaxerxes II or III there appears no reference to either a Jew or Phoenician, though nearly all other subject peoples are represented including an Egyptian and an Arab. Since there was no more room for a tomb at Naqš-i-Rustam, Artaxerxes had one hewn out on a high cliff above the southeast hall at Persepolis, where he cut an inscription, thus returning to the practice of Darius I (Ghirshman, *Persia,* p. 232, Fig. 280). Though he was continuously harassed by his Greek subjects, Artaxerxes II was favorably impressed by Hellenism as seen from his monuments. The jewelry in the Chicago collection is believed to have come from this period, notably the lion pendants and some plaques of gold (*JNES* XVI [1957] 1–23). Some of the same types have been found at Pasargadae (*Iran* III [1965], especially 33–40).

The Last Years
of the Persian Empire

The threat against the Persian empire ended in the autumn of 360 B.C. Before the death of Artaxerxes II, somewhere around 359 B.C., the crown prince Ochus undertook another campaign against Egypt, perhaps due to the unsettled state of affairs in the latter country at the time. It will be recalled that Tachos defected to the Persians, and perhaps because of this they thought the time was ripe to take advantage of their opportunity. But what it achieved is uncertain because Ochus had to return to the court upon the death of his father. The succession was again accompanied by murder and conspiracy. Artaxerxes II had three sons by the queen, Stateira—Darius, Ariaspes, and Ochus. The oldest son was found guilty of conspiracy and executed. Ariaspes killed himself after he was falsely persuaded that he had lost favor with his father. Another son, Arsames, now had the advantage but was murdered by an agent of Ochus, which act may have had much to do with the death of Artaxerxes II, the now aged father. Ochus took the name of Artaxerxes III and thus entered upon the scene of his official activities with blood-stained hands. Indeed that bespoke his character—ruthless, cruel, blood-thirsty. He ordered all his relatives to be slain.

The first uprising to confront the new king seems to have been a revolt of the troublesome Cadusians, which he apparently put down without too much difficulty (*Dio. Sic.,* 17:6); nor were the Greeks slow in testing him. When Artaxerxes peremptorily ordered the satraps of Anatolia to disperse, the satrap of Phrygia, Artabazus, with Athenian support and that of Orontes, now the satrap of the Ionian coastal region, raised the standard of revolt. But under threats of the king the Athenians withdrew their support and gave up their alliances with their rebellious comrades. Then the Artabazus move fell apart: Orontes submitted, and the leader was compelled to flee to Macedonia for refuge. Occupation with these matters and the consolidation of forces at home kept the new king from Egypt for a time. Meanwhile Nectanebo II revived support for the cult of Amon. At Ummabeda a temple was built for the god, as we know from an inscription from the hand of the builder. Many other buildings, structures, and other objects from this Pharaoh's time have come down to us. The news of this activity in Egypt did not rest well at the Persian court, for by 351–350 B.C. Artaxerxes at the head of a vast army set out for the Nile valley. But the effort seems to have collapsed once more (*Dio. Sic.*, 16:40; 16:44; 16:48), which the Sicilian historian attributes to the king's inexperience. The repercussions in the west were electric, for Isocrates in 346 B.C. spoke of the ease with which Philip of Macedon could overcome the inept Persian. The spark to ignite the Persian fuse came from Phoenicia, whose king, Tennes (Tabnit), destroyed the famous Persian paradise at Sidon that was kept for the provision of the king's cavalry and wiped out the officials who resided in his land. With the wealth acquired by trade, Tennes secured allies, built a huge navy, and provided for himself stores of all kinds against the coming siege. The Egyptians were ready to come to his aid. The Phoenician revolt triggered an uprising of nine of the rulers of city states in Cyprus who came to an understanding among themselves and an accommodation with the Phoenicians. Cilicia may also have been involved, although Diodorus says the satrap Mazios was at war with the Phoenicians (16:42). Syncellus preserves a report of Eusebius (Dindorf edition, I, pp. 486f.) to the effect that in connection with his campaign against Sidon and Egypt, Artaxerxes exiled some Jews to Hyrcania, others to Babylon. They may have become involved through Egypt. To the same sequence of events may belong the Solinus reference (35:4) to a tradition of a conquest of Jericho by an Artaxerxes, though some dispute it. It is also possible that the story of Judith belongs somewhere in this reign, though it may also be earlier (see below). In 346 B.C., in conjunction with the Persian preparations for an invasion of the west, the satrap of Syria and the governor of Cilicia (*Dio. Sic.*, 16:42) struck against Phoenicia, where Tennes, with the help of Egyptian troops under Mentor of Rhodes, defeated both and drove them out of his country. The Cyprus phase of the campaign was more fruitful but hardly decisive. Artaxerxes was not a man to be discouraged easily and so continued his preparations for the conquest of Egypt, this time by enlisting Greek help. His appeal to the Greek states was responded to somewhat indifferently though not in a way to offend the king. Sparta and Athens lent their advice, others a moderate number of troops. In 343 B.C., the Greeks and Artaxerxes began the march from their respective places of preparation. A year earlier Cyprus had come to terms, and even the king of Salamis gave up the struggle because of lack of support from Nectanebo. Discouragement on the part of the Cypriots was contagious, so that Sidon alone was left to face the great king. Tennes then resolved to betray his land to the Persians, leaving Mentor ostensibly to defend a part of the fortified city, which, when its leaders saw the collusion, burned its ships and immolated themselves rather than surrender. With the collapse of Cyprus and the Phoenician states, the first phase of the king's conquest of the west had finally succeeded. The next one began in the autumn of 343 B.C. when the Persian forces moved against Egypt. Just what the effect upon Palestine proper was of the internecine struggle between Artaxerxes III and Tennes is not quite certain. It has been pointed out recently (D. Barag, "The Effects of Tennes Rebellion on Palestine" in *BASOR* CLXXXIII [1966] 6–12) that archaeological discoveries at Hazor, Megiddo, Athlit, Lachish, and Jericho exhibit destruction at levels that appear to date around the middle of the fourth century B.C. If so, there must have been a rather serious upheaval all around the province of Judah.

Nectanebo was now left alone to defend his land against the invader on his own soil. He fortified the Delta areas, in particular Pelusium. He had two strikes against him—the knowledge of the fortifications of Mentor, who, with Tennes, had defected to the enemy, and dissension in his own forces. The Greek commanders failed to achieve full cooperation on the part of their troops. After a protracted effort by the invaders, Pelusium was at last reduced, and the way to the south lay open. That was the signal for further disagreements between the Greeks and Egyptians, and the cities of the Delta capitulated one by one. All this time, Nectanebo was at Memphis. When he realized that resistance was futile, he fled to Ethiopia, which left lower Egypt at the mercy of the Persians; and they were certainly not merciful. The walls of the great cities were leveled, the treasures gathered for the temples by Nectanebo and his predecessors plundered, and their records seized (*Dio. Sic.,* 16:51). The Demotic Chronicle (4:22,23) speaks of the mourning throughout the land and the empty houses due to the misfortune wrought by the Medes. The punishment visited upon Egypt was severe, but it was all for the purpose of teaching the Egyptians a lesson and of preventing the recurrence of rebellion in the future. Perhaps the determination of Artaxerxes to conquer Egypt and restore the empire reveals something of his character—a capable, ruthless, tireless, and gifted personality. Phrenedates was made satrap, and after rewarding his Greek allies, Artaxerxes returned to his homeland. Artaxerxes succeeded in restoring the empire to the proportions it possessed in earlier days. After the humiliation of Egypt, the reluctant Greeks of Asia Minor fell in line—largely through the efforts of Mentor, who even prevailed upon his brothers Memnon and Artabazus, both of whom had taken refuge in Macedonia, to return. There may even have been some sort of accommodation with Macedonia, which was not yet a first-rate power. But things were too good to endure for long. Once more the blow came from within. The trusted Bagoas poisoned Artaxerxes, had his whole family executed, and put Arses (339–336 B.C.) on the throne. Artaxerxes was apparently buried in a tomb on the cliff above Persepolis (Ghirshman, *Persia*, Fig. 280). A few building contributions of this king are known. He built a new palace at Persepolis overlooking the ruins; he completed the restoration work at Susa begun by his father; and at Ecbatana he set up the stone pillars of the apadana (palace). A number of coins come from this reign, some bearing the image of the king.

The short reign of Arses is marked by the resurgence of Macedonian power under Philip II. Almost at the time Artaxerxes was murdered, Philip established his supremacy over the Greek states by defeating them in the battle at Charoneia. Then he organized a Greek league, and when the Persian king rejected Philip's demand for reparations, the latter set out to free the Greek cities of Anatolia from Persian control. He had little trouble in winning them over, and the die was cast against Persian hegemony. Meanwhile Arses attempted to rid himself of the rigid control of Bagoas but himself became the victim, and the eunuch was compelled to enthrone the nephew of Artaxerxes II, Darius III. In the maneuvers, Bagoas, who because of the new king's vigorous activity attempted to poison Darius, was himself made to drink of the cup he had prepared for the king.

Events at the Persian court did not escape notice in Egypt. A Nubian prince by the name of Khababasha had been crowned at Memphis as the Pharaoh (338 B.C.). He officiated at the Apis rites in his second year. He restored the temple lands taken away by Artaxerxes III. He also attempted to fortify the Delta against the contingency of a Persian punitive campaign but without success. By 335 B.C. we find the Persians in control of Egypt, and Darius was recognized as "Pharaoh" from 335 B.C. to 333 B.C. Kienitz (*Die politische Geschichte*, p. 110) cites an inscription of a high-ranking official who gives thanks to his god for bringing him safely through the disturbed period inas-

much as he was favored by a native Pharaoh and at the same time
stood in well with the Persians. Evidently many of the Egyptian
princes and principalities knew how to accommodate themselves to the
rapidly changing times much like the Jewish garrison at Elephantine
did in the time of Cambyses and later.

Alexander the Great took over the kingship of Macedonia in 336
B.C., after the murder of his father, possibly with Persian complicity.
Before he could carry out the ringing commission of his father to conquer Persia, Alexander had to calm the troubled seas around him. It
looked as if the Grecian league would fall apart, and the peoples from
the north were showing signs of restlessness. The Macedonian army
was not having too much success in Asia Minor, where serious defections to Persia were taking place. There were some negotiations between Athens and Darius, spurned by the latter until it was too late.
In disregard of the opposition of Demosthenes, the Athenians came
over to the side of Alexander after the latter's crushing defeat of
Thebes. Plans had been made by the Macedonians for a Darius-
Xerxes operation in reverse, and to that intent the young king crossed
the Hellespont in the spring of 334 B.C. At Troy, Alexander paid
homage to the Greek heroes of the past and poured out a libation to
Athena. Then he moved on and met the Persian forces on the banks
of the Granicus river, where he won his first great victory because of
the hasty stand of the enemy. The Persians were sent away, but the
Greek mercenaries were harshly treated. Alexander immediately reorganized the conquered territory along Persian lines since that would
create the least problems. Then he overran the cities bordering on the
Aegean followed by an invasion of Phrygia. Had not the Persian general Memnon died, he might have expected real trouble. Further mis-
takes in Persian strategy prevented the reconquest of the territory so
speedily overtaken by Alexander's army, and in the following year he
was on his way to Cilicia. One after another, the states of Anatolia
submitted. Just as he was ready to crash the Cilician gates, the Persian
defenders fled. After breaking up all possible resistance of the Persians
in Cilicia, Alexander was in control of all Anatolia. Meanwhile Darius
had collected a vast army of his own and had encamped in Syria at
Sochi. Both armies were halted at their respective locations. The advisers in each camp interpreted the pause as weakness in the other.
Darius made the first move by taking Issus and thus attacking the
Greeks from the rear. Alexander wheeled around, and the two armies
collided in reverse position. Darius' forces were defeated, his family
captured, and he himself barely escaped. A new master had taken over

in the Persian world. Henceforth hegemony of that world was to be exercised by western Indo-Iranians as it had been hitherto by the eastern. All was now in readiness for the march south through Syria and Phoenicia to Egypt. The king of Arvad arrived first with his officials and surrendered his city with its holdings. In the interim Darius dispatched a letter to Alexander offering him all of Asia west of the Halys river in return for a treaty of friendship. It was spurned by the Macedonian, and Darius was compelled to assemble another army to do battle on another day.

Alexander now continued his march south toward Egypt. One by one the Phoenician states offered their submission. Byblos and then the party of Sidon that was against Persia and Cyprus brought their tokens of surrender. Tyre too offered to submit, until Alexander insisted upon offering sacrifice in the temple of Baal Melqart, whereupon the Tyrians withdrew their proposal and prepared for siege. After a difficult operation involving the construction of a mole between the city and the mainland, the city was finally reduced after seven months of hard and costly operations. Alexander crucified all the men of Tyre who survived and sold the women into slavery. After the fall of Tyre (332 B.C.), Syria came over to the side of the Persians. Once more the Macedonians began their movement south along the coast, all going well until they reached Gaza, which was by now a great emporium dealing in gems, incense, and spices from Arabia. It was the western end of the great South Arabian trade routes. Betis, the governor of the city, is described as having exceptional loyalty to the king, and hence he put up a stiff resistance against the Grecian invaders. Alexander was wounded in the course of the siege, which put a severe strain on his army. When it finally capitulated, the population was treated the same as that of Tyre. Betis was subjected to the most senseless cruelty. (For description of the siege of Gaza, see Curtius, *History of Alexander*, 4:6:7–30 and Arrian, *History*, 2:25:4–2:27:7). It is significant that both Curtius and Arrian mention Arabs as the defenders of Gaza. Since the Persians did not subdue the Arabians, Gaza may have remained independent throughout the Persian period. The Minnaeans were in control of South Arabia by 400 B.C. In the time of Nehemiah, Geshem was an important Arab prince as we know from bowl inscriptions from Tell el-Muskhuta near Ismailia. By the time of Alexander, the Arabs had firmly entrenched themselves in the former territory of Edom and doubtless saw their trade-expansion threatened by his conquests (see *ZAW* 74, 1962, pp. 186–190). (For internal developments in Arabia see J. Ryckmans, *L'institution monarchique en Arabie méri-*

dionale avant l'Islam [Louvain: Institut Orientaliste, 1951], and R. Dussaud, *La pénétration des Arabes en Syrie avant l'Islam* [Paris: Geuthner, 1955], Chap. I.) Now the way to Egypt was clear; Gaza was the last city between Palestine and Egypt. Although Sabaka, satrap of Egypt, had taken part on the Persian side in the battle at Issus where he lost his life, there was no effort in Egypt to resist the invasion of Alexander; we do not know the reason. Perhaps the new satrap, Mazaces, was convinced of the futility of resistance (Arrian, *History*, 3:1:2), or he may not have had the will to oppose the inevitable. Resistance to the Persians was always inspired by some native prince; this time there was none to stir up trouble for the invader. There had been a short plundering expedition around Pelusium by Amyntas, which was suppressed by Mazaces before the arrival of Alexander. When the Macedonian came, he was greeted by the satrap on friendly terms. That marked the end of the Achaemenid empire in the west.

After Alexander's famous visit to the oracle of Ammon in the oasis of Siwah where he was acclaimed as the son of Zeus-Ammon, he set his course eastward. Meanwhile he ran into opposition with the Samaritans, who had cremated the Syrian satrap Andromachus for which they were severely punished (see F. M. Cross, "The Discovery of the Samaria Papyri," *BA* XXVI [1963] 110–121). The tradition of Alexander's visit to Jerusalem at this time is probably apocryphal (Josephus, *Ant.* 11:7:5)—there is no other evidence for such a visit. However, the Jews seem to have been friendly toward him, perhaps because he was thought of as the successor of the Persians, for Alexander everywhere posed as their successor.

The final contest between Alexander and the Persians took place at Arbela (331–330 B.C.), where the battle once more went against Darius. This time when he fled, the empire was lost and Alexander became the undisputed master of the world. To be sure, Darius was not dead yet. He fled to Bactria, where he hoped to organize further resistance but was slain by the local satrap Bessus (330–329 B.C.). Alexander was received with open arms at Babylon, where he commanded at once the restoration of the temples, especially that of Bel Marduk. On his way to Susa he was informed of the surrender of the capital with its treasures. Persepolis resisted but was taken without too much difficulty. The magnificent monument of the Persian empire was ruthlessly destroyed and its treasures plundered. Here the supposedly literate and perceptive Greeks acted like barbarians, as seen from the still splendid ruins after more than two millennia. Alexander's degeneration began on the day he set the torch to the most artistic city ever built. His great plan to weld the two cultures of Greece and Persia, symbolized by his marriage of the daughter of Darius and the connubium of 10,000 Greek soldiers with Persian maidens, failed because his successors soon forgot the east. Yet the world after the conquest of Alexander was but a continuation of Persian patterns. Their impact upon it had its effect on many facets of life in the west. The contrast between the organizing genius of Cyrus and his successors and Alexander and his is striking indeed. The empire of the former lasted two centuries, the latter's little more than a decade. (For further observations see W. S. Smith, *Interconnections in the Ancient Near East* [New Heaven, Conn.: Yale University Press, 1965], p. 58.)

The contribution of the Persians to the future history of the world was phenomenal, considering the fact that what we know about them has come largely from the writings of their enemies. They initiated the provincial system of government that was copied by later world rulers. They did levy taxes for their own uses, sometimes misuses, but they used a large measure of them to improve certain areas of the empire from which they came. One thinks of the Jews as outstanding recipients of their assistance in the time of Nehemiah and Ezra. They taught the world the use of a less cumbersome method of writing than cuneiform by making Aramaic the language of diplomacy and communication. They must have promoted or at least put no impediments in the way of trade and commerce as evident from the establishment of flourishing trading posts all along the Palestinian coast from the mouth of the Orontes river to Pelusium in Egypt. Their road system and rapid methods of communication were the forerunners of the Roman road system, perhaps even the beginnings of the very roads now traveled in the Near East. Even the medieval Arab organization was reminiscent of that of the Persians. They did make few distinctive art contributions, although they adapted what they borrowed to their own designs and purposes. The world of the restoration was one of change and one that opened ways of progress, especially in communication, that in a real sense was a preparation for the dissemination of culture and later on the spread of Judaism and Christianity.

Whether Zoroastrianism made any impact on the early Persian kings is not clear, but it is doubtful if it had any direct influence on the religion of the Jews in this period. Indirectly, however, the religion of the Persian monarchs did prove of immense significance. Earlier kings required the submission of their subjects to their gods (see 2 Kgs 16,10ff.), although they seem to have permitted local cults in addition. Whereas the Persian kings were ardent devotees of Ahuramazda, they did not force their national cult upon their subjects. As we know from other sources, they even encouraged and supported the religions of the various nations who came under their national control. That attitude and practice prevented them from coming into religious collision with the Jews; it worked to great advantage for them. Not only were the Jews free to observe such cult ordinances as they could at Babylon, but they were permitted to return to their ancestral home where they were supported in the reconstruction of their sacred institutions. In that way the Persians had a tremendous influence on the perpetuation and development of the Jewish religion. God was at work in that world. (For further observations see A. J. Arberry, ed., *The Legacy of Persia* [Oxford: Oxford University Press, 1953].)

Judah
and the Jews

Just when things began to look up for the *golah* in Judah and Jerusalem, political conditions in the world around them began to deteriorate, and a cloud settled over the land and people so that much of what actually went on was almost totally obscured. What must have concerned them greatly, and perhaps interfered with their internal development, was the almost constant upheaval in Egypt that brought the Persians to the west again and again. Although there is no evidence of their traversing the land itself, they did pass nearby, and there must have been rumors of war floating through the air almost constantly. So far as is known, the Jews were not directly involved in any of these military preparations or expeditions.

There is some evidence that they occupied themselves largely with internal affairs, probably with cultic practices. The well-known *Yahud* stamps point to local self-administration, the gathering of local taxes, and the maintenance of the status quo. For example, four stamps with this legend were found at Ramat Rahel in IVB (= Persian period): *yhwd/yhw'zr/phw'* (= "Judah"/"Jehoazar"/"governor"—approximate translation); five stamps with this legend: *yhwd/l'hyw* or (*l'hzy*)/*phw'* (= "Judah"/"to Ahio" (or "to Ahzai")/"governor"; one with *yhwd/hnnh* (= "Judah"/"Hannah") written in two lines with a horizontal dividing line. Another stamp from Jericho with the reading *yhwd/'wryw* (= "Judah"/"Urio"), and other *yhwd* stamps from Bethany and Tell Nasbeh were discovered. The abundance of the Judah (*yhwd*) stamps would seem to indicate a semiautonomous religious state whose government was directed by ecclesiastical officials. The stamps were authentications from the Jerusalem temple treasury, which was the repository for civil and ecclesiastical affairs, from which local expenditures were discharged (see Neh 13,12f.). This method of operation may, incidentally, have created the climate favorable to noninvolvement in the disturbances of the fourth century B.C. The little religious principality was a threat neither to the neighbors nor to the great powers vying for supremacy. Perhaps the new layer of clouds that settled over the community at the time were a real blessing in that they kept their little realm from the sight of destructive forces. It must be remembered that many other communities and cities suffered annihilation during the course of events that overtook Palestine in the fourth century. The little settlement at Kadesh-barnea in the Persian period appears to have been destroyed in the Hellenistic age (*IEJ* XV [1965], p. 143). The citadel at Tell Arad was also leveled in the construction of a Hellenistic tower (*ibid.*, p. 250). The residency at En-gedi was demolished around 400 B.C. (*ibid.*, p. 258). These southern cities were probably involved in the westward pressures exerted by the Arab movements of the latter years of the fifth century so that their disappearance was gradual and could only be remotely connected with the events noted above (cf. *IEJ* XIV [1964] 126f. and esp. note 8). The heavily populated coastal areas (*IEJ* XV [1965] 263) must have suffered in the see-saw Persian-Egyptian conflicts of the fourth century. Perhaps we shall have a better idea of the course of events when the Persian levels at Ashdod have been sifted.

Other Matters of Interest in the Fourth-Century World

This was not so productive an era as that of the preceding century. It was the period of the great orators, who hurled their words around the marketplace at Athens—Aeschines, Demosthenes, and Isocrates. It was the century of Aristotle, whose ideas are still prevalent, and of Diogenes the cynic. At the beginning of that century Ctesias, the private physician of Artaxerxes II, wrote his history of Persia, and Xenophon penned his Cyropaedia and Anabasis and the Memorabilia of Socrates and the Hellenica. The great comic poet Aristophanes lived for twenty years in this century. So did Hippocrates. In the second quarter of the fourth century Praxiteles, one of the foremost sculptors of Greece, flourished at Athens.

We do not have much of a definitely datable character from the Jews. There are the seals, stamps, some ostraca, and a few other inscribed materials that are mostly datable by archaeological context. It now appears that the book of Tobit may come from the fourth, perhaps the fifth, century (Albright, *New Horizons in Biblical Research* [New York: Oxford University Press, 1966], p. 38). It has been assumed by many scholars that the story underlying the book of Judith belongs to the reign of Artaxerxes III (Eissfeldt, *Introduction,* 586f.), but we must reckon with an even earlier date in view of Claus Schedl's recent study, which attempts to connect the Nebuchadnezzar of the story with the Araka in the Darius Behistun inscription (*ZDMG* CXV [1965], 242–54; see also A. M. Dubarle, *Judith: formes et sens des diverses traditions* [Rome: Pontifical Biblical Institute, 1966] who now thinks it came from the Persian period—Tome I, p. 136, note 23. Others date it much later; e.g., *The Jerusalem Bible* [New York: Doubleday & Co., Inc., 1966], p. 603 and R. J. Faley, *The Bible Today,* No. 8, November 1963 [Collegeville, Minn.: The Liturgical Press], 505–10). Some scholars think the Chronicler did his work some time in the first half of the fourth century, but that appears to the writer to be too late. At the very latest he could hardly have done his work much after 400 B.C. (See *I Chronicles: Anchor Bible* 12, pp. LXXXVIIff.).

Selected Readings

Bright, J., *A History of Israel,* Chap. 11. New York: Harper & Row, Publishers (Harper Torchbooks), 1963.

Heinisch, P., *A History of the Old Testament,* Chap. 44. Collegeville, Minn.: The Liturgical Press, 1963.

Olmstead, A. T., *History of the Persian Empire,* Chaps. 26–36. Chicago: The University of Chicago Press, 1948.

Ricciotti, G., *The History of Israel,* 2nd ed., II, 140–68. Milwaukee: Bruce Publishing Company, 1958.

Abbreviations

Old Testament

Genesis	Gn	Song of Solomon	Song
Exodus	Ex	Wisdom	Wis
Leviticus	Lv	Sirach	Sir
Numbers	Nm	Isaiah	Is
Deuteronomy	Dt	Jeremiah	Jer
Joshua	Jos	Lamentations	Lam
Judges	Jgs	Baruch	Bar
Ruth	Ru	Ezekiel	Ez
1 Samuel	1 Sm	Daniel	Dn
2 Samuel	2 Sm	Hosea	Hos
1 Kings	1 Kgs	Joel	Jl
2 Kings	2 Kgs	Amos	Am
1 Chronicles	1 Chr	Obadiah	Obd
2 Chronicles	2 Chr	Jonah	Jon
Ezra	Ezr	Micah	Mi
Nehemiah	Neh	Nahum	Na
Tobit	Tb	Habakkuk	Hb
Judith	Jdt	Zephaniah	Zeph
Esther	Est	Haggai	Hag
Job	Jb	Zecariah	Zech
Psalms	Ps(s)	Malachi	Mal
Proverbs	Prv	1 Maccabees	1 Mc
Ecclesiastes	Eccl	2 Maccabees	2 Mc

New Testament

St. Matthew	Mt	1 Timothy	1 Tm
St. Mark	Mk	2 Timothy	2 Tm
St. Luke	Lk	Titus	Ti
St. John	Jn	Philemon	Phlm
The Acts of the		To the Hebrews	Heb
Apostles	Acts	The Epistle of St. James	Jas
St. Paul to the Romans	Rom	1 St. Peter	1 Pt
1 Corinthians	1 Cor	2 St. Peter	2 Pt
2 Corinthians	2 Cor	1 St. John	1 Jn
Galatians	Gal	2 St. John	2 Jn
Ephesians	Eph	3 St. John	3 Jn
Philippians	Phil	St. Jude	Jude
Colossians	Col	The Apocalypse of St.	
1 Thessalonians	1 Thes	John the Apostle	Ap
2 Thessalonians	2 Thes		

Other Source Material

AI	R. de Vaux, *Ancient Israel*, John McHugh, trans. (New York: McGraw-Hill, 1961)
AJSL	*American Journal of Semitic Languages and Literatures* (Chicago)
Alt, KS	A. Alt, *Kleine Schriften zur Geschichte des Volkes Israel*, I–III (München: C. H. Beck, 1953–59)
Ant.	Josephus, *Antiquities of the Jews*
AP	W. F. Albright, *The Archaeology of Palestine* (Baltimore: Penguin Books, Inc., 1960)
Aramaic Papyri	A. Cowley, *Aramaic Papyri of the Fifth Century B.C.* (Oxford: The Clarendon Press, 1923)
BA	*Biblical Archaeologist* (New Haven)
BANE	G. Ernest Wright (ed.), *The Bible and the Ancient Near East: Essays in Honor of William Foxwell Albright* (New York: Doubleday, 1961)
BASOR	*Bulletin of the American Schools of Oriental Research* (New Haven)
BMAP	Emil G. Kraeling, *The Brooklyn Museum Aramaic Papyri* (New Haven: Yale University Press, 1953)
BP	W. F. Albright, *The Biblical Period from Abraham to Ezra: An Historical Survey* (New York: Harper Torchbook, 1963)
Dio. Sic.	*Diodorus Siculus*
HTR	*Harvard Theological Review* (Cambridge, Mass.)
IEJ	*Israel Exploration Journal* (Jerusalem)
ILN	*Illustrated London News* (London)
JBL	*Journal of Biblical Literature* (Philadelphia)
JNES	*Journal of Near Eastern Studies* (Chicago)
JTS	*Journal of Theological Studies* (Oxford)
KB	*Keilinschriftliche Bibliothek* (Berlin)
Meyer, KS II	E. Meyer, *Kleine Schriften*, 2nd ed. (Halle: Max Niemeyer, 1924)
LXX	Septuagint
MT	Masoretic Text
QDAP	*Quarterly of the Department in Antiquities of Palestine* (Jerusalem and London)
RB	*Revue Biblique* (Paris)
ZAW	*Zeitschrift für die alttestamentliche Wissenschaft* (Berlin)
ZDMG	*Zeitschrift der deutschen morgenländischen Gesellschaft* (Wiesbaden)

The following references are to the Persian Inscriptions in R. G. Kent, *Old Persian Grammar, Texts, Lexicon*, 2nd ed. (New Haven: American Oriental Society, 1953)

A^2 Sa	Artaxerxes II, Susa a
A^2 Sd	Artaxerxes II, Susa d

A² Hb	Artaxerxes II, Hamadan b
DB	Darius, Behistun
DNa	Darius, Naqš-i-Rustam a
DNb	Darius, Naqš-i-Rustam b
DPd	Darius, Persepolis d
DPh	Darius, Persepolis h
DSe	Darius, Susa e
DSf	Darius, Susa f
DSo	Darius, Susa o
DSp	Darius, Susa p
DSs	Darius, Susa s
XPa	Xerxes, Persepolis a
XPh	Xerxes, Persepolis h

Index

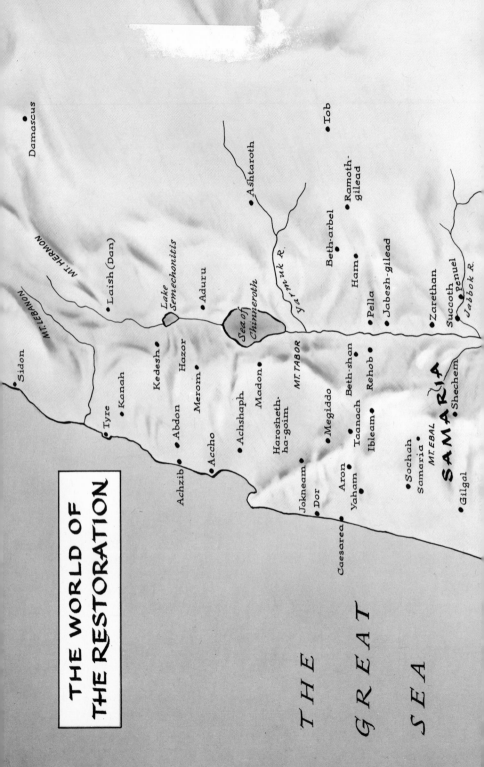

THE WORLD OF
THE RESTORATION

THE GREAT SEA

SAMARIA

MT. HERMON

MT. LEBANON

Yarmuk R.

Jabbok R.

MT. TABOR

MT. EBAL

Damascus

Sidon

Tyre

Achzib

Accho

Kanah

Abdon

Kedesh

Hazor

Merom

Laish (Dan)

Lake
Semechoniitis

Aduru

Sea of
Chinneroth

Ashtaroth

Iob

Ramoth-
gilead

Beth-arbel

Ham

Pella

Jabesh-gilead

Zarethan

Succoth

Penuel

Achshaph

Madon

Harosheth-
ha-goiim

Megiddo

Beth-shan

Rehob

Taanach

Ibleam

Shechem

Jokneam

Dor

Aron

Yaham

Sochah

Samaria

Gilgal

Caesarea